Psychotherapy: Portraits in Fiction

Psychotherapy
Portraits in Fiction

Edited by
Jesse D. Geller, Ph.D.
and
Paul D. Spector, M.A.

𝒜

Jason Aronson Inc.
Northvale, New Jersey
London

10 9 8 7 6 5 4 3 2 1

Library of Congress Cataloging-in-Publication Data

Psychotherapy: portraits in fiction.

   1. Psychotherapy—Fiction. 2. Short stories, American.
I. Geller, Jesse D.   II. Spector, Paul D.
PS648.P77P79 1987   813'.01'08353   87-17528
ISBN 0-87668-935-7

Manufactured in the United States of America.

Contents

Introduction

What *really* happens in psychotherapy? Therapists and patients alike have difficulty describing their experiences. Moreover, when people read academic textbooks in an attempt to learn about the intimate and unique nature of the psychotherapeutic experience, they often come away dissatisfied; perhaps, like psychoanalyst Helmuth Kaiser, they feel as though they are "trying to decipher a melody by looking at the grooves on the record."

This book presents nineteen stories about psychotherapy. These fictional portrayals offer insights useful for experienced psychotherapists, those in training, and people who are now or have been in, or are contemplating entering, psychotherapy. Works of the imagination, they make palpable the atmosphere, rhythms, nuances, and tensions of the psychotherapeutic exeprience. Both the fiction writer and the psychotherapist are commentators and interpreters, reconstructing the past through the telling of stories. The metaphors created by artists may stand closer to the experience of a lived psychotherapy than do the elegant abstractions of scientists.

The idea for this anthology began with our reading of "My Love Has Dirty Fingernails" by John Updike. Updike's story eloquently captures the *feel* of an actual therapeutic relationship. Our encounter with this story encouraged us to seek out other such accounts about psychotherapy. We were surprised to learn that hundreds of such stories have been published.

Although there exist today approximately one hundred and thirty "brands" of therapy, psychoanalytically oriented practice occupies a monolithic position in the fiction describing psychotherapy. We found no stories dealing with alternative schools of therapy (for example, Gestalt, Reichian, or behavioral therapy) or with alternative forms derived from the creative arts (such as dance, music, art, or drama therapy). In the short stories we read, male and female patients appear in equal numbers. In reality, there are three to five times as many women as men who seek treatment. In fiction, as in the scientific literature, less has been written about the work of women therapists with male patients than about any other gender pairing.

While many of the stories we have chosen for this anthology show the successes of therapy, some reflect the difficulties and failures. These stories neither propagandize for the effectiveness of therapy nor present an idealized image of the psychotherapist. (Some demonstrate the potential destructiveness of psychotherapy and the shortcomings of the therapist.) In general, these stories focus on the neurotic and character problems and the crises of everyday living—the inability to love, blocked creativity, the incapacity to mourn—that people bring to psychotherapy. (Psychotic symptomatology is portrayed in such works as *Lilith, David and Lisa, One Flew Over the Cuckoo's Nest, I Never Promised You a Rose Garden, Woman on the Edge of Time, Equus,* and *Marat/Sade.*) All but two of the therapy relationships described in this collection take place in professional offices. These stories succeed in reflecting the complex ways in which patients and therapists interact, as well as the inner life of therapy sessions. The accounts are rich in a variety of central therapeutic issues; for example, the universality of transference reactions can be discerned in every story.

Our prefatory remarks are meant to be evocative rather than exhaustive. The stories themselves are exciting and clear pictures of the therapeutic interaction.

"Mending" by Sallie Bingham

Individuals experience recurrent transference reactions, perceptions of others that, without the individual's awareness, are influenced by feelings and responses originally experienced in relation to significant people from the past (usually parental figures). All relationships are a blend of realistic and transferential elements. Psychotherapy distinguishes itself by providing patients with ongoing opportunities to work through the transference and eventually experience the therapist as a "real person," apart from transferential distortions.

There is a cliché that women patients invariably fall in love with their male therapists. This so-called love is usually depicted mockingly. Risking intimate exposure of the sexual and romantic feelings stimulated by the therapist's caring concern may be the first step toward overcoming a chronic sense of alienation. "Mending" portrays, respectfully, the childhood origins, meanings, and consequences of a young woman's felt need to be loved by her male therapist. We are given a sense of the skill and emotional maturity required to manage and harness the healing potential of what is called the erotic transference.

"My Love Has Dirty Fingernails" by John Updike

The roles of therapist and patient are not tightly scripted. In many respects, psychotherapy changes with each new relationship. Like jazz musicians, psychotherapists must be capable of improvising, gracefully. Much of the work of psychotherapy consists of exploring the unique ways in which patients respond to the complexities and ambiguities woven into the therapeutic interaction.

In "My Love Has Dirty Fingernails" the therapist pulls together the unconscious themes of the session with a transference interpretation. But the interpretation is overly theoretical and too lengthy—an attempt to "convince" the patient. The story masterfully recreates the uncertainties and power struggles, and the emotional atmosphere, of a psychotherapy in which a central question is: Who is seducing whom?

August by Judith Rossner
Ordinary People by Judith Guest

The excerpts from the novels *August* and *Ordinary People* dramatically highlight the work of two therapists. The patients in both cases are adolescents, suicidal, and coming for their first sessions. The therapists differ radically in approach and style. In the selection from *August*, Dawn meets a female psychoanalyst, Dr. Schinefeld, whose interventions are shaped by attention to abstinence, neutrality, and objectivity. In contrast, Judith Guest's Dr. Berger is informal, personable, and talkative.

Asking which of these two styles indicates the better therapist is like evaluating whether jazz is better than classical music. Successful therapy depends on the elusive fit between therapist and patient. The chemist can predict how two elements will interact; there is no comparable science of human chemistry.

"Emergency" by Helmuth Kaiser

What constitutes the primary healing ingredients of psychotherapy? Some emphasize the cathartic discharge of unexpressed emotions, others the widening of consciousness, and still others the experience of discovering oneself in the process of communicating authentically.

The quality of relatedness in an authentic dialogue transcends words. "Emergency," by Helmuth Kaiser, dramatizes the author's conviction that a therapist free of restrictive theoretical preoccupations and techniques and rigid roles will maximize the healing potential of genuine communication. Implicit in Kaiser's view is the belief that patients can have a healing influence on their therapists.

"Understanding Eva" by Elizabeth Brewster

Therapists vary in the extent to which they are self-revealing. The focus of the psychoanalytically oriented therapist on the transference necessitates limiting self-revelation in order to approximate a "blank screen" for the patient's projections. Other therapists are guided by the belief that self-revelation begets self-revelation. In turn, patients struggle with how much they want to know about their therapists' personal lives, and how they will go about gratifying their curiosity. "Understanding Eva" draws our attention to the implications of one patient's coming to know the very human aspects of her psychotherapist.

"The Girl Who Couldn't Stop Eating" by Robert Lindner

From its inception the "talking cure" has existed on the boundary between science and art. Some gifted psychotherapists, like Robert Lindner, have written "case histories" that are both scientific works of art and artistic works of science. In "The Girl Who Couldn't Stop Eating," Lindner challenges the misconception that analysts are, at all times, scientific—objective and emotionally detached from their patients—and demonstrates how psychotherapy can be an experience of engagement, commitment, and caring concern. On occasion, therapists have raw and primitive feelings toward their patients. Some patients, like Laura, would tax any therapist's emotional maturity and competence and provoke agonizing self-examination. It is these patients who also strengthen Lindner's view that therapy "is a vital art that demands more of its practitioners than the clever exercise of their brains. Into its practice also goes the heart, and there are occasions when genuine human feelings take precedence over the rituals and dogmas of the craft."

"The Success" by John Logan

Resistance in the treatment situation refers to the ways, conscious and unconscious, in which patients obstruct the aims and process of therapy. Silence, discussing trivia, missing appointments, avoiding charged topics are but a few of its concrete expressions. Whatever styles patients use to protect themselves from painful self-awareness, resistance is self-defeating and a major obstacle to therapeutic progress unless worked with appropriately. The central focus of "The Success" is a particular style of resisting therapeutic involvement. Here, psychologizing and intellectualizing are used by an obsessional patient to avoid authentic feelings and direct contact with the therapist. In Logan's story, the patient succeeds in his quest for failure.

"It Never Touched Me" by Ann-Marie Wells

Most forms of therapy are premised on the assumption that the acceptance and expression of the contradictory and painful feelings provoked by grief are essential to emotional health. When we choose to forget or deny the legitimate suffering in our lives, we sacrifice our capacity for pleasure as well. In this story the therapist makes an intervention and the patient responds. Her silent associations demonstrate a strangely distanced flood of painful memories, vague fears, and morbid fantasies that must more explicitly be felt in the course of therapy.

"The 1930 Olympics" by H. L. Mountzoures

Deception, self-deception, and the fallibility of memory are central issues in psychotherapy. Freud first accepted and then rejected the literal truth of patients' childhood memories, concluding that these accounts were fantasies that the patients believed to have actually happened. "The 1930 Olympics" takes the issue of remembering-what-never-happened even further. It presents a patient who, as a form of resistance, consciously lies to—and deceives—his therapist.

"An Astrologer's Day" by R. K. Narayan

In "An Astrologer's Day," R. K. Narayan dramatizes the work of an ancestor of the healing professions. Gurus, witch doctors, shamans, astrologers, fortune tellers, and faith healers derive their authority and their capacity to influence others from both rational and nonrational sources. The rational basis of authority derives from the knowledge, experience, and skill that practitioners bring to their work. The charismatic origins of their authority can be traced to the child's faith in and obedience to powerful parental figures. No one completely relinquishes the primitive belief in the possibility of merging with the calmness, infallibility, and omnipotence of perfect parental figures. In this story, Narayan demonstrates the artfulness, common sense, exquisite timing, and luck that this astrologer shares with psychotherapists.

"The Fairy Godfathers" by John Updike

Patients cast their therapists into diverse and contradictory roles—parent, guide, mediator, healer, friend, confessor, provocateur, spy, voyeur, teacher, guru, advocate, conscience, moralist. Whatever role psychotherapists are assigned, or assume for themselves, their influence is felt between sessions and long after termination; patients create and hang on to multipurpose images of the therapeutic relationship. Sometimes seen as approving, sometimes seen as forbidding, the felt presence of the therapist, in reality and fantasy, shapes patients' perceptions and may give them a tool to use in their relations with others. "The Fairy Godfathers" portrays just how pervasive therapists' influence can become.

"The Ordeal of Dr. Blauberman" by Lillian Ross

Lillian Ross's short story reveals a psychoanalyst's flaws and shortcomings. Dr. Blauberman's personal alienations and his envy of the patient result in controlling, judgmental, intrusive therapeutic work. Under the guise of meeting his patient's needs, Blauberman tries to gratify his own. He rationalizes his failures as a therapist by blaming the patient for being passive and resistant. This story highlights how difficult it is to extricate oneself from even a destructive therapeutic relationship. Dr. Blauberman's negative impact may be short-lived; his patient's capacity for love and creative work exceeds the therapist's, and the patient ends therapy.

"Black Angels" by Bruce Jay Friedman

The profession of psychotherapy originated within the entrepreneurial context of the private practice of medicine, and, like all other professionals, psychotherapists charge fees. Psychotherapists can be paid directly by their clients, reimbursed by insurance companies, or salaried by institutions. No matter how payment is handled, there is some tension between the practical concerns of commerce and those of humanitarianism in the practice of psychotherapy. Some critics view psychotherapy as a form of purchasing friendship. Questions concerning the price tag of caring and listening inevitably arise during the course of therapy. "Black Angels" is a fantasy about the business aspects of therapy.

"The Hidden Oracle" by Crystal Moore

"The Hidden Oracle," written under a pseudonym, is autobiographical. Whether the incidents described by the author are fictional or actually happened, they express an essential truth. Individuals who, like Crystal, dread intimacy yet intensely crave closeness cannot avail themselves of the healing potential of human relationships and have difficulty with the possibilities for relatedness in the psychotherapeutic relationship. Psychotic patients withdraw from and may respond with hostility to caring concern and intimacy. In this story a young woman who invites rejection encounters a paraprofessional who "stays with" her, thereby opening up the possibility of recovery.

"Mr. Prinzo's Breakthrough" by Bruce Jay Friedman

Facing the limitations of what psychotherapy can actually accomplish, and determining realistic criteria to assess a patient's readiness to terminate, pose problems for therapists and patients alike. The relief of "symptoms" is probably the most widely accepted criterion of readiness for termination. The wild parody "Mr. Prinzo's Breakthrough," by Bruce Jay Friedman, dramatizes a patient's pervasive distrust and frantic testing of the ground rules and boundaries of the therapeutic relationship. In his seventh year of treatment, Mr. Prinzo longs for his dramatic therapeutic "breakthrough" and pushes the issue of basic trust to an absurd and darkly humorous conclusion.

"Psychiatric Services" by Joyce Carol Oates

Countertransference, the therapist's emotional reactions to the patient, is potentially one of the therapist's richest sources of information. The therapist-in-training learns through sound supervision that understanding personal feelings can clarify the meaning of the therapeutic process. The supervisory relationship, like the therapeutic relationship, is fraught with hazards and requires a sense of safety and trust if problematic feelings are to be brought to full awareness, accepted, and used therapeutically. In this story a psychiatric resident is anxious and confused because of her empathic involvement with a patient. Her supervisor, instead of helping her to understand that these feelings are the price one pays for practicing the "impossible profession," increases her sense of powerlessness by his arrogance and presumptuousness.

"The Patient" by Barbara Lawrence

Like "The Patient" in Barbara Lawrence's short story, many of us seek and invariably find some personal flaw that justifies devaluing ourselves or others. Stereotyping the self or others as unlovable and inferior is just one negative expression of the tendency to create categories of people. With the help of his therapist, "The Patient" gradually relinquishes his elaborate scheme for pigeon-holing people, and in so doing achieves greater self-acceptance.

"End of a Game" by Nancy Huddleston Packer

The course of individual psychotherapy, by its very nature, excludes significant others in the patient's life. The excluded spouse, especially, is vulnerable to feelings of anxiety and uncertainty. In "End of a Game," Nancy Huddleston Packer depicts the anguish of a spouse, Charles Andress, who is outside the therapy experience. He agonizes over his wife's relationship with her therapist and, like a jealous lover, envisions the therapist as a competitor. As can often happen when the outsider consults the therapist, Andress feels demeaned, ignorant, and embarrassed. With his wife he feels inadequate, plagued by the question "Why isn't *my* type of love healing?"

1

Mending

Sallie Bingham

On Fifth Avenue in the middle fall, the apartment buildings stand like pyramids in the sunlight. They are expensive and well-maintained, but for me their grandeur stems not from the big windows with the silk curtains where occasionally you can see a maid dusting with vague gestures but from the doctors' names beside the entrance door. Whether those doctors are more magical than the ones who are proclaimed in the windows is one of the puzzles I amuse myself with as I ply my trade up and down the avenue.

My trade is not the trade which might be expected from the height of my red-heeled sandals or the swing of my patent-leather bag. I am, after all, a good girl, a fairly young girl, although I have a few lines and a tendency to wake up at five in the morning. Taxi drivers still comment on my down-home accent, and although for a while I tried to dispel that impression by buying my clothes at Bloomingdale's I have given up the effort.

My trade is doctors, and it is essential. I have a doctor for my eyes and another for my skin; I have a special man for my allergies—which are not crippling—and I also have a specialist for the inside of my head.

For a while it seemed that my head was as far as he would go, with an occasional foray down my throat. Finally a choking sensation forced me to cancel my appointments. I suppose I should not expect anyone to take that at face value. He was a very handsome man; he is still, and it is still painful for me to imagine the man whose lap I longed to sit on presiding behind his profession, gazing with those curious green, unshadowed eyes at the women (why are they all women?) – the young ones, the old ones who hang their coats on his rack and sling their bags beside their feet as they sit down, with sighs, or in silence, on his couch.

My childhood was made to order to produce a high-heeled trader in doctors on Fifth Avenue, although my childhood would never have provided the money. My mother was blond and a beauty, and she had a penchant for changing men. My favorite was a truck driver from Georgia who used to let me ride with him on all-night trips down the coast. Mother didn't approve of that, but it took me off her hands. He would sing and I would doze in the big high cab, which seemed to me as hot and solid as a lump of molten lead – as hard to get out of, too, as I discovered when I tried to open the door. Oh, that truck was ecstasy. That was as close as I could come. My mother lost interest in him when I was six and replaced him with a white-collar worker. She thought Edwin was a step up, but for me, he never had any kind of appeal; he was the first of her men to carry a briefcase, and I learned an aversion then I have never been able to overcome to men who tie their shoes with very big bows and carry cow-smelling leather briefcases.

There were many others after Edwin, but they washed over me and I do not remember disliking them at all. They did not make much of an impression, as my mother would say; that was left to my first doctor, a personable Cincinnati gynecologist. My mother, who had settled in that town with a railroad man, made the appointment for me. She wanted me to know the facts, and she did not feel up to explaining them. Of course by then I knew everything, as well as the fact that if you turn down a boy, he will suffer from an excruciating disease. I did not really need to know that to be persuaded, since the interiors of those 1950 Chevrolets smelled just like the cab of Ronny's truck.

The gynecologist armed me with a strange rubber disk that flew across the room the first time I tried to insert it. The second time I was successful, but I was never able to find the thing again. It sailed like a moon through the uncharted darkness of my insides. I knew it was not right to have a foreign body sailing those seas, but it took me a month to summon the courage to call the gynecologist. I was so afraid he would be disappointed in me. He rescued the thing the next day as I lay down on his long table; he was disappointed, and the thing had turned bright green.

After that my mother married an Air Force man who was going to be stationed in Honolulu. I still think of her little black boots when I think of brave women leaving for parts unknown. She tripped up the steps to the airplane, an indomitable little mountain climber, with tears in her eyes. The Air Force man was in tears, too, and smiling as though their future lay shining on the tarmac. There was no room in that arrangement, and so I was farmed out to my mother's only prosperous relative, a hard-working doctor who lives in Greenwich and had the luck to marry my aunt.

I was nineteen, too old to be educated, too young to be employed. It made sense for me to do what I could to help Aunt Janey run her large house. There were people to do everything that needed to be done, but no one to organize them. Often the window washer arrived on the same day as the man who put up the screens, or the children needed to be picked up at friends as Aunt Janey was going to bed with her second cousin. (He was no relative of mine: another briefcase man.) So it was vital to have someone she could rely on to make telephone calls and draw up schedules.

Since I was not being paid in money but in good food and a fine room with roses on the wallpaper, Aunt Janey felt responsible for finishing me. She had been a brilliant woman once, and she still had her books from those days. She wrote my assignment every morning while I started the telephoning. I had to do it before I could do the bills. I can't say the reading meant a great deal to me, but the swing of the sentences—*Jane Eyre*, for example—seemed to carry me out of my ordinary way. I had thought that life was quite plain and obvious, with

people coupling and breaking apart like the little snot-colored dots I
had seen under the microscope in fifth-grade biology. The only lesson I
had learned so far was to stay out of the way of those dots. After I read
about blind Rochester's cry, I began to want some of that for my own.

I had not been demanding until then. No one could have complained that I made a fuss over a quick one in the back hall—that was
the furnace repairman—or took it more seriously than the roar of the
crowd at a construction site. I was never a prude, and my body did not
do me that kind of helpful disservice. At home, in the upper South, in
the Midwest, in Florida, they talked about boobies or the swing on my
back porch. Greenwich is more refined, even New York City is more
refined, and the repairman used to praise my eyes. When it came to
seeing one of the men twice, I would shy away, not only because I was
waiting for the voice across the miles but because I did not want to
spend any time with a man who might begin by praising my eyes and
then go on to feeling things himself—I did not mind that—but then
would expect me to feel things, as well.

In feeling, I was somewhat deficient. It had not mattered before. I
could remember the smell of Ronny's cab and glory in it, but I was not
able to enjoy the particular flavor of a man's body. A naked man, to
me, was like a root or tuber. I can't say I was afraid. But I never could
see the gleam, the light before the dawn, the pot at the end of the rain-
bow when a naked man stood in front of me. It seemed to me that
women were seemlier, more discreet, without that obtrusive member I
was always called on to admire. I could not touch it without conscious
effort, and that showed in my face. For a long time, it did not matter to
me, but it mattered to those men. They wanted me to admire, they
wanted me to feel something. Even the man who came to prune Aunt
Janey's forsythia insisted that I had to feel. "What's wrong with you?"
he complained, when we were lying under the bare branches of the big
bush. I knew he was feeling that it was somehow his fault.

I have never wanted to hurt anyone. I have wanted to help, if possible. And so I decided I would stop going out with men.

The trouble was that I wanted a pair of arms. I needed a pair of
arms with a pain that even now I can't bring myself to describe. That,

of all things, I had carried out of my childhood. When my mother was between men and feeling the ache, she would call me into her bed and squeeze me until suddenly she would fall asleep. I was more the holder than the holdee. It did not matter. The warmth of her thin arms, the wrists hardly wider than milk-bottle necks, the bones as fine as glass splinters, would last me through the next day and the next. Chronic cold was one of my chief complaints. But after she had held me, I didn't even need to button my school coat. I would walk down whatever gray street we were living on in whatever more or less depressed small-city neighborhood in whatever indistinguishable section in the middle of this country with no scarf over my head, no gloves on my hands, and the wind that comes from the Great Plains or the Mississippi or the Rockies or some other invisible boundary lifting the ends of my mouse-colored hair like a lover. Of course the trick was that my mother didn't expect anything of me, except not to wet the bed. She didn't expect me to feel anything in particular or to praise the way she looked in her nylon slip. She gave me the warmth of her long, skinny arms, and I gave her the warmth of mine, and before I was ten years old, I was addicted.

When the new man moved in, I had to spend the night in my own bed with my fist in my mouth, not because the sounds they made frightened me—they were no more frightening than the chittering of the squirrels in the little-city parks—but because there was no more warmth for me. Mother got into the habit of buying me bunny pajamas and wooly sweaters before she installed a new cousin.

After the forsythia man and my decision to do without men, I started to get cold in the old way. Aunt Janey noticed the gooseflesh on my arms one morning when I brought up her breakfast tray. She made me sit down on the satin blanket cover. "We haven't had a talk in I don't know how long." She was the prettiest woman I'd ever seen—the best, the brightest, with her jewelry box turned upside down on the pillow and her list of the day's duties, prepared by me, balled up and thrown on the floor. I could think of her only in silly ways—still that's the best I can do—because when I think of her eyes and the way her lips curled when her second cousin rang the doorbell, I know I will always be lonely for her. So I describe her to myself as a fickle woman who cheated on what my mother (who never had her luck) called, reverently, a perfectly good husband, and fed her children peanut butter out of the jar when I made the mistake of leaving a meal to her, and was happy. So happy. Outrageously happy. She had my mother's long, skinny arms—the only family resemblance—and although she very seldom held me in them, I knew she had the same heat. The difference a diamond wristwatch and a growth of fine blond hair made was not even worth thinking about.

(And he, the second cousin, did she make him groan with happiness, too? She used to come downstairs afterward in her Chinese kimono with her pearls hanging down her back, but I never saw much of him.)

We had our talk that morning. It was fall and Jacob the gardener was burning leaves. I insisted on opening the window, although Aunt Janey hated fresh air, and so I was able to flavor her words with the leaf smoke. She told me that I was unhappy, and there was no way I could deny that. So for once she took the pad and the telephone book and asked for the telephone, which had a crook on the receiver so that it could perch on your shoulder. And she began to make me appointments.

She had noticed my teeth, she said between dialings. Was there an implication about my breath? She had noticed that I squinted a good deal over the print in the telephone directory, and so she was sending me to have my eyes checked. She was also not certain that I should be as thin as I seemed to be growing, and so she was making an appointment with her own internist on upper Fifth Avenue. Unfortunately in his office I felt my old enemy, tears rising like an insurrection of moles, like a walking army of termites. When I cried on the leatherette chair, the doctor, who was as friendly as the repairman my mother had left after six months of too much loving, suggested that I ought to go and see the other kind.

That was all right, too, as far as I was concerned. I was ready to take anyone's advice. It did not seem possible to go through the rest of my life trying to get warmth from the eyes of construction workers; it did not seem possible to go on spreading my legs for men who took it personally that that part—"down there," as my mother called it—had no more feeling than the vegetable it so closely resembles: a radish, fancy cut.

The next waiting room was soft and beige, like the tissue inside of an expensive shoe box, and I could have lain there forever, till the robins covered me with magazine leaves. Of course I had to get up and go and lay myself down when the time came—why this eternal lying?—on an even softer, browner couch in a smaller, safer room. I asked the doctor right away to let me stay forever. He held my hand for a moment, introducing himself, and my cold began to fade. Can it fade from the hand up and will the heart in the end be heated, like a tin pot on a gas burner turned high? I had always assumed that my body warmed up independently and that my heart, at the end, would always be safe and cold. He did not want anything from me—you can't count money in a desperate situation like this—except my compliance, so that he could try and help. And I believed him.

My mother would have said there is no such thing as a disinterested man; she would have gone on to add that since he had green eyes, he must have other things in view. He did have green eyes, pale, finely lashed, and a pale, tired face. He seemed to have spent himself warming people up. By the second session, I hated the idea of any particle of him going to other people, and I ground my teeth when I passed the next patient—always a woman—in his little hall. I wanted him all to myself and it seemed to me that this was my last chance. My day was flooded with sights I had never seen in my life, views of my lean body folded up on his lap or the back of my neck as I knelt to kiss his feet. I had been cross and mean all my life and now, like a three-year-old with a lollypop, I was all syrup and sunshine. Shame had no part in it. As I went my rounds to the other doctors, letting them fill my teeth or put contact lenses in my eyes, as patiently as I have seen horses stand to be bridled and saddled, I imagined myself in my doctor's arms. Of course he did not respond. How could he respond? He wanted to help and, as he explained, holding me in his arms for a while or even for fifty minutes could not do me anything but harm. It is true that afterward I would never have let him go.

I thought I could push him. After all, other men had always wanted me. So I started to bring him little presents, bunches of chrysanthemums from Aunt Janey's garden, jars of my own grape jelly, poems on yellow paper that would have embarrassed a twelve-year-old. He made me take them all away, always neutral, always kind, always ready to listen, but never won or even tempted. My wishes were making me wild and I wanted to gather myself up and wrap myself in a piece of flowered paper and hand myself to him—not for sex or compliments, but only to be held by him.

Aunt Janey caught me crying after three months of this and offered a trip to Paris as a distraction. I told her I couldn't go because I couldn't bear to break a single appointment with my doctor; she was taken aback. We had a long talk in the late-night kitchen where Uncle John had been making pancakes. She told me that analysis works but not in that way. "I can understand you wanting to go to bed with him, that's what everybody wants, but I can't understand you letting it get so out of hand."

"I don't want to go to bed with him," I said. "I couldn't feel him any more than I could feel the furnace repairman. I want him to hold me on his lap and put his arms around me."

"Yes, that's childish," she said, tapping her cigarette out.

"If I can't persuade him to do it, I'll die. I'll lie down and die." It was as clear to me as an item on the grocery list.

"You will not die," she said firmly. "You will go to Paris with me and we will shop for clothes and visit the museums and we will find you a nice free man."

"With green eyes and rays around his eyes and long hands with flat-tipped fingers?"

"That I can't promise," she said. "But he'll be free."

"I won't go if it means missing an appointment."

She started to figure how we could leave late on a Friday and come back on a Sunday, but then she saw it was no use and decided to go for a longer time with the second cousin.

So I was left alone for two weeks, except for Uncle John and the children. He was gone most of the time, coming back at night for his ginger ale and his smoked salmon and a spot of conversation before the late news. He wouldn't let me fix real coffee in the morning; I think, being old and tired, he was afraid of the obligation. (The quid pro quid, my mother called it; nothing was free in her world, especially first thing in the morning.) The two girls spent most of the day in school and when the bus brought them home, I would have our tea picnic ready and we would take it out to the field behind the house. Late autumn by now and not many flowers left to pick, so we found milkweed pods and split them into the air. The little girls sat on my lap, either one at a time or both together, and when I kissed them, their hair smelled of eraser dust. I was in pain because the hours between my appointments were the longest hours of my life, and yet I never saw anything as beautiful as that field with the willows at the far end and the two little girls in their navy skirts and white blouses running after the milkweed parachutes.

By then I had discovered that my doctor had a wife and three children, and they all loved one another and managed well. More than that he would not tell me, and I was forced to believe him. After all, the owners of pale green eyes and flat-ended fingers tend to find the wives and get the children they can enjoy, the way a girl I met in one of my many schools knew exactly—but exactly—what to say to win a smile, and what flavor of milkshake would bring out the angel in her.

As my mother used to say, "Those that know what they want, get it." But she had feeling all over her body, not just lodged here and there in little pockets.

Meanwhile my doctor was trying to take the bits and pieces I gave him and string them together to make me a father. I had never known or even asked which one of the cousins was my father, and so I gave him all the pieces I remembered from the whole bunch of them. Ronny and his truck. He had thick thighs that rubbed together when he walked and made him roll like a seafaring man. He liked to hold me between the thighs and comb my hair. Edwin with his briefcase that reminded me of my doctor's (although Edwin's was more expensive) and which he once told me, held a surprise. The surprise, it turned out, was my cough medicine. Louis the railroad man who said he would take me with him on the train except that white girls brought bad luck; it was just like in the mines. The Air Force regular who yelped with joy and hugged me the day my mother said she would go to Honolulu.

My doctor wanted to know which one was my father and he proposed that I write my mother and ask. I wrote her because I did everything he even hinted at and I would have as soon slit my own throat. Word came back a week later; she thought I had known all along. My father had been a Kansas boy stationed at Fort Knox one summer when she was working at a diner called the Blue Boar. I remembered then that she had always kept a picture of a big-faced smiling boy on the mantelpiece, when there was one, or on the table by her bed. She said he had been killed in Korea.

My doctor did not try to do much with that scrap. Probably my father never even saw my mother's big stomach; if he had, he might have told her what to do about it, as a farm boy familiar with cows. So we had to start all over again with the scraps and pieces, trying to undo the way my memory simplified everything, trying to get behind the little pictures I wanted so desperately to keep: the shape of men's hands and the ways they had let me down.

We were still at work when Aunt Janey came back from Paris and she made me get on the scales that first evening. I told her the work we were doing was wearing me down; it was like ditch digging, or snaking out drains. She knew I was better, and she told me not to give up now with the end in sight. I wasn't sure what she meant, but I knew I had to keep on. There was some hope for me somewhere in all that. At my doctor's, the sweat would run down my face and I would have to pace the floor because there were months and even years of my life when all I could remember was the pattern a tree of heaven made when the sun shone through it on a linoleum floor. My doctor thought some of the scraps might have forced me into bed, but I only remember being tickled or chased with the hairbrush or locked in the car while they went into a road house. Nothing high or strange but only flat and cold. Something killed off my feeling, but it wasn't being raped by Ronny or Edwin or any other others. Mother had sense enough to find men who wanted only her.

I told my doctor I believed I had been an ugly, squalling baby who kept my mother up at night, screeching for more milk. That was the only thing Mother ever said about me, and she said it more to criticize herself. She hadn't had sense enough, she explained, to realize I was hungry and to give me more bottles. Instead she slapped me once or twice. That wasn't enough to kill off much feeling, although it is true that if I were asked to draw a picture of myself, I would draw a great mouth.

By then I was almost in despair about getting what I wanted from my doctor, even a kiss or a lap sit or holding his hand. I kept having faith in him, the kind he didn't want, the kind that keeps you from eating and wakes you up at night. That faith woke the saints with visions of martyrdom and woke me with visions of lying in his arms. I kept believing that nature and its urges would triumph over the brittle standards of his profession; I kept believing that his calm attention was the marker for a hidden passion. I also believed that if he would take me, I would begin, magically to feel. Or lacking that, light up like a torch: joy, like Aunt Janey with her pearls hanging straight down her back.

But he would not.

So for me it was a question of quitting—which of course I would not do, because at least during the sessions I saw him—or of going on with the work, keeping to the schedule, getting up in Greenwich in time to dress and catch the train. It was a question of opening my mind to the terrible thoughts that flashed through it like barracuda through muddy water. It was a question of making connections between one thing and another that did not come from the expression in his eyes— the looks I called waiting, eager, pleased—but from some deep, muddy layer of my own, where the old dreams had died and lay partially decayed.

The result was that I lost what ability I had. The children went back to eating peanut butter out of the jar although I had gotten Aunt Janey to lay in a supply of bread. The little skirts and tops we had bought at Bloomingdale's began to stink with sweat, and I stopped washing my hair. It did not seem possible to stand under the shower and come out feeling alive and new. It did not seem worthwhile even to try.

I didn't care anymore about getting better—that was a sailing planet—but I did care about the little fix of warmth which I got from sitting next to my doctor. I cared about his words, which were for me and not for all the other women, and after a while I began to care about the things he said that hurt me and seemed at first unacceptable. There were, in the end, no answers. Yet he seemed to see me, clearly, remotely, as I had never seen myself, and he watered me with acceptance as regularly as he watered the sprouted avocado on his windowsill. Is it after all a kind of love? By January, I was back inside my own bleached mind; I knew it the day I went out and bought myself a bunch of flowers.

Aunt Janey washed my hair for me and insisted on new clothes and a trip to Antigua; when I said I would go, she hugged me and kissed me and gave me a garnet ring. Uncle John told me I was looking like a million dollars, and the little girls, who had been scared off by my smell, began to bring their paper dolls again so that I could cut out the clothes. I was still, and always would be, one of the walking wounded; I was an internalized scab, and when I looked at myself in the mirror, I understood why people call naked need the ugliest thing in the world. I broke two appointments with my doctor and went to Antigua with Aunt Janey, and one night, I danced with an advertising man. I was no queen, but I was somebody, two legs, two arms, a body, and a head with a mouthful of choice words. I wouldn't sleep with him because I knew that I wouldn't feel a thing, but the next day we played some fine tennis.

When I came back to New York, the pyramids of Fifth Avenue were no longer shining. The gutters were running with filth and melted snow, and the doctors' names in the windows and on the plaques were only names, like lawyers' and dentists'. My doctor was on the telephone when I walked in, and I looked at his free ear and knew he would never be mine. Never. Never. And that I would live.

2

My Love Has Dirty Fingernails

John Updike

The man stood up when the woman entered the room, or, to be exact, was standing behind his desk when she opened the door. She closed the door behind her. The room was square and furnished in a strange cool manner, midway between a home (the pale-detailed Japanese prints on the wall, the thick carpet whose blue seemed a peculiarly intense shade of silence, the black slab sofa with its single prism-shaped pillow of Airfoam) and an office, which it was, though no instruments or books were on view. It would have been difficult to imagine the people who could appropriately inhabit this room, were they not already here. The man and woman both were impeccably groomed. The woman wore a gray linen suit, with white shoes and a white pocketbook, her silvery blond hair done up tightly in a French roll. She never wore a hat. Today she wore no gloves. The man wore a summer suit of a gray slightly lighter than the woman's, though perhaps it was merely that he stood nearer the light of the window. In this window, like the square muzzle of a dragon pinched beneath the sash, an air conditioner purred, a little fiercely. Venetian blinds dimmed the light, which, since this side of the building faced away from the sun, was already refracted. The man had a full head of half-gray hair, rather wavy, and scrupulously brushed, a touch vainly, so that a lock overhung his forehead, as if he were a youth. The woman had guessed he was about ten years older than she. In addition to the possibility of vanity, she read into this casually overhanging forelock a suggestion of fatigue—it was afternoon; he had already listened to so much—and an itch to apologize, to excuse herself, scratched her throat and made her limbs bristle with girlish nervousness. He waited to sit down until she had done so; and even such a small concession to her sex opened a window in the wall of impersonality between them. She peeked through and was struck by the fact that he seemed neither handsome nor ugly. She did not know what to make of it, or what she was ex-pected to make. His face, foreshortened downward, looked heavy and petulant. It lifted, and innocent expectation seemed to fill it. The cus-tomary flutter of panic seized her. Both bare hands squeezed the pock-etbook. The purring of the air conditioner threatened to drown her first words. She felt the lack in the room of the smell of a flower; in her own home the sills were crowded with potted plants.

"I saw him only once this week," she said at last. Out of polite habit she waited for a reply, then remembered that there was no polite-ness here, and forced herself to go on alone. "At a party. We spoke a lit-tle; I began the conversation. It seemed so unnatural to me that we shouldn't even speak. When I did go up to him, he seemed very pleased, and talked to me about things like cars and children. He asked me what I was doing these days, and I told him, 'Nothing.' He would have talked to me longer, but I walked away. I couldn't take it. It wasn't his voice so much, it was his smile; when we were . . . seeing each other, I used to think that there was a smile only I could bring out in him, a big grin whenever he saw me that lit up his whole face and showed all his crooked teeth. There it was, when I walked up to him, that same happy smile, as if in all these months . . . nothing had changed."

She looked at the catch on her purse and decided she had begun badly. The man's disapproval was as real to her as the sound of the air conditioner. It flowed toward her, enveloped her in gray coolness, and she wondered if it was wrong of her to feel it, wrong of her to desire his approval. She tried to lift her face as if she were not flirting. In another room she would have known herself to be considered a beautiful woman. Here beauty ceased to exist, and she was disarmed, realizing how much she depended on it for protection and concealment. She wondered if she should try to express this. "He sees through me," she said. "It's what made him so wonderful then, and what makes him so terrible now. He knows me. I can't hide behind my face when he smiles, and he seems to be forgiving me, forgiving me for not coming to him even though . . . I can't."

The man readjusted himself in the chair with a quickness that she took for a sign of impatience. She believed she had an honest gift for saying what he did not want to hear. She tried to say something that, in its frankness and confusion, would please him. "I'm suppressing," she said. "He did say one thing that if he hadn't been my lover he wouldn't have said. He looked down at my dress and asked me, in this shy voice, 'Did you put that on just to hurt me?' It was so un*fair*, it made me a little angry. I only have so many dresses, and I can't throw out all the ones that . . . that I wore when I was seeing him."

"Describe the dress."

When he did speak, the level of his interest often seemed to her disappointingly low. "Oh," she said, "an orangey-brown one, with stripes and a round neckline. A summer dress. He used to say I looked like a farm girl in it."

"Yes." He cut her short with a flipping gesture of his hand; his occasional rudeness startled her, since she could not imagine he had learned it from any book. She found herself, lately, afraid for him; he seemed too naive and blunt. She felt him in constant danger of doing something incorrect. Once she had a piano teacher who, in performing scales with her side by side on the bench, made a mistake. She had never forgotten it, and never learned the piano. But as always she inspected his responses conscientiously, for a clue. She had reverted, in their conversations, again and again to this rural fantasy, as if, being so plainly a fantasy, it necessarily contained an explanation of her misery. Perhaps he was, with this appearance of merely male impatience, trying to head her into acknowledgment that she was too eager to dive to the depths. His effort insofar as it was visible, seemed rather to direct her attention to what was not obvious about the obvious. He asked, "Have you ever worn the dress here?"

How strange of him! "To see you?" She tried to remember, saw herself parking the car, Thursday after Thursday, locking the door, feeding the meter, walking down the sunny city street of bakeries and tailor shops and dentists' signs, entering the dour vestibule of his building, and with its metal wall-sheathing stamped with fleurs-de-lis, seeing the shadow of her gloved hand reach to darken his bell. . . . "No. I don't think so."

"Do you have any thoughts as to why not?"

"There's nothing profound about it. It's a casual dress. It's young. It's not the identity a woman comes to the city in. I don't come in just to see you; I buy things, I visit people, sometimes I meet Harold afterward for a drink and we have dinner and go to a movie. Do you want me to talk about how I feel in the city?" She was suddenly full of feelings about herself in the city, graceful, urgent feelings of sunlight and release that she was sure explained a great deal about her.

He insisted, "Yet you wore this quite informal dress to a dinner party last weekend?"

"It was a party of our *friends*. It's summer in the suburbs. The dress is simple. It's not *shabby*.

"When you picked it to wear to this party where you knew he would see you, did you remember his special fondness for it?"

She wondered if he wasn't overdirecting her. She was sure he shouldn't. "I don't remember," she said, realizing, with a flash of impatience, that he would make too much of this. "You think I did."

He smiled his guarded, gentle smile and shrugged. "Tell me about clothes."

"Just anything? You want me to free-associate about clothes in general?"

"What comes to your mind."

The air conditioner flooded her silence with its constant zealous syllable. Time was pouring through her and she was wasting her session. "Well, he"—it was queer, how her mind, set free, flew like a magnet to this pronoun—"was quite funny about my clothes. He thought I overdressed and used to kid me about what an expensive wife I'd make. It wasn't true, really; I sew quite well, and make a lot of my things, while Nancy wears these quiet clothes from R.H. Stearns that are really quite expensive. I suppose you could say my clothes were a fetish with him; he'd bury his face in them after I'd taken them off, and in making love sometimes he'd bring them back, so they'd get all tangled up between us." She stared at him defiantly, rather than blush. He was immobile, smiling the lightest of listening smiles, his brushed hair silvered by the window light. "Once I remember, when we were both in the city together, I took him shopping with me, thinking he'd like it, but he didn't. The salesgirls didn't know quite who he was, a brother or a husband or what, and he acted just like a man—you know, restless and embarrassed. In a way, I liked his reacting that way, because one of my fears about him, when I was thinking of him as somebody I owned, was that he might be effeminate. Not on the surface so much as down deep. I mean, he had this passive streak. He had a way of making me come to him without actually asking." She felt she was journeying in the listening mind opposite her and had come to a narrow place; she tried to retreat. What had she begun with? Clothes. "He was quite lazy about his own clothes. Do you want to hear about *his* clothes, or just *my* clothes? Next thing, I'll be talking about the children's clothes." She permitted herself to giggle.

He didn't respond, and to punish him she went ahead with the topic that she knew annoyed him. "He was sloppy. Even dressed up, the collars of his shirts looked unbuttoned, and he wore things until they fell apart. I remember, toward the end, after we had tried to break it off and I hadn't seen him for several weeks, he came to the house to see how I was for a minute, and I ran my hand under his shirt and my fingers went through a hole in his T-shirt. It just killed me, I had to have him, and we went upstairs. I can't describe it very well, but something about the idea of this man, who had just as much money as the rest of us, with this big hole in his undershirt, it made me weak. I suppose there was something mothering about it, but it felt the opposite, as if his dressing so carelessly made him strong, strong in a way that I wasn't. I've always felt I had to pay great attention to my appearance. I suppose it's insecurity. And then in lovemaking, I'd sometimes notice—is this too terrible, shall I stop?—I'd notice that his fingernails were dirty."

"Did you like that?"

"I don't know. It was just something I'd notice."

"Did you like the idea of being caressed by dirty hands?"

"They were *his* hands."

She had sat bolt upright, and his silence, having the quality of a man's pain, hurt her. She tried to make it up to him. "You mean, did I like being—what's the word, I've suppressed it—debased? But isn't that a sort of womanly thing that everybody has, a little? Do you think I have it too much?"

The man reshifted his weight in the chair and his hands moved in the air diagrammatically; a restrained agitation possessed his presence like a soft gust passing over a silver pond. "I think there are several things working here," he said. "On the one hand you have this aggressiveness toward the man—you go up to him at parties, you drag him on shopping expeditions that make him uncomfortable, you go to bed with him, you've just suggested, on your initiative rather than his."

She sat shocked. It hadn't been like that. Had it?

The man went on, running one hand through his hair so that the youthful lock, recoiling, fell farther over his forehead. "Even now, when the affair is supposedly buried, you continue to court him by wearing a dress that had a special meaning for him."

"I've explained about the dress."

"Then there is this dimension, which we keep touching on, of his crooked teeth, of his being effeminate, feeble in tatters; of your being in comparison healthy and masterful. In the midst of an embrace you discover a hole in his undershirt. It confirms your suspicion that he is disintegrating, that you are destroying him. So that, by way of *repair* in a sense, you take him to bed."

"But he was *fine* in bed."

"At the same time you have these notions of 'womanliness.' You feel guilty at being the dynamic party; hence your rather doctrinaire slavishness, your need to observe that his fingernails are dirty. Also in this there is something of earth, of your feelings about dirt, earth, the country versus the city, the natural versus the unnatural. The city, the artificial, represents life to you; earth is death. This man, this unbuttoned, unwashed man who comes to you in the country and is out of his element shopping with you in the city, is of the earth. By conquering him, by entangling him in your clothes, you subdue your own death; more exactly, you pass through it, and become a farm girl, an earth-girl, who has survived dying. These are some of my impressions. It is along these lines, I think, that we need more work."

She felt sorry for him. There it was, he had made his little Thursday effort, and it was very pretty and clever, and used most of the strands, but it didn't hold her; she escaped. Shyly she glanced at the air conditioner and asked, "Could that be turned lower? I can hardly hear you."

He seemed surprised, rose awkwardly, and turned it off. She giggled again. "I'm just being masterful." He returned to his chair and glanced at his watch. Street noises—a bus shifting gears, a woman in heels walking rapidly—entered the room through the new silence at the window, and diluted its unreal air. "Can't earth," she asked, "mean life as much as death?"

He shrugged, displeased with himself. "In this sort of language, opposites can mean the same thing."

"If that's what I saw in him, what did he see in me?"

"I feel you fishing for a compliment."

"I'm not, I'm *not* fishing. I don't want compliments from you, I want the truth. I need help. I'm ridiculously unhappy, and I want to know why, and I don't feel you're telling me. I feel we're at cross-purposes."

"Can you elaborate on this?"

"Do you really want me to?"

He had become totally still his chair, rigid—she brushed away the impression—as if with fright.

"Well"—she returned her eyes to the brass catch of her purse, where there was a mute focus that gave her leverage to lift herself—

"when I came to you, I'd got the idea from somewhere that by this time something would have happened between us, that I, in some sort of way, perfectly controlled and safe, would have . . . fallen in love with you." She looked up for help, and saw none. She went on, in a voice that, since the silencing of the air conditioner, seemed harsh and blatant to her. "I don't feel that's happened. What's worse—I might as well say it, it's a waste of Harold's money if I keep anything back—I feel the opposite has happened. I keep getting the feeling that you've fallen in love with *me*." Now she hurried. "So I feel tender toward you, and want to protect you, and pretend not to reject you, and it gets in the way of everything. You put me into the position where a woman can't be honest, or weak, or herself. You make me be strategic, and ashamed of what I feel toward Paul, because it bothers you. There. That's the first time today either of us has dared mention his name. You're jealous. I pity you. At least, in a minute or two—I saw you look at your watch—I can go out into the street, and go buy a cheesecake or something at the bakery, and get into the car and drive through the traffic over the bridge; at least I loved somebody who loved me, no matter how silly you make the reasons for it seem. But you—I can't picture you ever getting out of this room or getting drunk, or making love, or needing a bath, or anything. I'm sorry." She had expected, after this outburst, that she would have to cry, but she found herself staring wide-eyed at the man, whose own eyes—it must have been the watery light from the window—looked strained.

He shifted lazily in the chair and spread his hands on the glass top of his desk. "One of the arresting things about you," he said, "is your insistence on protecting men."

"But I wasn't *like* that with *him*. I mean, I knew I was giving him something he needed, but I did feel protected. I felt like nothing when I was with him, like the—center of a circle."

"Yes." He looked at his watch, and his nostrils dilated with the beginnings of a sigh. "Well." He stood and made worried eyebrows. A little off guard, she stood a fraction of a second later. "Next Thursday?" he asked.

"I'm sure you're right," she said, turning at the door to smile; it was a big countryish smile, regretful at the edges. The white of it matched, he noticed with an interior decorator's eye, her hair, her suit, and the white of her pocketbook and her shoes. "I *am* neurotic."

She closed the door. The sigh that he had begun while she was in the room seemed to have been suspended until she had left. He was winning, it was happening; but he was weary. Alone, in a soundless psychic motion like the hemispherical protest of a bubble, he subsided into the tranquil surface of the furniture.

3

August

Judith Rossner

Dr. Lulu Shinefeld opened the door to her waiting room and said hello to the girl who was scheduled for a consultation. The girl, whose name was Dawn Henley, nodded coolly.

"Would you like to come into the office?" Dr. Shinefeld asked.

Dawn Henley stood. She was tall, even taller than Dr. Shinefeld, and quite beautiful, with dark brown, almond-shaped eyes, a startling, almost olive complexion, and honey blond hair cropped to shoulder length along a straight and severe line. It was July. Dawn wore white cotton pants, a white T-shirt, and sandals, but she might have had on a ball gown for the grace with which she preceded the doctor into the office, sank into the chair facing the doctor's, and inspected her surroundings.

The waiting room was nondescript, but the furnishings in the office were attractive, if spare. The walls were white; the couch, brown; the two chairs were covered in a splendid cherry red wool. A kilim rug with predominating colors of brown, teal blue, and red covered a portion of the wood floor. Aside from the rug, the artwork in the room consisted of a semi-abstract painting, in which shapes suggestive of hu-

mans seemed to be posing for what could have been an old-fashioned
family photograph, and a small sculpture resting on the table at the
foot of the couch that was reminiscent of one of Henry Moore's pri-
mordial shapes, an egg embraced by some delicious, unidentifiable object. On the doctor's desk stood a slender blue vase that held three
purple irises. Through an open door near the windows, it was possible
to see another, smaller room with a thick brown carpet. Visible in this
room were a bookcase containing various primary toys, a large doll-
house and a couple of yellow plastic beanbag chairs.

Dawn's eyes came to rest on the doctor.

No adolescent unease here. No suspicious glances or shifting in
the seat. The girl's expression was neutral.

"So," Dr. Shinefeld said with a smile, "let me think of what you've
told me. I know that you're eighteen years old, that your home is in
Vermont but you've been going to boarding school in Westchester,
and that you're entering Barnard College in September."

Dawn nodded.

From her canvas shoulder bag, which she'd placed on the floor,
she extracted a small cassette recorder, which she placed on her lap.

"Do you want to tape our conversation?" the doctor asked.

"It seems like a good idea, don't you think?"

"Why's that?"

"Well," Dawn said coolly, "then one can be clear later about what
was said . . . and anyway, if something should happen to one of us . . ."

"Yes?"

"Well, then, everything wouldn't be lost."

When the doctor didn't reply, Dawn turned on the recorder.

"What is it?" she asked in response to a flicker of expression on the
doctor's face. "You don't mind this, do you?"

"I don't know," Dr. Shinefeld said. "I'm certainly not accustomed
to it."

"Well," Dawn said calmly, "if it really bothers you, I'll turn it off.
But see if you can't get used to it."

Dr. Shinefeld was disconcerted. While many patients attempted
to control sessions from the moment they entered the room, the re-

corder added a new dimension. Anyway, control in that sense might not even be what Dawn was after.

"All right," the doctor said. "Well, then . . . perhaps you'd like to tell me why you're here."

"I have no reason," Dawn said without animosity. "That is, while I don't mind being here, I wouldn't have chosen to see another analyst if Vera . . . my mother . . . hadn't asked me to."

"Why do you think she asked?"

"It's actually quite clear why she asked. I had an automobile accident in which I nearly killed myself. That had happened to me once before. I mean, it was a bicycle that time. I was thirteen, but I went into a car in such a way that I really had to take full responsibility for what happened. My neck was broken, and one arm and leg. As soon as I could move around again Vera sent me to an analyst. Dr. Leif Seaver. I know you must know him, since he gave me your name. As I told you on the phone."

For the first time a hint of feeling showed through Dawn's extraordinary facade.

The doctor nodded.

"I saw Dr. Seaver for four years," Dawn said. "Until the beginning of June, when I also graduated from high school. He was . . . extremely helpful to me."

This last had an almost rote quality. The doctor waited.

"Then, a couple of weeks ago . . . I had another accident. I was driving the car this time. I was in Vermont, near Marbury. Where Vera is. Where I grew up. Anyway, I fell asleep at the wheel. It would've been the end except the boy who was with me grabbed the wheel, so we went into some bushes instead of a tree." She smiled. "He thinks he's in love with me. You'd think if someone nearly killed you, you'd never want to see her again . . ." Her tone had grown abstract. "A few people *think* they're in love with me."

"Both times you said *think* they're in love," Dr. Shinefeld pointed out. "Is that different from *being* in love?"

"No," Dawn said. "Not really. I guess. I mean, if you think you're in love, then you're in love. Anyway, who can say you're not?"

"Have you ever thought you were in love?" the doctor asked.

"Oh yes," the girl said without hesitation. "I was in love with Dr. Seaver."

"What was the difference in the way you felt about Dr. Seaver and the way these boys feel about you?"

"That's easy," Dawn said. "They're in love with the way I look. I have the kind of looks you're supposed to have in this country. Blond hair, long legs, all that junk. None of it has anything to do with *me*, with who I *am*. If I showed any of them what's inside my head they wouldn't want to have anything to do with me. Dr. Seaver—Dr. Seaver didn't care what I looked like. He barely looked at me when I talked to him. I remember that right from the start. Nothing I said ever surprised him because he didn't even *see* the Outside Me. And I didn't care what he looked like. I knew some people would think he was ugly, sort of knotty looking, and with that funny little hunch to his back so at first when you see him you think he's just sort of scrunched over on purpose. I didn't care about any of that."

There were tears in Dawn's eyes. She didn't bother to wipe them.

"Why do you think you had the accident?"

"Because he left me."

"You finished the analysis?"

"He thought I was finished. I was sort of okay. He didn't understand I could only do all the things I was doing because I had him."

"Did you tell him that?"

"I tried to, but I must've not said it right because I can't believe he would have done it if I had. I was in a trance a lot of the time. Maybe that sounds crazy, but it's true. From the day he started to talk about ending, I was in a sort of trance . . . The same thing happened after the first accident. For a few minutes I was so numb, I didn't even know anything was broken. They said I was in shock. Well, this was the same sort of thing, where I didn't exactly feel what was happening, only it lasted for months and months instead of for minutes."

Dr. Shinefeld was silent. She was already deciding to find the time to see Dawn if the girl wished. Her history even before Seaver was fascinating, from what Vera Henley had told her on the phone. Seaver himself was an interesting man; his reputation, most particularly as a diagnostician, was superb.

"Why do you think you had the first accident?" the doctor asked.

"Because my parents got divorced. I imagine you know about my parents."

"My conversation with your mother wasn't very long. I'd prefer that you tell me whatever you think I should know."

Dawn smiled. "Well, there's a lot, and it's pretty crazy. At least most people would think so. I grew up taking it for granted."

Vera Henley wasn't Dawn's natural mother, but her aunt. Her mother had committed suicide when Dawn was six months old and her father had drowned the following year when his sailboat capsized in a storm off the northern Massachusetts coast. Dawn had no memory of either of her two unfortunate parents. When she spoke of her parents she meant Vera and—well, Vera was actually a lifelong lesbian who had lived, since before Dawn's birth, in what was essentially a marriage with another woman, Tony (Antonia) Lubovitz. Vera and Tony were who Dawn meant when she talked about her parents, and it was their "divorce" that had been the precipitating factor in her first accident.

This was where life became confusing, because while Dawn had just referred to Vera as her mother, she had actually called Vera Daddy during their first years together. Tony was the feminine of the two women, wore makeup, jewelry and skirts, although it was also Tony who left each morning to work as chairman of the mathematics department in a Vermont high school three towns away. Vera didn't work and had never made any pretense at being other than who she was. Although (Dawn smiled shyly) this was New England they were talking about, and her aunt obviously hadn't gone around town proclaiming that she wasn't just a rather athletic old maid. Not that anyone would ask. One of the reasons Dawn loved Marbury was that really, whoever you were was all right as long as you followed the rules for public behavior. Upon coming to live with Vera, Tony had taken the name Henley, and the two women were assumed to be relatives. Dawn herself had never thought about the matter of their sexuality until she was in analysis with Dr. Seaver. Like a lot of other kids she knew, she'd rather taken it for granted that her parents, who shared a bedroom, had no sex life to speak of.

None of the children had ever questioned Dawn about her household, although at the beginning of school there had been nomenclature problems with the teacher. In the previous year, Vera, anticipating some such problems, had tried to train Dawn away from Daddy and toward Aunt Vera. What had remained with Dawn was that she was to call Daddy Aunt Vera when she was talking to other people. In first grade (Vera hadn't sent her to the optional kindergarten) Dawn had begun to read, learning from the primer that Daddy went to work and Mommy stayed home and took care of the children. The book was quite clear on this. Daddy might leave for a variety of places—bank, office, store, etc., but Mommy's work was done at home. It would not have occurred to Dawn's friends to support her claim that the opposite was true in her home because that would have involved arguing with the teacher, but as it turned out their support would have been useless. Dawn explained to the teacher that it was her daddy who stayed home and her mommy, Tony, who went to work. The teacher's task became clear. The child had suffered some elementary confusion and would have to be straightened out with drills. The drills were not done in a punitive manner, and by the time Parent's Day arrived, Dawn was calling Vera Mommy and Tony Daddy—in school. By the time she had acquired the conceptual vocabulary that would have enabled her to explain to her teacher that both her mommy and daddy were women, the class was absorbed in Vasco da Gama and the multiplication tables and no explanations were called for.

Dawn seldom invited other children to her home. The few who lived nearby remained her friends throughout eighth grade, but she rarely sought them out. After a full day at school she wanted only to return to the bosom of her family. The long New England winters that horrified so many people represented love and warmth to Dawn Henley.

The walk from school was about half a mile, and Dawn would make it with the other children unless they dawdled, in which case she would break away from them in her eagerness. Sometimes she and Tony, who would be driving from three towns away, reached home at the same time and raced, giggling, for the door. Dawn still recalled with pleasure arriving once before Tony's car was in sight, hiding behind a bush, then dashing to the front door just in time to beat Tony up the steps.

Afternoons were occupied with homework, sewing, baking. Tony gave Dawn piano lessons. In the evening they read, knitted and played cards, chess, and checkers. The television was in a little room of its own. No one watched it very much.

Dawn supposed the most important thing to say about Vera and Tony was that for all she'd learned of their problems, she adored them both and felt they'd given her much more than average parents gave their children, in time alone. In her analysis with Dr. Seaver, she had come to see that there were periods in her life when, like any child, she'd wished for one of her parents to "disappear" so that she could have the other to herself. That was, as Dr. Shinefeld must already know, why she'd had the accident when they separated; it was guilt over getting that old wish, for she still had them both but they didn't have each other anymore. With Dr. Seaver she'd understood that loving them both so much hadn't balanced out her jealous, hostile feelings but had tended to make them more intense, harder to bear.

They had been an extraordinary couple. What one lacked, the other possessed in abundance. Vera was your prototypical New England WASP patriarch—large and strong, with features almost identical to those of her brother and their father. What she lacked in warmth (the cuddling of little Dawn was left to Tony) Vera made up in strength, bravery and a broad range of talents. Aside from being a superb skier and horsewoman, she knew more about animals than most veterinarians, and she could fix, or build, for that matter, almost anything in the house. She was an excellent cook and a nearly miraculous gardener.

Tony was dark, pretty and plump. Her grandparents had emigrated from Russia, but she'd grown up in a Brooklyn ghetto that mirrored to a considerable extent the conditions of the old country. It was only when, over her parents' objections, Tony accepted a scholarship at a college outside New York that she finally lost the accent foreign to her English. Tony's clothing was marvelous, exotic even by New York standards in those days just before the sixties. Embroidered Roumanian blouses with drawstring necks and full sleeves. Full skirts of trimmed velvet in the winter, cotton when it grew warmer. Huge earrings and pendants set with turquoise and other stones; delicately wrought rings and bangle bracelets that rattled and clanked on her wrists as she gestured. Her shiny black hair, which came down to her waist, she braided, knotted, and swept up with an array of golden barrettes, tortoiseshell combs, and special hairpins with enameled heads that Dawn had never seen anywhere else, even in Europe, where she'd been sent on a graduation trip just this past June. Tony didn't like to cook, although she could do it if the occasion arose. She was a dressmaker and made most of her own clothes and Dawn's; Vera's attire consisted of men's shirts with jeans in the summer and slacks in the winter. All of them had sweaters knitted by Tony. Her mathematical abilities went beyond mere proficiency, and Tony had told Dawn a few years earlier, after the divorce, that she had sacrificed a fellowship to leave Boston because she'd promised Vera (they had met in Vermont the previous summer and fallen in love; Vera was twenty-one years her senior) that when she finished college she would get a job that would enable them to live together. It was inconceivable to Vera that they could be comfortable under the scrutiny of a university town.

Dawn smiled.

So Tony had given up a more interesting career for love. Just like a lot of other women.

The doctor returned Dawn's smile. They had gone past the full hour she allowed for consultations. The buzzer had sounded and a patient was waiting.

"How old were you when the women actually separated?" she asked Dawn.

"Fourteen," Dawn said. "It was my first year in boarding school."

Dr. Shinefeld hesitated. "I'm reluctant to end now because I have other questions I'd like to ask. But there's someone waiting. Would you like to come back later this week?"

Dawn shrugged. "Sure. If you want me to." She switched off the tape recorder and returned it to her satchel.

For a moment Dr. Shinefeld considered asking her to come without it the next time. Then she decided the moment wasn't opportune. The truth was that she would have liked to ask Dawn for a copy of the transcript.

As it turned out, the request was unnecessary. Dawn began the next session, at two o'clock on Friday afternoon, by offering the doctor a copy. "In case you should find it useful."

"Thank you," the doctor said. "That was very thoughtful."

Dawn had an overnight bag with her as well as her satchel. She was going from the doctor's office to Penn Station, where she would board an Amtrak Metroliner to Boston. She was going to visit Tony and her husband.

"A man?" Dr. Shinefeld asked.

Dawn nodded.

"Was he the reason for the divorce?"

Well, Dawn thought, yes and no. Vera claimed that Tony had left her for Leonard Silverstein, but Tony said it wasn't true and that *Vera* had really left *her*, in spirit if not in body, years before. Where once Vera had met her eagerly at the door, Tony claimed, now her "housewife" barely seemed to notice her arrival. Where once Vera had listened with reasonable interest and unwavering support to Tony's stories of her day among students and faculty, now Vera seemed uninterested in Tony's life and increasingly turned in on herself. Restless. Vera had started talking about going to Europe at the very beginning of that school year—just as it became impossible for Tony to do so.

And Vera was drinking. Liquor had been a problem in the Henley family, and for a long time Vera had refused anything stronger than beer. But gradually she'd begun to drink whiskey, and by the time Dawn was preparing to leave for boarding school Vera was drinking quite heavily.

Dawn herself, by the way, had never really accepted the boarding school decision, although she didn't argue because she took it to mean that Vera and Tony didn't want her with them anymore. She'd been

over all that a good deal with Dr. Seaver . . . Strangely enough, she'd
felt the same way about her graduation trip to Europe. That she was
being sent away. Some sort of collusion between Vera and Dr. Seaver.
So she wouldn't notice that her sessions had ended.

For a while Dawn had believed that Vera's decision to send her to
boarding school had nothing to do with her—Dawn's—developing
sexuality, with the fact that she was growing breasts, had begun to
masturbate, and so on. Lately she'd become uncertain again. It was the
punishment aspect. While she was with Dr. Seaver she'd lost the sense
of having been sent away as a punishment, but now it was back . . . as
though she'd never really believed his version. It was only that his ideas
had been more powerful than hers in her own mind while she continued to see him.

Dawn was quiet. For the first time in the hour she seemed uncertain of what she wanted to say next. Perhaps she was waiting for a
response.

"How did you find boarding school?" the doctor asked.

"Oh, it was all right. At first I was miserable, but then I got used to
it. Like the others. But when I went home for . . . I couldn't wait to go
home for Christmas, and when I got there, it was awful. Tense and unpleasant. Different from ever before. I should've known something was
up. Then, when I went home again at Easter . . . Tony was gone."
Dawn paused where perhaps her voice had once broken as she remembered. "The whole house was quiet. Tony was the one who made noise,
who talked, who played music. I still . . . when I remember . . ." She
shuddered. "The only important thing that happened to me at Sidley
was the art classes. I learned to make lithographs. Art class was the
only reason I wanted to go back after the accident. What I didn't want
. . . Vera rented our house and moved down to Westchester to be near
me at Sidley. That hurt me almost as much as the divorce. It was the
only house I'd ever lived in."

"The only house?"

"Mmmm." Dawn seemed barely to notice the question. "But once
Vera made up her mind . . . She took an apartment near school, and I
had home study until I could walk again. I still lost half a year. I

couldn't concentrate on my work and I was having terrible dreams. It was worse after the casts came off. And even worse when I was finished with the crutches and the neck brace. They were so awful, they gave me some kind of focus. Once they were off I became aimless. I didn't want to do anything. That was when Vera started bringing me to New York to see Dr. Seaver. Later she went back to Marbury and I came in on the railroad."

"Do you think Vera chose a male analyst on purpose?"

"I think she got a few names from the guidance people at school and talked to them all. He sounded the smartest to her. Actually, I think they were all men. She just took it for granted that I should . . . He *was* terribly smart, as you probably know. I should say, he *is*."

Dawn laughed, a little embarrassed.

"Anyway, it was that year that I started making prints. Someday I'll show you . . ." She laughed again, embarrassed again. "I forgot. This is a consultation. If you think I should continue, you're going to send me to someone else."

"Not necessarily," Dr. Shinefeld said. "I know we began on the phone on that basis, and I'll be happy to refer you elsewhere if you want me to. But if you'd rather work with me, as long as you have a certain flexibility in your hours, I can see you when I return from vacation. After Labor Day."

Dawn smiled sadly. "Labor Day. When all the analysts come back to New York and give birth to their patients."

But her manner had altered radically in that moment after Dr. Shinefeld's offer to continue seeing her. She had become almost childlike, and there were tears in her eyes.

A few moments passed.

"When are you leaving?" she asked after a moment.

"The end of July. Two weeks," the doctor told her.

"Will I see you until then?"

"It can be arranged."

Dawn nodded.

"You remind me of Tony . . . except that you're bigger. And not so fluffy."

Dr. Shinefeld smiled, and they paused together in that restrained mutual good feeling that was so essential to satisfactory treatment while raising such difficult issues for those involved in it.

"What I was going to tell you before," Dawn said after a while, "was that I did a series of lithographs, in my last year at Sidley. My last year with Dr. Seaver. I was making the best one to give to Dr. Seaver on my birthday." She smiled. "I wanted to give it to him on *his* birthday, but he wouldn't tell me when it was." Amusement didn't keep her from falling into sadness, now. "Anyway, he didn't want me to give him anything on my birthday *or* his. He'd already begun talking about the end of treatment. That was why I made that series in the first place . . . That whole year was a nightmare. Not exactly a nightmare; I just didn't feel anything most of the time. I don't understand what happened to me. He thought I was all right, but I wasn't."

"Have you considered seeing Dr. Seaver again—rather than another analyst? Or at least talking to him before you see someone else?"

"Oh, yes," Dawn said. "Of course. It was the first thing I thought of when I woke up. I was knocked unconscious and I bruised my head on the steering wheel, but I wasn't hurt, just shaken up. There was something else that happened, actually. Before the accident. But I don't know if I can talk about that yet. It may have to wait until September."

The doctor nodded.

"When I came back from Europe three weeks ago and I knew . . . something was wrong . . . I called and said I needed to talk to him. He said it was too soon and I guess I pleaded with him but . . . Anyway, I called again last week, after the accident, and when I told him he said he'd see me . . . Vera didn't think it was a good idea. I think she knew that I loved him too much. She thought I should see a woman and I liked that idea, in a way, but first I needed him to know what had happened to me . . . I'd brought the print. Not to give him. I just needed him to see the message. The words were very important. I showed it to him, thinking of all the times we'd argued about it, and I kept waiting for the light to go on. He was finally going to understand this terribly important thing and explain it to me, and then I'd feel better. Instead

he said, *Nice work, Dawn. You're doing some really nice work. Keep it up.*
He didn't even remember the arguments! I felt as though I had no importance to him at all, and never had. I was less than a patient. I wasn't even a person!"

"Was that when you decided to see a woman?" the doctor asked after a moment.

"You'd think so," Dawn said with a wry smile, "but not quite. I was still . . . You have to understand something. Vera was my father until I met Dr. Seaver. Then he became my father. He didn't stop being my father just because he wouldn't see me anymore."

Dr. Shinefeld glanced at the clock.

"Is it time for me to go?"

"We have another minute or two."

"I don't remember what I was saying."

"We were talking about when you decided to see a woman."

"Oh. Yes. Well, I told him I was thinking of doing that. And he said I had to make the decision myself. He could refer me to some good women analysts if that was what I wanted. Or, he said, perhaps it would be just as well to work it out with him. I was about to thank him. Or to cry. And then he added . . ." She paused, trying to get over the words. ". . . that since he knew me already, if I came to him the work would go much faster." Her voice trembled, and her lips twisted so she wouldn't cry.

"And that was the end for you."

"Of course. I could see that the same thing would happen all over again."

Dawn stood and stretched, then put the cassette player in the satchel.

The doctor picked up her appointment book and they arranged times for the following Tuesday and Friday. At Dawn's request, regular appointments were scheduled for the additional week in July. Dawn was staying in Westchester with a friend from Sidley. She would spend August with Vera in Vermont.

The hour was at an end. They walked together to the door, which the doctor opened.

"Dawn?" the doctor asked on impulse as the girl passed over the threshold, "what were the words at the bottom of the lithograph?"

"Dylan Thomas," Dawn said. "*After the first death there is no other.*"

At the outset of her third visit, Dawn offered Dr. Shinefeld a transcript of the second, then seated herself, as she had previously, in the chair facing the doctor's. Dr. Shinefeld hadn't spoken again with Vera Henley. The matter of Dawn's continued visits had been arranged between the girl and her aunt.

"In your analysis with Dr. Seaver," Dr. Shinefeld asked as Dawn reached for the tape recorder, "did you lie on the couch?"

"Yes, sure," Dawn said, momentarily distracted from the machine.

"Would you like to do that now?"

Dawn glanced at the couch uneasily.

"I feel as though I hardly know you," she said, then laughed. "I know that's not the only reason, because Dr. Seaver asked me the second time and I did it right away. I guess I feel as though . . . if I lie down, I'll get attached to you. And I don't want to get attached when you're just going away for the longest time."

"Tell me about the longest time."

"No," Dawn said after a moment. "I don't want to talk about that now. I'll do it when I come back."

She had been looking toward the couch, avoiding the doctor's eyes, which she now met. "You know that I'm not a lesbian, don't you?"

"Actually," the doctor said, "I don't know anything about your sexual preferences."

"Well then, we're even," Dawn said. "Because neither do I." She giggled. "I mean, I don't actually have any at the moment. Yes, that's what I mean. I prefer at the moment not to have any sexual preferences."

Dr. Shinefeld smiled. There was a lengthy silence.

"I had an abortion when I came back from Europe."

"Oh?"

"I never slept with my boyfriend until April. My *then* boyfriend. Alan Gartner was his name. Not that it matters. I never even worried

about getting pregnant, that was the weird part. Before that, I didn't
sleep with him just because I didn't feel like it. I never slept with anyone
before him, either. He thought I was on the pill but I wasn't on anything. I'm chattering like this because the whole business made me
crazy and still does."

"When did you have the abortion?"

Her eyes filled with tears. "Three weeks ago. A week before the
accident."

"Don't you think you might feel a little less crazy if you talked
about it?"

Dawn studied the doctor's face. "You know what I'm thinking?
That I still haven't turned on the tape recorder and you don't want me
to turn it on."

The doctor was silent.

"I wish I could understand why you don't like it."

"It might be more useful to understand why you *do* like it."

"Are you going to make me put it away?" Terribly anxious and
childlike.

"No, but I'd like to keep talking about it."

Dawn laughed. "Okay. Go ahead. Talk." There was a nervous,
slightly hostile edge the doctor hadn't heard in her voice before. Dawn
switched on the recorder.

"You could die," Dawn said after a moment. "Or get sick. Or go
away on vacation and never come back. Or maybe get sick of seeing
me. The first year or two I was seeing Dr. Seaver he never went away
for more than a week at a time. Then suddenly . . . everything
changed. August! Easter! Christmas! I don't know what else. The first
time he went away for August I really thought I was going to die before
he got back. I went up to be with Vera, but then I couldn't stand being
there. She was so unhappy. But that wasn't it. Dr. Seaver ruined me for
people like Vera. It wasn't just that she didn't understand anything
that had happened to me. She doesn't *want* to understand things like
that. She's all closed off. It was worse than being alone. . . . It wasn't
just because Tony was gone. Tony was right, Vera was the same only
more so. Before Dr. Seaver, I thought that was just the way men were
. . . Anyway, Vera couldn't even stand it when I played the radio. I

think music reminded her of Tony, so she just decided to shut that out of her life, too."

Dawn shuddered. "I left after four days. I felt guilty but . . . I told Vera I'd taken a couple of incompletes and I had to work in the school library. I was really going to Boston. To Tony. But I didn't want to tell her that. She'd have felt worse. Not that she ever let me know how she felt. . . . Anything I know about what happened between them I know from Tony. I figured I'd be able to talk to Tony about how I felt, but even she didn't really understand. Not the way Dr. Seaver did. Sometimes I didn't even have to explain things to him . . . He spoiled me for other people, you see . . ." A long pause, and then, her voice breaking: "That was the worst of it. He spoiled me for everyone else in the world and then said I had to get along without him."

Dawn had picked Alan Gartner because he was older than the boys from school and looked a little like Dr. Seaver. He had black hair and he was very tall and skinny, with tortoiseshell glasses. And he was reasonably intelligent. Boys, as Dr. Shinefeld had probably noticed, were terribly *boring*, and Alan was somewhere in between Dr. Seaver and the boys of the world. He had a doctorate in literature but was acting with an improvisational group at a café in the Village. During the last year she'd tried to explain to Dr. Seaver about the difference between going out with a Young Man and a Man. Dr. Seaver had told her a lovely story, as a matter of fact, about his daughter. (She hadn't known until then that he had a daughter and she'd been horribly jealous; she had a dream in which his real daughter died and he adopted her to take the real daughter's place.) Anyway, when Dr. Seaver's daughter was in nursery school, she'd asked one day who she could marry who wasn't already taken. He had explained that by the time she was ready to marry, there would be many boys who were ready too, and he'd mentioned two or three from her nursery school whose names he knew.

"Oh, no!" the little girl had protested vehemently, "I don't want a boy! I want a man!"

Dawn had understood very well the point of that lovely anecdote. But she was quite old enough to understand that people grew up and changed. Boys, on the other hand, didn't change fast enough.

There might have been a time when it made sense for girls to wait for them. But in this world, why would you wait for someone to grow up when the chances were he'd leave you for someone else when he did? Of her three best friends at school, the parents of two had been divorced during the last three years because the man left for a younger woman. The third—that was Bevvy Gartner, actually, Alan's younger sister—her parents' marriage had been what you might call open at one end from the beginning. Bevvy's father had always done pretty much what he wanted without having to pay for two households. Probably he'd leave, too, once Mrs. Gartner got old and pathetic enough so she really needed him. Alan still lived at home when he wasn't traveling or living with some girl who had her own apartment. It seemed to Dawn that more and more kids weren't exactly leaving home, and maybe it was because they didn't have real homes to leave.

The office was quiet. The sounds from Central Park West were muffled by the air conditioner's hum. Briefly Dr. Shinefeld had a sensation familiar to her from other moments of intense absorption in patients' lives—that the office wasn't in a large building but was floating around freely somewhere in space with the two of them inside. It was at times like this that she most missed cigarettes. For a while after she'd stopped smoking, she had kept a saucer of rock candy on her little table and sucked on a piece when she felt in danger of being sucked too thoroughly into a patient's psyche. Occasionally, though, forgetting herself, she'd crunched on the candy, and once a patient had leaped off the couch, at once frightened and angry, demanding to know what she was doing. It was all very well to analyze the patient's fear of being devoured, but of course one wasn't allowed to be the active catalyst for such associations. Pencils weren't bad to chew, but pens were better for taking notes, which she found herself doing now. She had the wry thought that she was going to miss the transcriptions once she'd persuaded Dawn to leave the recorder at home.

"So," Dr. Shinefeld said, "if I die while I'm on vacation, you will have a piece of me in the transcriptions."

"You're not sick, are you?" Dawn asked, clutching the arms of the chair.

"Not that I know of."

"I don't suppose you'll tell me how old you are."

"No."

"You're not that old. You look about Tony's age and she's . . . forty. Much younger than Vera . . . Vera's healthy as anything . . . You can't even promise me"—but she seemed almost to be trying to find a way to bear to do what the doctor wanted her to do—"that you won't get sick."

"No," the doctor said. "Although I'm also a rather healthy person."

Dawn didn't speak or move.

"There is one promise I can make to you," Dr. Shinefeld said after a while. "That I won't ask you to leave here until you're ready. In other words, you can be the one to decide when you're finished."

"Finished." Dawn's eyes filled with tears and her voice quivered. "That has such a funny sound. People don't get finished. They're not jobs. Or books." But she relaxed in the chair.

"It's the analytic work that gets more or less finished."

"But what if I finish and I leave and then a week or a month or a day later something terrible happens to me? Something I have to talk to you about?"

"Well, in that case you'd call me up and come back and we'd talk about it."

"Why wouldn't Dr. Seaver let me? What was such a big deal?" Dawn cried. "He said I was going out into the world, that I had to really be finished. Then, when I found out I was pregnant and came home to have the abortion, I called him up and . . . He was still . . . In my mind . . . I don't really want to tell you this . . . If Alan's sister wasn't my best friend, if I hadn't needed her help, I never would've told him. In my mind Alan had nothing to do with the baby. I mean, he was barely in my mind at all. It was Dr. Seaver who was there. I kept thinking, now he'd *have* to understand. I really don't know what I thought he'd understand. Except . . . This is awful. I don't know if I can say it . . . I delayed. The abortion. This is very hard for me to talk about. In my house . . . I didn't know about menstruation until I got to boarding school. Which was before I got my period, fortunately. Even Tony didn't like to talk about those things. Anyway, I didn't want to have the abortion right away. The truth was, I'd been feeling sort of nice while I was in Europe, and I'd thought to myself, Dr. Seaver was right, it was really hard for a while but I'm getting over him. It never occurred to me that . . . It was as though Dr. Seaver had left a big hole right in my center and somehow it had gotten filled up. I didn't know—at least I didn't know I knew—it was only that I had his . . . the baby . . . It was his baby in my mind, not stupid Alan Gartner's, and that was why I was all right." Dawn was crying. "I didn't want to give it up. At least not until I was ready. I didn't want to lose the baby just because I wasn't supposed to have it in the first place!"

Now she was crying in earnest, the only sign that she wasn't oblivious to the world outside herself, Dr. Seaver, and her aborted baby being that at some point she clicked off the recorder.

"No sense recording seventeen hours of me crying my eyes out," she said when the tears had finally abated. "I hardly ever cried until I got to Dr. Seaver's. Vera and Tony used to tell me how when I was little, if I fell and hurt myself, I never cried."

"Why do you think that was?"

The question surprised Dawn. "I don't know. They thought I was brave. I might've talked about that a little with Dr. Seaver. I remember telling him I just didn't mind if I hurt myself a little. What's the big deal if you fall off a bike and scrape your knees." There was no bravado in her voice. She was puzzled at how easily girls cried. "Crying is worse than most of the reasons people cry."

"Why?" Dr. Shinefeld asked.

Dawn turned on the tape recorder. "It can make you choke, for one thing. Especially if you're lying down. Dr. Seaver said I choked to cut off the bad feelings . . . as though I were afraid of getting them out of my system . . . but I don't think that was right. It's more that I can't help it. I choke if I cry a lot."

"Why did you turn on the tape recorder just now?"

"Because I could tell I was going to cry."

"But after you cried, you didn't turn it right back on."

"What were we talking about?"

"You said that crying was more unpleasant than most of the reasons people cried, and I asked you why."

"And that's when I turned it back on." Dawn laughed. "Well, I can believe it. Just thinking about the question . . . It makes me uncomfortable. It makes me wish I had a friend here."

"I guess that's why I don't like the tape recorder," Dr. Shinefeld said.

"Cassette player," Dawn corrected.

"I feel as though it's your friend and it comes between us."

Dawn laughed but then quickly became serious. "It's not that I don't like you. I don't even *want* anything to be between us. I want to feel better. If I didn't like you . . . Dr. Seaver gave me three names. I picked yours first. But if I didn't like you I would have tried the others."

"Was my name the first on the list?"

"No, the last. But he said there was no order of preference."

"Why do you think you picked mine?"

"I don't know. I liked the sound of it. It sounds like water gurgling. Lululululu." Dawn giggled. "And Shinefeld. A shining field. It sounds so wonderful. I thought you must be beautiful. I had to see what you looked like. You are beautiful, you know. I can't tell if you're one of those people who can tell she's beautiful, because it's not in the conventional way. Not where I come from, anyway." A long pause. "I remember when I was looking at the piece of paper he gave me." Slow and thoughtful, now—Dawn was trying to remember the details. "The other two were on the East Side, so they were less convenient to school. On the other hand, with the Number Five bus, that's no big deal. And they were both in Dr. Seaver's neighborhood, so I'd maybe see—Oh, my God! I know what it was. It was your initials. They're the same as Dr. Seaver's! I remember how they struck me when I was looking at the piece of paper, because he makes his capital letters five times as big as the small ones." Dawn turned off the cassette player. "You see," she said, "I really couldn't bear not to see him anymore. But I couldn't see him, either. It was too frightening. So I picked someone safer. A woman with his initials. I was hoping from the beginning you'd say I could keep seeing you. I didn't know what I would do if I had to try the others."

Lulu Shinefeld turned the corner of Seventieth Street onto Central Park West. It was ten to two and she'd just finished lunch. The day was crisp and sunny, and she was minding that she had to go back indoors. As she walked toward her building, Lulu became simultaneously aware of the doorman grinning at her and the girl with her face hidden behind a camera—of course it was Dawn—snapping pictures of her.

Dr. Shinefeld smiled grimly and proceeded into the building. Dawn ran after her.

"Are you angry with me?"

"Let's talk upstairs," the doctor said.

Dawn's mood in the office was contrite and extremely anxious. She was willing to apologize, to analyze, to do anything, in fact, that might appease the doctor short of offering to give up the film, which the doctor did not suggest she do.

"I'm going to make a series of prints," Dawn said. "Of you, sort of. While you're on vacation. But I need a photo to look at. Even if the print doesn't end up having anything to do with the photo . . . I didn't bring the cassette . . . I didn't even transcribe the last tape . . . You're angry with me."

"I was a little annoyed," the doctor said. "Not because you wanted to take a picture of me. I'm willing to talk about that. It's more about your not asking. And with the fact that we weren't in the office."

"But I couldn't do it indoors. I don't have the right equipment. My flash is in Vermont. And if we'd talked about it, you would only have wanted to analyze me out of it. And if you had, then I wouldn't have the photo!"

It was an unproductive session. Dawn was defensive and angry with the doctor for being angry when it was clear to her that the need to take the picture had been an absolute if she was going to give up the cassette recorder. It had seemed pointless to the doctor to deny an irritation that had been palpable to all concerned, but there were moments when she wished she had tried. Dawn spoke less freely than she had during previous visits, as though she were all too aware of the power of free association and was afraid that in the unraveling of the meaning of her act she would find herself giving up the film without really wanting to. On the other hand, it was surely self-defeating to deal with a girl who thought that crying was more painful than pain by pretending not to be annoyed at her acting out. In any event, Dr. Shinefeld was certain that the bond already established between them was strong enough to withstand this early storm and that Dawn would return as scheduled.

At their next meeting it turned out that Dawn had believed Dr. Shinefeld might refuse to see her again. Her own anger during the previous session had been a conscious preparation for being cast out in disgrace. She and the doctor discussed on a rather elementary level the various degrees of anger, ending with that rage so powerful as to make one abandon another. Dawn said that neither Tony nor Vera had ever really gotten angry with her. Vera was very firm and had no problem giving orders or forbidding various activities. But there was little visible change of emotion if Dawn did occasionally, very occasionally, disobey. Tony was light and gay, tending to respond to both good and bad with little jokes and laughs and wasn't Dawn a wonderful girl? Dawn had never experienced the feeling she knew was common among her friends, that a benevolent parent had turned into a raging beast. Bevvy Gartner said that when she was younger she'd called her mother the Hulk, after the comic strip man who, when he was angry or in pain, metamorphosed into a great green monster.

"Did I turn into a great green monster?" Dr. Shinefeld asked.

"Well, no," Dawn said, "but I thought that if you let even that much show, there must be much worse somewhere. Analysts don't usually show anything at all."

"You generally see us in the office. Away from our offices we're just like other people."

"I wonder," Dawn said. "I wonder if that's possible."

The snapshots of Dr. Shinefeld had been overexposed and came back from the drugstore with the doctor's face blurred. Dawn was in a panic.

"Are you thinking it's just as well?" she asked, sitting on the edge of the couch. She didn't want to lie down. "Maybe I did it on purpose.

Set the meter for the wrong exposure. I had to fail because I knew you wouldn't want me to do it. But I needed them. I still do. I'd be afraid to go through that whole routine again and make you angry again, but that doesn't mean I need them less than I did before."

"Tell me."

"I *have* told you." The girl was wild-eyed. "I'm sick of saying the same thing over and over again."

"Why?"

"It's like a kind of whining. I don't like to whine. I get sick of myself. And it doesn't *help*."

"Sometimes," the doctor pointed out, "as you repeat yourself, new elements are added."

"I can't."

"Can't what?"

"I don't know. I can't go past a certain point. It's as though there's a wall. Once or twice I tried to find out what was behind the wall, but . . . It's solid . . . Oh, my God, every time I think of the photos I want to run out of here screaming."

"Talk about that."

"I can't. I'm at the wall."

"I know that it might be difficult for you to lie down just now," the doctor said, "but if you could do it anyway, and say what comes to mind, something useful might come up."

Dawn lay down, but her body didn't relax at all.

"My mind is a blank. I mean it. I'm not saying it just to . . . Even the normal things aren't there . . . Usually when my mind wanders, I make up stories about the rug. About the people who wove it, say, or the dyes they used for the colors. Now when I say *dyes,* I think about *dying* without the *e* and then I'm right back at the wall."

"Is the wall about dying?"

"No. It's just a wall that keeps me from getting anyplace."

"A place you want to go?"

"No. There's no place I want to go."

"So the wall is sort of protective. It serves as—"

"Don't you see?" Dawn burst out. "We're sitting here talking about walls and all I can think of is that I don't have a picture of you!"

"Then maybe you'd better talk about what you'd planned to do with it."

"First I was going to make copies and put them in different places so I couldn't lose all of them. Then I was going to enlarge the best ones, maybe one up to poster size if the image held. Then I was — What's the sense of all this? I don't have it! I don't have anything of you!"

"Don't you have me, in a sense, even when I'm not here?"

"No! I don't! Certainly if I can't be sure you'll ever be here again! I was going to do a lithograph . . . not just one, another whole set . . . something with the rug. You and the rug." She rambled on about various projects she'd considered in connection with the photographs, but when she stopped talking, she was as rigid and upset as she'd been all along.

"Tell me," the doctor said after a long pause, "about *After the first death there is no other*."

There was a moment when the tension in the room was as powerful as an electric charge. Then Dawn's body went through a remarkable series of motions, beginning with a violent shaking of her head, back and forth on the pillow, the movement then extending to her hands, her torso, and finally her legs, all thrashing around in a series of violent, rigid motions that resembled nothing so much as the convulsions of severe colic. Finally she relaxed, quite thoroughly. Her body took on the air of a beatified saint. Several minutes passed.

"Uh . . ." Dawn said, ". . . What were we talking about?"

The doctor debated whether to answer the question. Finally she said that they'd been talking about the lithographs Dawn had done.

"Oh, yes," Dawn said easily. "You mean, the *First Death* series? What about it?"

When the doctor failed to respond, Dawn sat up and turned around. "If you don't answer I can't tell for sure that you're there."

The doctor smiled. "I'm here."

"I *know*. But when I can't see you I don't always feel as though you are . . . You know, when I was a little kid I could never stand to play hide-and-seek. I couldn't stand to be It. And if I was hiding I was too worried about how It would feel, so I'd let her see me or make some noise so she'd find me . . . Something happened to me just now but I don't know what it was."

The doctor waited.

"Did you know something happened to me?"

"Yes."

"Good. Because I don't know what it was, but it was pretty weird. And it would be weirder if you thought everything was normal."

"Mmmm. I can understand that."

"But what happened?"

"Maybe you can tell me what you remember."

"I don't remember anything," Dawn said. "That's the funny part. I was in a *white space*. Once or twice with Dr. Seaver I was in a white space, but it wasn't complete because the words *white space* were printed in it. This was total." She shuddered. "What's that about?" But she was fairly calm. "I'm not scared now," she said after a moment. "But if I don't know what happened I'm going to be scared later."

"In fact," the doctor said. "I think that's what happened. You got scared."

"Of what?"

"Well . . . of something I said. It's possible that I was too abrupt with you."

"Too abrupt? How? What did you say?"

"I referred to the caption of the lithographs."

"*After the first death?*" Dawn was incredulous. "But how could that bother me? I've been trying to find out . . . For most of the last year I was with Dr. Seaver I was trying to get him to . . . I *need* someone to tell me what it's about."

"Sometimes," the doctor said, "a patient wants to know what something's about in order to gain mastery over it with words . . . without actually living through the painful feelings that meaning involves . . . She may be terribly eager to learn some *why* but also quite frightened to know. It makes sense if you realize that virtually every aspect of life that's been buried has been buried for what the self considered to be an excellent reason. In other words, she's trying very hard to find out something she already knows but wishes she didn't."

Dawn giggled. "I like that."

The doctor was silent.

"But if I didn't want to know, why did I keep trying to find out?"

"Did you?"

"You know that I kept asking."

"Asking what?"

"To bring him the lithograph."

"Why?"

"I needed him to see it. Part of it was showing off, but also I needed him to see what was written on the bottom."

"Why?"

"So he could tell me what it meant."

"Did you ever just say the words to him?"

A long silence. "I'm trying to remember. I must have. I'm not sure. I think . . . The truth is, sometimes I tried and I couldn't. I got all choked up. That's why I wanted to show it to him. I couldn't say the words."

"Why do you think that was?"

"I don't know," Dawn said. "I remember I was very excited about the whole series. I went around high all the time. Kids at school asked me if I was *on* something, but I was just naturally high. Of *course* I talked to him about it. I talked to him about everything. He was a part of everything I did . . . First I was doing this series of prints, then . . . I remember I felt mischievous when I said it was going to be for my birthday . . . Anyway, by then nothing I said got to him. You probably think I knew *that*, too. But I don't think so. I think it was that I was desperate by that time. Nothing else worked. I don't know what I mean by that. Yes I do. The part of what you're saying that's true . . . It wasn't that I was afraid to know. It was more that I was afraid to unlock the last secret. I mean, I didn't *feel* afraid. I hardly felt anything. But it kept passing through my mind that if I knew what that line meant, I'd know all I had to know, and then we'd *really* be finished." She began to cry.

At their final session she had explained to Dr. Seaver that there was something terribly important they hadn't figured out, a great secret of her life. He had said that many patients had that feeling at the end of an analysis, that if they'd only unlocked one more door, everything would be all right. In reality, life was difficult, and there was seldom a time when everything was all right. There were many secrets and many doors, and one didn't stop opening them because one ceased having analytic sessions. She had learned a new system of thought, Dr. Seaver had told her, and she would continue to think that way, and to learn.

And Dawn had lain quiet on the couch, thinking, *Don't argue. It will feel worse if you argue. Don't cry. You'll get hysterical. You'll choke.*

Anyway, he'd been wrong. Because she hadn't been able to think that way at all since he'd left her. That way of thinking was about him and therefore too painful. She hadn't been vaguely analytic about anything she'd said or done since the first week of June. She still found herself reluctant to think analytically unless she was right here in the office.

Dawn had forgotten the catalyst for her brief "fit" of amnesia. Indeed, she appeared to have forgotten the fit itself, although she was eager to discuss the issue of whether she'd been unfair to be angry with Dr. Seaver. She was looking for a way to return to her former state of untempered adoration.

The issue was a complex one for Dr. Shinefeld. A misstep might send the girl back to Seaver, apologetic at having "blamed" him for not understanding what he hadn't been told and eager to resume the transference romance. Not only was the doctor reluctant to lose her patient, but she suspected that Seaver had been somewhat blinder than the circumstances dictated. She was coming around to the belief that like a number of other analysts, he had a deep resistance to exploring that period of life before the relatively comfortable and specific Oedipal attachment began. This was the most difficult and frightening period of life for the obvious reason that words did not exist that were adequate to describe the over-powering feelings engendered in an infant who did not yet have words to describe and sort out those feelings. If that were the case, then, Dr. Shinefeld thought, she might be more helpful to Dawn than Dr. Seaver could be at this stage.

Dawn spent considerable time evaluating the merits of female as opposed to male psychiatrists and eventually held fast in her determination to return to regular treatment with Dr. Shinefeld. The matter of the first death seemed to have vanished and would not reappear until August had come and gone and the bond between Dawn and the doctor had been reestablished.

4

Ordinary People

Judith Guest

The building is shabby, and inside, the lobby is hot and dark. He glances at his watch; too dark in here to make out the numbers. The crisp and sunny day he has left outside has nearly blinded him. A directory on the far wall; he goes to it; scans the list of names. Eleven in all; seven with M.D. after them. The top name on the list is the one he is looking for: T. C. BERGER M.D. 202. Would any of these guys be of use in an emergency? All specialists—podiatrists, optometrists, psychiatrists—but what if an accident were to happen in front of the building? Or a mugging? It looks like a great neighborhood for muggings.

Glancing at his watch again, he finds his eyes have adjusted to the dim light. Four o'clock. Exactly. *Well then get on it no backing out now* an idea he has toyed with all week not going just not showing up won't work. He is to meet his father at his office at five-fifteen. "Don't be late. I've got a meeting tonight. I'd like to get out of there as close to five as I can." Translated: "Don't let the guy upset you, show up when you're supposed to, it only takes ten minutes to walk from Sherman and Tenth to the Plaza, I have clocked it." No. Not fair. Not necessary to take everything so personally. He probably does have a meeting tonight. Everything's all right, everything's fine, keep it that way. On an even keel, as his grandfather would say.

Stuck between the directory and the wall is a small white business card:

> I love you.
> Is this okay?
> Jesus C.

The edges of it are furred; curved slightly inward. As if it has been there a long time. He shakes his head, making for the staircase; forces a growl from the back of his throat. He is being strangled.

In the narrow hallway on the second floor, a single light bulb burns, helpless against the invading gloom. High, old-fashioned doors, with windows of bubbled glass in them; all dark on both sides of the hall, and looking as if they haven't been used for years. Any people in this building? Is this an emergency? Even a podiatrist would do. Panic begins to settle in around him.

At the end of the hall is a doorway with light behind it. He goes to it. The letters, stuck to the opaque glass with adhesive backing, spell out T C BERGER M D. They slant upward, crooked rectangles, like a kid would print them on unlined paper. He pushes experimentally at the door, but it works on a heavy spring mechanism. Even when he turns the knob, it doesn't give. He pushes harder this time, and it opens. He steps inside. The door closes sharply behind him.

He is in an entry, empty of people, longer than it is deep, with a chair in it, a floor lamp, a small table strewn with magazines, a green metal wastebasket. Barely furnished, the room still seems cluttered. Opposite him is a doorway; an overturned chair blocks it. From inside the other room mysterious, shuffling sounds are issuing. A scene of total disorder confronts him as he moves toward the door. Books, magazines, loose piles of paper are everywhere; empty plastic cups, pieces of clothing, a cardboard box, THE BAKERY lettered in script on its lid, all tossed together in the middle of the floor. Several ashtrays are dumped, upside down, on the rug. A gooseneck lamp lies, like a dead snake, beside them. In the midst of it, a man stands, bent over, his back to the doorway. As Conrad approaches, he turns. About him there is the look of a crafty monkey; dark skin, dark crinkly hair sprouting in tufts about his face, a body that hunches forward, an elongated question mark.

"Wait," he says, "don't tell me. Jarrett."

The eyes, a compelling and vivid blue, beam into whatever they touch. They touch Conrad's face now, and the effect is that of being in an intense blue spotlight.

He snaps his fingers. "Yeah. You look like somebody Crawford would send me. Somebody who's a match for my daring wit and inquiring mind."

Conrad, cool and polite, asks, "Am I seeing you? Or are you seeing me?"

He laughs, delighted. "That oughta be easy. This my office, or yours? No. No good. Lotsa guys in this business make house calls now. Let's see your appointment book." He steps over to his desk, rummaging fiercely for a minute; he comes up with a gray stenographer's notebook. "Here. Tuesday, four o'clock. Conrad Jarrett. Ah. I knew it." He grins, then.

Conrad is not easily charmed. Or fooled. Eccentricity. A favorite put-on of psychiatrists. He does not trust them. Too many oddballs floating around the hospital. Only Crawford had behaved as if he knew what he was doing. He bends to pick up the overturned chair.

"Bring that over here," Berger directs him. "Sit down."

He continues to prowl around the room, lifting books, setting them aside, retrieving papers from the floor, stacking up empty plastic cups. On further examination, he resembles a compact, slightly undersize gorilla. Conrad cannot take his eyes off him.

"I think I was ripped off this afternoon," he says. "Or else the cleaning lady did one hell of a job on me. Place didn't look this bad when I left. Somebody was after drugs, I guess. What a neighborhood. Nothing but placebos here. Use 'em myself for quick energy sometimes. Just sugar." He smiles, arms raised, palms turned up in an attitude of perplexity.

"You were robbed?"

"Looks like."

"You going to call somebody?"

"Who? You mean cops?" He shrugs. "What's missing? Maybe nothing. Maybe they even left something, who knows?" He moves to the small sink, half-hidden in the corner behind a huge pile of books. "You want some coffee? Listen, do me a favor, look on the desk there, see if you can find a data sheet—you know, name, age, date of birth, et cetera—fill it out for me, will you? Gotta keep records, the state says. Rules." He sighs. "Now what am I supposed to do with those poor bastards lying on the floor, I ask you?" He indicates the overturned filing cabinet, its contents scattered. "Did you say yes or no?"

"What?"

"Coffee. Yes or no? Sit down, sit down."

"No. Thanks." Obediently he goes to the desk; searches through the papers on top of it until he comes up with a blank information card. He begins to fill it out. Berger empties the other chair of debris and drags it over to the desk.

"How long since you left the hospital?"

"A month and a half."

"Feeling depressed?"

"No."

"Onstage?"

"Pardon?"

"People nervous? Treat you like you're a dangerous man?"

He shrugs. "Yeah, a little, I guess."

"And are you?"

"I don't know."

Berger grins, then. "You look sensible enough to me. At least, you looked sensibly disgusted when you walked in here. God, it is disgusting, isn't it? The second time this year. What do you think I oughta do about it?"

He is used to this technique; he looks for psychological design in the question. No. Too farfetched. Nobody would go to this much trouble just to set up a test for him.

He says, "I guess I'd just clean it up and forget about it."

"Yeah, you're right. Christ, what a gigantic pain in the tail though, huh?" The man sits back, fingers curved around his coffee cup, watching as Conrad finishes filling out the card. "Sure you don't want any coffee? I've got clean cups around here somewhere."

Conrad shakes his head; hands him the card.

He reads it quickly. "Good, strong print. Neat. Like an engineer. So. What're you doing here? You look like a healthy kid to me."

"What I'm doing here," Conrad says, "is that I had to come."

Berger nods. "Uh huh. Rules again. Authority reigns." He tosses the card onto the desk. "So, suppose you didn't have to come. What would you be here for?"

"I wouldn't."

He finds himself firmly enveloped in the piercing blue gaze; shifts uncomfortably in the chair.

"How long were you there?"

"Eight months."

"What did you do? O.D.? Make too much noise in the library?"

"No." Looks steadily at the bookcase in front of him; floor-to-ceiling, jammed with books. "I tried to off myself."

Berger picks up the card again; studies it as he blows on his coffee. "What with? Pills? Gillette Super-Blue?"

He sees the way to handle this guy. Keep it light. A joker. Slide out from under without damage. "It was a Platinum-Plus," he says.

The eyes are fixed upon him thoughtfully. They hold him still. "So how does it feel to be home? Everybody glad to see you?"

"Yes. Sure."

"Your friends, everything okay with them?"

"Fine."

"It says here, no sisters, no brothers. Right?"

"Right," he says. *Don't squirm don't panic release is inevitable. Soon soon.*

Berger leans back in the chair, hands behind his head. It is hard to figure his age. He could be twenty-five. He could be forty. "So, what'd you want to work on?" he asks.

"Pardon?"

"Well, you're here. It's your money, so to speak. What d'you want to change?"

He thinks, then, of his father; of their struggle to keep between them a screen of calm and order. "I'd like to be more in control, I guess. So people can quit worrying about me."

"So, who's worrying about you?"

"My father, mostly. This is his idea."

"How about your mother? Isn't she worried?"

"No."

"How come?"

"She's—I don't know, she's not a worrier."

"No? What does she do, then?"

"Do?"

"Yeah, what's her general policy toward you? You get along with her all right?"

"Yeah, fine." He is abruptly uncomfortable. An endless grilling process, like it was in the hospital. He forgot how it tightened him up; how much he used to hate it.

"You've got a funny look on your face," Berger says. "What're you thinking?"

"I'm thinking," he says, "if you're a friend of Crawford's you're probably okay, but I don't like this already. Look, what do you know about me? Have you talked to Crawford?"

"No." The blue high-beams have switched to low. The smile is benign. "He told me your name, that's all. Told me to look for you."

"Okay, I'll tell you some things." He turns his head slightly, taking in the narrow window at the left of the bookcase. Sunlight streams in from the slot, cutting a bright path across the carpeting. "I had a brother. He's dead. It was an accident on the lake. We were sailing. He drowned."

"When?"

"Summer before last."

Staring now at the bookcase, he tries to make out the titles of the books from where he is sitting. He cannot. They are too far away.

"I suppose you and Crawford talked about it," Berger says.

"Every day."

"And you don't like to talk about it."

He shrugs. "It doesn't change anything."

A pigeon, dull-gray, lights on the cement window sill. It pecks inquiringly at the window for a moment; then flies off.

"Okay," Berger says. "Anything else?"

"No," he says. "Yeah. About friends. I don't have any. I got sort of out of touch before I left."

"Oh?"

He does not respond to this technique; the comment in the form of a question. He had cured Crawford of it by telling him it was impossible to concentrate on what a person was saying if you were listening for his voice to go up at the end of the sentence.

"Well, okay," Berger says. "I'd better tell you. I'm not big on control. I prefer things fluid. In motion. But it's your money."

"So to speak."

"So to speak, yeah." Berger laughs, reaching for his notebook. "How's Tuesdays and Fridays?"

"Twice a week?"

He shrugs. "Control is a tough nut."

"I've got swim practice every night."

"Hmm. That's a problem. So, how do we solve it?"

A long, uncomfortable silence. He is tired and irritated. And again, there are no choices; it only looks as if there are.

"I guess I skip practice and come here twice a week," he says.

"Okeydoke."

It is over, and Berger walks him to the door. "The schedule," he says, "is based on patient ratings. A scale of one to ten. The higher I rate, the fewer times you gotta come. Example: You rate me ten, you only have to see me once a week."

Conrad laughs. "That's crazy."

"Hey, I'm the doctor." Berger grins at him. "You're the patient."

The worst, the first session has been gotten through. And the guy is not bad; at least he is loose. The exchange about the razor blades reminded him of something good about the hospital; nobody hid anything there. People kidded you about all kinds of stuff and it was all right; it even helped to stay the flood of shame and guilt. Remembering that day at lunch when Stan Carmichael rose from his chair pointing his finger in stern accusation: "Profane and unholy boy! Sinner against God and Man, father and mother—" Robbie prompted him "—and the Holy Ghost, Stan—" and he ranted on "—and the Holy Ghost! Fall on your knees! Repent of evil! Ask forgiveness for your profane and evil ways, Conrad Keith Jarrett!" and he had nodded, eating on, while Robbie leaned across the table, and asked, "Stan, may I have your gingerbread? Just if you're not going to eat it, buddy." And Stan broke off his ravings to snarl petulantly, "Goddamn it, Rob, you're a leech, you scrounge off my plate at every meal, it's disgusting!"

So, how do you stay open, when nobody mentions anything, when everybody is careful *not* to mention it? *Ah, shit, Jarrett, what do you want? Want people to say, "Gee, we're glad you didn't die?"* Poor taste, poor taste.

He is suddenly aware of the other people on the street, hurrying by, intent upon their business. See? No one's accusing. They don't even seem repelled. As a matter of fact, they don't even notice. So. No need to be affected by them, either, right? Still, as they pass him, he carefully averts his gaze.

5

Emergency

Helmuth Kaiser

SEVEN DIALOGUES REFLECTING THE ESSENCE OF PSYCHOTHERAPY IN AN EXTREME ADVENTURE

Prologue

Just as the normal function of an organ or an organism is frequently illuminated by pathologic events, so the views of a therapist on the essential nature of his daily work may become unusually lucid when they are applied to an extreme and unusual case which is theoretically possible but has never occurred in real life.

The following seven dialogues sketch such an unusual case. The views of the therapist in the story are my views. They are not easy to present or to transmit, not because they imply a complicated theory, but because they are simple where one expects the elaborate. When they are expressed in abstract terms, as a textbook would do, the reader is likely to miss their meaning, as if he had to decipher a melody from the grooves of a gramophone disk.

The sequence of scenes contains, in condensation, interaction between the therapist and his patient. However, I do not intend to prove, but only to show.

Scene 1

Dr. Terwin's office. Dr. Terwin is in the process of clearing his desk, as he usually does before leaving for the day. He picks up a letter and gets caught up in reading it through.

Secretary: Dr. Terwin—Dr. Terwin!

Dr. Terwin [*his eyes still on the letter*]: Yes, Linda?

Secretary: You didn't forget that you still have to see a patient?

Dr. Terwin: A patient?

Secretary: You know—the lady who phoned this afternoon, Mrs. Estella Porfiri.

Dr. Terwin [*hardly remembering*]: Oh yes, something urgent, didn't you say?

Secretary: Right, Doctor, she made it sound very urgent indeed!

Dr. Terwin [*good-naturedly*]: You never know; it might be a real emergency.

Secretary: Anyway, she seemed dead set on seeing you today, no matter what. But I can tell you now: When she complains about lack of will power, general apathy, and no interest in life—don't believe a word of it!

Dr. Terwin: Who knows?

Secretary: I know! May I leave? Or—

Dr. Terwin: By all means! Enjoy yourself!

Secretary: Thank you. Good-bye, Dr. Terwin!

Dr. Terwin [*after another look at the letter*]: O.K. [*He opens the door to the waiting room.*] Mrs. Porfiri, I assume?

Mrs. Porfiri [*entering*]: How do you do, Dr. Terwin!

Dr. Terwin: How do you do! Will you sit down here, Mrs. Porfiri?

[*Mrs. Porfiri sits down and looks attentively at Dr. Terwin, who takes a chair facing her. She seems surprised by his appearance.*]

Mrs. Porfiri: You look so different from what I had expected!

Dr. Terwin [*with a little smile*]: Maybe you came to the wrong person. I am *Simon F.* Terwin.

Mrs. Porfiri: No, no! Dr. Simon F. Terwin. There is no other Dr. Terwin in the whole city. You know Dr. Redstone, do you?

Dr. Terwin: Dr. Oliver Redstone? He was one of my teachers.

Mrs. Porfiri: I know! [*She lapses into a thoughtful silence.*]

Dr. Terwin: I understood you were in a kind of emergency?

Mrs. Porfiri: Because I insisted on seeing you as soon as possible? I have been in fear for a long time—especially in the last four months. And I did not know what to do. And then, suddenly, I learned that you were in the city—that you have been in this very city for something like a quarter of a year. [*With a faint smile*] So I felt I should not lose any more time!

Dr. Terwin: I am not sure that I understand you fully. Do you mean to say that Dr. Redstone referred you to me?

Mrs. Porfiri: He did, but I should rather say he confirmed my opinion. I'll explain in a minute! [*Tensely*] May I ask you a question first?

[*Dr. Terwin looks somewhat astonished and waits.*]

Mrs. Porfiri: It is very important to me. All depends—

Dr. Terwin: Of course! What do you want to know?

Mrs. Porfiri: About half a year ago I read an article of yours—I forget the title—was it "Talking to People" in the *Clinical Psychologist*?

Dr. Terwin: That's right.

Mrs. Porfiri [*quickly*]: There you said something like, "In order to treat a person, nothing more is required than that the therapist meets this person regularly for a sufficient time in his office. There are no rules for the patient. He need not talk about any specific topics or talk at all." I want to know whether you mean this literally. [*She looks at Dr. Terwin in great suspense.*]

Dr. Terwin [*smiling*]: The answer is yes.

Mrs. Porfiri [*repeating his word*]: Yes. Good—that's very important. [*She seems to rest from the effort of settling this question and to ponder about the next step.*] You—you don't think that it matters where the doctor sees the patient?

Dr. Terwin: I don't know what you have in mind. I would not want to see a patient in—let's say, a restaurant.

Mrs. Porfiri: Of course, of course! That's not what I meant. There is really no point in trying—

Dr. Terwin: Trying what?

Mrs. Porfiri [*impatiently*]: Oh, my God, to trap you! Can't you see? To get you to commit yourself by answering my general questions, so that you cannot back out when I beg your help in my special case! But it won't work! If you are a coward, you will back out anyway!

Dr. Terwin: That might be. But I can neither back out nor accede to your request as long as I am completely in the dark as to what it is you are asking for.

Mrs. Porfiri [*proudly*]: I am not going to ask for a favor. I'll tell you what my fears are and you will either help or refuse to do so! You know who I am?

Dr. Terwin: I understood, Mrs. Estella Porfiri!

Mrs. Porfiri [*waving her hand impatiently*]: I mean, do you know my husband?

Dr. Terwin: You expect me to know him? Don't forget that it's been only three months since I moved to this city!

Mrs. Porfiri: Good, very good! I thought you might have heard the name: Dr. Emilio Porfiri, psychiatrist.

Dr. Terwin: I am sorry. The name sounds only vaguely familiar to me. I would not have known that he is a psychiatrist and lives in this city, if you had not said so.

Mrs. Porfiri: He is not very well known. He is 36, in private prac-tice, and he hasn't published anything—oh, in the last five or six years. We have been married almost eight years. It may sound strange to you when I say that it has only been during the last two or, perhaps, three years that I have come to understand how unhappy Emilio really is. Or maybe it is not my better understanding—it might also be that in the beginning of our marriage he was not so unhappy or disturbed as he became later. I know that during the last four months a change for the worse has taken place.

Dr. Terwin: You would say that your husband is severely depressed?

Mrs. Porfiri: Oh, God yes! Severely depressed! I don't mean that he goes around groaning and moaning; but there is no sparkle in his eye any more. He doesn't complain—or only very rarely. Seeing him from afar you wouldn't notice much. He is well controlled, has always been. He goes to his office, sees his patients, goes to meetings, and even gives speeches occasionally. But it is as if he were far away in his mind, only going through the motions of life.

Dr. Terwin: And you say all this has become more pronounced in the last—I think, four months you said?

Mrs. Porfiri: Yes—as far as I can tell; it began gradually, yet—

Dr. Terwin: Yet?

Mrs. Porfiri: I wanted to say that in the last four months he has become very restless, which he had not been before at all. You know, he used to design furniture; he was quite good at it. When we needed something he did the design. He liked to work it out carefully, and it always took him a long time to do it exactly the way he wanted to. Yet he always finished what he had started. Now he seems unable to stick with anything which is not absolutely necessary.

Dr. Terwin: When you say that there was a deterioration in the last four months, are you only making an estimate of the time, or can you think of an event which occurred four months ago?

Mrs. Porfiri: The latter, Dr. Terwin. There was an event which caused Emilio great concern and distress. And I don't doubt that it contributed in some way to the deterioration. Only, as you will see, it cannot be the clue to everything!

Dr. Terwin: You seem hesitant to describe this event.

Mrs. Porfiri [*thoughtfully*]: I *am* hesitant. It's silly, I know! I feel that this incident will bias you against Emilio, but, as you will see, there was really nothing he could have done to prevent it. It was simply hard luck. This is what happened: Emilio had a patient, a Mr. Dorand, whom he had seen for approximately two years. An addict! Four months ago, the patient, who had improved and seemed decidedly on the way up, had to interrupt treatment for two weeks. Some family problem. When he came back, a few days later than anticipated, he

called my husband, as we learned from the answering service which
had picked up the call. We got the message late on a Sunday afternoon.
My husband called the patient's number several times, but there was
no answer. He tried again in the evening; again no answer. The same
happened Monday morning. But as soon as Emilio had left for the office, Mr. Dorand called. I told him that Dr. Porfiri had tried to reach
him, and that Mr. Dorand should call him at his office in fifteen minutes. The patient remained silent a few seconds, but I could hear him
clear his throat. Then the line went dead. I called his apartment, but
there was no answer. Apparently he had called from somewhere else,
and he never got back home. Somebody found his dead body Monday
night in a little motel. Suicide! I have told all the details to show that,
as far as I can see, Emilio had done all that could be done under the circumstances. It seemed natural that Emilio was terribly upset when he
learned about the suicide. He canceled some of his hours; he went to
the police, to the coroner, and to the morgue. He got in touch with the
relatives. And for a week or so this unhappy event kept him occupied. I
have asked myself, of course, and have asked Emilio more than once,
whether his worrying on Sunday evening was completely accidental or
whether he had any reason to suspect that something had gone wrong
with the patient. "No reason," he said, "not the slightest bit of a reason.
But, look, in spite of the lack of any reason I *was* worried, and you
know I was. I must have made a mistake and must have known it without knowing when or how."

Dr. Terwin: What followed?

Mrs. Porfiri: Well, to the best of my recollection, Emilio recovered from the shock, I would say, within a week or two. But then—I
cannot tell how it started. There must have been a slow transition or—
well, I don't know. But he must have slid into his present behavior,
this—what should I call it: aloofness, restlessness, silent despair—oh, it
is uncanny!

Dr. Terwin: It frightens you?

Mrs. Porfiri: It does! Oh, my God, it does!

Dr. Terwin: I understand your husband is working as before
the—the accident?

Mrs. Porfiri: I think so. He keeps his hours, sees his patients. However, during these four months or so he has lost some other patients—not in the same way, of course, but two or three quit prematurely, as I understood. Emilio has mentioned that occasionally, but not as he would have done before—in former times, I mean. It used to concern him a good deal if a patient left without too good a reason, but now he doesn't seem to care. No, that's not right! He does care, but something has changed in him. I think sometimes that he takes the other side, Mr. Dorand's side—he used this expression once, in a different context, but it sticks in my mind.

Dr. Terwin: I see—

Mrs. Porfiri: Dr. Terwin, can you say anything? Can you help?

Dr. Terwin: Possibly! I would certainly be glad to talk to your husband. Isn't that what you have in mind?

Mrs. Porfiri: [*after sighing and then remaining silent for a few seconds*]: I had it in mind. Of course, I had it in mind. I had it in mind a year ago, and during these last four months I've had little else in my mind. But, you know, he does not want to. Calmly and firmly, he refuses to see anybody.

Dr. Terwin: His reasons?

Mrs. Porfiri: I'm not sure that I can answer this question. He says it won't help him—something like that—but this can't be the real reason. How could he know without trying? I have asked, begged, implored him to try. But he seems unassailable.

Dr. Terwin: You know, your husband might simply need more time to make his decision. A psychiatrist has, perhaps, more serious obstacles to overcome than many who are not of the faculty.

Mrs. Porfiri [*intently*]: You tell me to wait?

Dr. Terwin: Let me ask: What is it you are so afraid of?

Mrs. Porfiri [*in a low voice*]: Suicide!

Dr. Terwin: I assume your husband moves in a circle of psychiatrists. It would be strange if not one of his friends had noticed the change in him which you have observed?

Mrs. Porfiri: I can't tell whether anybody has noticed. Nobody has said anything to me about it—with the exception of our maid. She asked me, oh, some weeks ago: "Is Dr. Porfiri ill? He doesn't seem to feel well." Dr. Terwin—believe me, oh, *do* believe me, it *is* urgent!

Dr. Terwin: Mrs. Porfiri, you will understand that I am in no position to confirm or deny the urgency of the case. [*As he notices a look of despair on her face, he goes on.*] Do not misunderstand me! I am ready to act on the assumption that there *might* be urgency. But I have to get some idea that my action would at least not make things worse! I refuse to act simply for the sake of giving you, or myself, the feeling that action has been taken! Let me ask: What do you think would happen if you told your husband that you had asked me to come and see him? Presenting him with a *fait accompli,* as it were? [*As she makes a gesture to interrupt and even starts to say something, he raises his hands to make her listen.*] Please, don't feel you have to decide in a hurry. Such a *fait accompli* method has an advantage and also a disadvantage, and which prevails depends essentially on the patient's personality. I want you to consider as calmly as you can these two sides. Look, when you want psychiatric help for your husband, you imply that his refusal to go to see somebody is unreasonable and its motivation irrational. You follow me?

Mrs. Porfiri: Yes, but—

Dr. Terwin: All right, listen: We may then assume that what prevents him from consulting a colleague is something like shame or pride. More generally, he might consider it as wrong in some sense or other for him to admit to a colleague his worry, depression, or whatever it is. This would not exclude the possibility that he would like to have somebody help him, but his countermotivation overrides the desire. If this were so, it might help to present him with a *fait accompli.* He would not feel so keenly that he himself is asking for help, because you had taken all the initiative. He might tell himself that not to talk to me, when I had been summoned by you, would be rude. So it would not be his doing if he talked to me, but rather yours.

Mrs. Porfiri: But, Dr. Terwin—

Dr. Terwin: Allow me a minute more—we are not *that* much in a hurry. I said that there is a disadvantage, too, in the *fait accompli* method. I take it that he has no close friends. You are probably the only person at the present moment he feels close to and has some confidence in. Your calling in a psychiatrist, behind his back, as it were, your putting before him a *fait accompli* and trying to force him into treatment, might impress him most of all not as a sign of your caring for him and loving him, but as a sign that you have lost confidence in him—that you, well, declare him incompetent to look out for himself and are now acting like a guardian who forces onto his helpless ward what *he*, the guardian, thinks is best.

Mrs. Porfiri: That is exactly what I am afraid will happen! That's what I wanted to say all the time. Emilio is terribly sensitive about what he calls "people with the best intentions." He would cancel the appointment or, if it were too late for that, he might even leave the house. No, that *fait accompli* method has no chance and would be very, very dangerous.

Dr. Terwin: Hm! Your estimate as to your husband's reaction might be completely correct. But I am baffled! I thought you would take the opposite view. What, then, is it that *you* suggest? I understood you wanted to make a suggestion, didn't you?

Mrs. Porfiri: I *do* want to make a suggestion. It is not by chance that I came to see *you* and no other psychiatrist. [*There is a short pause. She is highly conscious that this is the moment of decision.*] I called you the minute I learned you were here—or rather, I wired Dr. Redstone and called you as soon as I had heard from him. I have a very definite idea how you could help. You remember my question—the one I asked right at the beginning? Well, the answer you gave me confirmed what I had thought. Listen, Dr. Terwin, I can see that you can't simply take my word that there is danger. But, as you admitted—and I appreciate very much that you did—you also can't say for sure that I am in error. I know that I am going to ask something unusual from you—something, let's say, that is not usually done by a professional man. But, please, listen to me with an open mind! [*A little pause*] Let me say something more: Dr. Oliver Redstone is a friend of mine. I had talked with him earlier, over the phone. We had a long discussion. He is very old, but his mind is as sharp as ever. Well, his verdict was: "Not impossible! But who would dare to do it, and be able to do it?" Your name was mentioned. But you lived far away then. Now you will understand how I felt when I heard that you were here in this very city of ours—just now, when I need help more than ever. [*She pauses to catch her breath.*]

Dr. Terwin [*in a low, almost dreamy voice*]: Oliver Redstone! How strange! [*Without raising his voice, but very firmly*] And your suggestion, Mrs. Porfiri?

Mrs. Porfiri: It can't matter where you see your patient. Emilio is a therapist. So you could go and see him as his patient! [*Her voice is faltering.*]

Dr. Terwin: See him as his patient, you say?

Mrs. Porfiri [*bravely*]: As his patient. You would call him and make an appointment. He has sufficient time open. You wouldn't have to use another name. I know that psychiatrists occasionally ask colleagues for their professional help. [*She smiles breathlessly.*]

Dr. Terwin [*in a controlled voice*]: But he would ask how I came to consult him, wouldn't he?

Mrs. Porfiri: I thought of that. You could mention Dr. Redstone. He doesn't know Emilio personally very well, but he thinks well of him as a psychiatrist. And anyway he would agree to your using his name. He says so in his letter!

Dr. Terwin: As you have read my article so carefully and talked to my teacher and friend, Dr. Redstone, about me, you certainly must know that it is my conviction that treatment can't accomplish anything substantial as long as the therapist keeps pretending, lying, play-acting.

Mrs. Porfiri: I thought of that! Your objections against lying and pretending in such a case are not based, I understand, on moral principles. Are they?

Dr. Terwin: Correct! They are not!

Mrs. Porfiri: But on the thought that lying and cheating would interfere with treatment?

Dr. Terwin: Indeed, they would.

Mrs. Porfiri: Now, listen, Dr. Terwin, I thought of that too. It is true you will have to tell lies in the initial interview—you will have to say or indicate that you want treatment, and probably also why you want treatment. You will have to pretend, invent, lie, and cheat. But as soon as treatment starts, once you are accepted as a patient, you have the inalienable privilege of the patient to say what you like. And it is up to you to limit yourself to truthful statements and leave unsaid the essentially conventional formalities as to whom *you* consider to be the patient and whom *you* consider to be the therapist. [*She looks at him with the courage of desperation.*]

Dr. Terwin: Mrs. Porfiri, you suggest that I, a psychiatrist, call a colleague of mine, another psychiatrist, and ask him for his professional help, ask him to take me into treatment for some real or invented troubles of mine, while, in reality, I am hired by his wife to treat him. Do you realize what that means?

Mrs. Porfiri [*proudly*]: I know what it means! It means doing the only thing which could probably save him!

Dr. Terwin [*with a faint smile*]: That is your point of view, which I certainly respect. But it is not the only possible one. I listened to you, as you asked me to, with a fairly open mind. Now I would like you to return the favor! [*He looks her straight in the face; she answers in the affirmative with a minimal nod.*]

Dr. Terwin: If everything goes well and we get over the point [*he wants to say*, which I shudder to think of, *but suppresses this remark and replaces it by taking a deep breath*] when I can tell your husband what it's all about, and we can continue the treatment in a more – usual way – it won't matter so much if the thing becomes known – it can be played down. My colleagues will call me a screwball, no doubt, but nothing succeeds like success. As long as neither you nor Dr. Porfiri complains, nothing much can happen. But it would be childish – or worse, it would be ludicrous, megalomaniacal, idiotic, irresponsible – not to consider the possibility of failure. Let's say that after three months or so I come to the conviction that I am getting nowhere. Please realize that something like that may happen under absolutely normal conditions of treatment, while here the conditions would be extremely unfavorable. In a normal case I would not worry. I know that it frequently takes more time to tune in, to hear the patient accurately, to acquire the necessary precision of perception. Yet in this case, which would be as new to me as doing psychotherapy with the pet wife of an Arabian sheik whose prisoner I was, I wouldn't know where to look for a helpful idea. I would never know whether it was only I who was not perceptive enough, or whether it was the damned situation I was in which limited my means of expression. If I got desperate enough, I would back out. It wouldn't be too hard to make my withdrawal plausible—at least as plausible as the quitting of most patients who stop prematurely, where nobody can ever tell for sure just what made them quit. But worse might happen. We cannot exclude the possibility that Dr. Porfiri might become suspicious. And then what?

Mrs. Porfiri: Oh God! You are right. We cannot exclude every danger. But you can be sure that as long as *you* didn't confess about our agreement, and I didn't, Emilio would always respect you as a patient and would rather accuse himself of a paranoid delusion and break off the treatment than accuse you of—of—being an impostor. I can assure you of one thing. Come hell or high water, neither I nor Dr. Redstone will admit as much as even the thought of our agreement, whoever might ask us about it.

Dr. Terwin [*murmuring*]: Crazy, crazy! So what if—your suggestion—

Mrs. Porfiri: Dr. Terwin, let me ask this: When you, for a moment, disregard the unusualness of my suggestion and the trouble it might cause you with your colleagues or your conscience, do you think it could have a chance of success?

Dr. Terwin [*looking at her thoughtfully*]: A chance of success? Heavens, what do you think I am arguing about? The answer is: Yes, a chance! [*For a whole minute the two stare at each other, sometimes frowning, sometimes smiling, obviously intent on reading the other's mind.*]

Mrs. Porfiri [*starts crying. After 20 seconds she manages to say between sobs*]: Excuse me, Dr. Terwin! I have no words any more.

Dr. Terwin [*confused and embarrassed*]: But—but—I—I did not say anything yet! You, you—don't—have to feel so—desperate.

Mrs. Porfiri [*with a faint smile through her tears*]: I don't cry out of despair. I—I am so—grateful!

Dr. Terwin: Who of us is the therapist? How could you know? Anyway, you are right. So cry if you feel like it!

Mrs. Porfiri [*somewhat recovered*]: I—I have this letter from Dr. Redstone—it might help some.

Dr. Terwin [*taking the letter without looking at it*]: Is there anybody besides Dr. Redstone to whom you have talked about your plan?

Mrs. Porfiri: Nobody!

Dr. Terwin: Good! Don't talk to anybody, no matter what happens. And don't get in touch with me as long as the experiment lasts. No need to complicate matters. Should I find it necessary to back out, I'll let you know. Do you think you can agree to that?

Mrs. Porfiri: I agree. About the fee—will you read the letter first?

Dr. Terwin [*reads mumbling to himself for a while, then aloud*]: "I declare that if Dr. Terwin should decide to undertake it, he has my full approval. I ask him in this case to send his statements for the time he will spend and the money he pays as fee to Dr. Porfiri to me. I'll take full financial responsibility for the whole treatment." So that takes care of that. Do you have any more questions?

Mrs. Porfiri: No, I can't think of any. You know how grateful I am!

Dr. Terwin: That's all right. Let's see what happens. I'll call your husband tomorrow. [*Both get up.*] Good luck, Mrs. Porfiri!

Mrs. Porfiri: I feel hopeful!

Scene 2

Dr. Terwin's office. He is dictating a letter to his secretary, Linda.

Dr. Terwin: "Dear Oliver: This is not the usual thank-you-for-the-referral note with the additional information that I have seen the patient and treatment has been arranged. You will know very well, dear Oliver, that things are somewhat different. My feelings are different, my expectations are different—so this letter will be different, too. It is more like a letter one writes before boarding a ship for an adventurous exploration of the unknown—a farewell letter. Big words! They may seem out of proportion to the unspectacular occasion. What, after all, is the big issue? An attempt at therapy under unusual circumstances? But every patient is unusual. There is always the risk, there is always a lot of unknown factors. Maybe it is the starting with a lie? Yet I shouldn't be too impressed by this bit of initial play-acting. I guess it is rather the challenge which goes with your expression of confidence! I have made an appointment with Porfiri for this afternoon, an hour from now. I liked his voice. I didn't find it difficult to talk to him—at least over the phone. But I still cannot imagine how it will go. I have a few sketchy ideas of what I am going to say. But I know that no preparation at all would be just as good—or better! Mrs. Porfiri referred to the inalienable privilege of the patient to say what he pleases. She is right; for a long time there will be no danger of arousing suspicion. The danger is rather of behaving too much like a patient. If for one reason or another the plan has to be abandoned or changed, I'll let you know! Wish me luck and thanks a lot! Yours. . . ." I would like to sign this letter before I leave and have it mailed before I come back.

Linda: O.K.

Dr. Terwin: I don't want to be tempted to add something after I meet Dr. Porfiri.

Linda: I see. You'll have it in a minute!

Scene 3

Dr. Porfiri's office. Dr. Porfiri is sitting at his desk and talking into the telephone.

Dr. Porfiri: Sorry, I have to stop. I'm just about to see a new patient and I'm already late. 'Bye, Bob! [*He puts the receiver down, slumps somewhat in his chair, and sighs. Then he looks at his desk, begins straightening out the things on its surface, interrupts himself, gets up, and wanders about the room, like someone who is trying to bring about order, but is not attentive to what he is doing. Finally he pulls himself together and goes over to the door of the waiting room and opens it.*] Dr. Terwin?

Dr. Terwin [*entering*]: How do you do, Dr. Porfiri? Very glad to meet you.

Dr. Porfiri: How do you do, Dr. Terwin? It is certainly—well, will you sit down? [*He steers Dr. Terwin to the chair at the side of his desk, then sits down behind the desk and takes up a pen.*]

Dr. Terwin: Thank you very much for arranging a meeting so soon after my call! [*He stops somewhat abruptly and looks toward the window.*] Very nice view!

Dr. Porfiri: Thank you, quite pleasant! Did I understand correctly—you wanted to consult me?

Dr. Terwin: Yes! Yes, I mean I would like to ask for your professional help—for myself!

Dr. Porfiri [*frowning*]: May I ask what made you pick me?

Dr. Terwin: I am new here, as you probably know. I relied on the recommendation of an old teacher of mine. [*Dr. Porfiri looks questioningly at him.*] Dr. Oliver Redstone. He was your teacher, too, I understood, though this must have been some years before my time.

Dr. Porfiri: 1937 to '39.

Dr. Terwin: Well, I met him for the first time in—I think '42. [*Pause*] I have been in treatment once, during my training. I thought then that I did it in the first place for learning purposes. I now see it differently. Anyway, I thought I should be used to it by now, but I find myself quite uncomfortable when it comes to discussing my troubles. Mind if I smoke? [*Before Dr. Porfiri can answer, Dr. Terwin pulls out a package of cigarettes and lights one. Then he offers Dr. Porfiri the package.*]

Dr. Porfiri: No, thanks! When did you start this treatment?

Dr. Terwin: During my residency—I think in '43.

Dr. Porfiri: And how long did it last?

Dr. Terwin: Close to three years, I guess.

Dr. Porfiri: Why was it terminated?

Dr. Terwin: Let's say mutual agreement. There were some improvements.

Dr. Porfiri: Improvements? In what?

Dr. Terwin: In what? A good question, Dr. Porfiri. I suppose in my symptoms. I—I had felt all kinds of anxieties, and after three years I felt them less, or less frequently, or I felt more ashamed to mention them. You see, I was then an advanced patient and a budding psychiatrist and—and felt under a kind of obligation to respond to treatment properly—that is, with improvement.

Dr. Porfiri: I see! And now?

Dr. Terwin [*more seriously*]: Now? Now I feel less obligated, or I have lost my power of imagination, my talent for self-deception. In a word, it doesn't work any more! [*Pause*] You probably are going to ask me what my symptoms are at the present time. You know, I often wonder to what degree the symptoms we hear so much about in our initial interviews are really the things our patients are bothered with most. In a way, I feel tempted to enumerate a whole lot of complaints, just because they have names. It is easy to say: I am suffering from insomnia of medium severity. Or to say: When I have to meet new people, I try to delay it, I feel an aversion to talking to them. I have to force myself into a conversation and usually fall silent after a short while. I don't work as persistently as I would like and frequently I waste time. Or, I am irritable with my wife and my children. And so on and so forth. All that would be true. All these things bother me—occasionally—I could even say frequently. And yet—I wonder whether these and, maybe, a dozen similar complaints have made me come and look for help. [*He pauses and looks at Dr. Porfiri in a kind of impersonal evaluation, and then his glance goes toward the window and his face takes on an expression of absent-mindedness.*]

Dr. Porfiri [*after having waited for a minute or so*]: What, then, made you come?

Dr. Terwin: What made me come? Perhaps the fact that two obsessional thoughts creep into my mind every so often. Sometimes they both appear together. The one runs: ". . . and so it will go on forever and ever! How awful!" And the other goes: "Somewhere, at some moment, it will stop and it will be as if there never was anything, as if nothing ever had happened." And that is just as terrible!

Dr. Porfiri: Would you say that these thoughts are—at least sometimes—concomitant with experiences of depersonalization?

Dr. Terwin: I think you understand what I mean. "Concomitant with experiences of depersonalization," very good! I would venture to say that these thoughts or feelings *are* experiences of depersonalization.

Dr. Porfiri: Hm, I see. Can you say anything as to the time when these obsessive thoughts, to use your expression, first appeared or reappeared—or, maybe I should say, when they became so obnoxious that you started to think of—of consulting somebody?

Dr. Terwin: A year before we moved here we lost a child, my oldest daughter. She was 12 and died of a congenital heart disease. The long-drawn-out alternation of hope and despair which preceded the final event was hard on all of us and left my wife, after all was over, in a state of depression or exhaustion which was very disquieting. So, after four or five months had gone by without any noticeable change, I thought that it might help to change our surroundings. It took some time to make the decision and another six months before we actually moved. Well, as far as I can see, it really helped. From the moment the decision was made and the preparations started, there was a marked change for the better. Well, to answer your question: During the time when the decision to move had been made, but the move itself had not taken place, it occurred to me for the first time that it might be sensible for me to go into therapy again.

Dr. Porfiri: Can you say that at the time you thought of returning into therapy your wife's condition had already improved?

Dr. Terwin: I am not too sure, but it could be.

Dr. Porfiri: The illness and death of your oldest daughter must have been a highly traumatic experience, not only for your wife, but also for yourself. And yet you seem in no way to connect your symptomatology with these tragic events.

Dr. Terwin [*after a short pause*]: I do not feel any connection.

Dr. Porfiri: That's what I assume. But isn't it astonishing that you did not even *think* of a connection?

Dr. Terwin: There aren't so many things left which I can find truly astonishing!

Dr. Porfiri: You told me that your wife felt better after the decision to move, and I take it that she has improved even more since the move, but you—you seem to feel worse here than in the other city, don't you?

Dr. Terwin: I have no way to tell, except that here I am arranging for treatment while there I managed without. But that doesn't prove anything. [*Pause*] By the way, when could you take me? Once I made this decision— [*He finishes the sentence by a silent gesture.*]

Dr. Porfiri: Well. as a matter of fact—I have hours open; you could start any time.

Dr. Terwin: Very good! If it's O.K. with you I'll come twice a week. As to the hours, the later in the day the better.

Dr. Porfiri: How about Monday and Friday at 7 P.M.?

Dr. Terwin: Friday is fine; could we make it Tuesday instead of Monday?

Dr. Porfiri: I guess that will be possible. I'll find out before our next meeting.

Dr. Terwin: Oh—well—what is your fee?

Dr. Porfiri: Twenty dollars the hour.

Dr. Terwin: All right; so I'll see you—

Dr. Porfiri: There is plenty of time left. I am free until six. If you want to start right now?

Dr. Terwin [*after a short hesitation*]: All right.

Dr. Porfiri: Let's sit over there! [*They move to other chairs.*]

Dr. Terwin: It sounds ridiculous, but I feel as if I had really done something—spectacular!

Dr. Porfiri: Well, you made a decision.

Dr. Terwin: No, my mind was made up before I came that I would give it a try anyway. [*Pause*]

Dr. Porfiri: I know so little about you yet. Won't you tell me something about your background, your upbringing, and so on?

Dr. Terwin [*a bit sadly*]: Come down to business? So that work can start? Is that what you mean?

Dr. Porfiri [*with friendly reproach*]: Of course; you know as well as I that I need a lot of information!

Dr. Terwin: Be it as you wish! I am forty-two now. Of my parents I remember only my father. My mother died when I was two years old.

I have a picture of her in my mind, but when I describe it to my sister she says it's all wrong. As she is eight years my senior she must be right, and I must have confused our mother with some other female. . . .

Scene 4

Dr. Terwin's office. Linda is sorting some papers.

Dr. Terwin [*entering from the hall*]: Hello, Linda!

Linda: Hello, Dr. Terwin! Back already? Cured?

Dr. Terwin: Almost, almost, Linda—of my megalomania. What I let myself in for! Likeable person, Dr. Porfiri, very likeable. But I feel lost. You can't make a plan. I mean, I made a plan; but I couldn't stick to it. At the end I felt very exhausted. Not that it had been difficult to talk, on the contrary! I would never have thought before that it could be that attractive to the patient! This inalienable right to say what one pleases!

Linda: What, then, was so exhausting? Did you have difficulty in sounding convincing?

Dr. Terwin: As a matter of fact, I was not concerned with sounding convincing. The thought never entered my mind. It rather took an effort to keep alert to the purpose of my visit.

Linda: You know, you sound quite excited!

Dr. Terwin: It is exciting and—confusing; and very different from what I expected.

Linda: Did the lying bother you much?

Dr. Terwin: I am ashamed to admit that no, it didn't; certainly not much. Once or twice, when I had to invent a bit in answering a direct question, I felt some pangs. But otherwise—no! I must be more used to it than I thought. But, then, there weren't so many lies required. Since the other guy assumes that you are coming for treatment, every little idea which goes beyond "Hello" and "How are you?" will appear to him as a symptom. When I come to think of it—I was more truthful in this one hour than any member of the faculty ever is in any staff conference, myself included. You know: The patient's inalienable right. It includes—strange as it may sound—the right to say the truth.

Linda: I knew it! It musn't be bad at all to be a patient! What would you think of extending this right to other people too—let's say, to secretaries?

Dr. Terwin: God forbid! What a subversive idea!

Scene 5

Dr. Porfiri's office. Dr. Porfiri is talking through the half-open door to a patient who is just leaving.

Dr. Porfiri: We'll talk about that day after tomorrow—at 10 A.M. Good-bye!

Woman's Voice: Tell me only one thing: You really think that I wanted to hurt him?

Dr. Porfiri [*against his will*]: I can't know what you wanted. *I* did not say that you wanted to hurt him—only *you* said so!

Woman's Voice: But Dr. Porfiri, you know very well that I can't really know. *You* have to tell me!

Dr. Porfiri [*pained and without a smile*]: But not before day after tomorrow at 10 A.M. Good-bye!

Woman's Voice: You are cruel! [*The door is slammed shut.*]

[*Dr. Porfiri almost falls into his chair, drops his arms lifelessly, and lowers his head until his chin touches his chest. He murmurs:* In a way she is right—she is damned right! *He sits motionless, staring at the floor. There is a knock at the door. Startled, he jumps up and for a moment faces the door, uncertain what to do. Another knock makes him unlock the door carefully and open it a bit. He says:* Oh, it's you! Come in, quick! [*Mrs. Porfiri enters.*]

Dr. Porfiri: I am sorry. I have hardly any time. What is it?

Mrs. Porfiri: Hi Emilio! I was just at Cynthia's. Her husband, Phil, came home early and we thought it would be nice if the four of us could eat out together. So I ran over to ask you—I thought you had this hour free—would you like to come?

Dr. Porfiri: Too bad! I can't. The hour has been filled again. You're quite right, it has been free. But now it isn't.

Mrs. Porfiri: Can't you skip it?

Dr. Porfiri: No, the patient must be already here, and besides, he's a new patient and a colleague to boot.

Mrs. Porfiri: What a pity! Maybe you can cut the hour short?

Dr. Porfiri: I tell you, I'd like to! The man is a nightmare!

Mrs. Porfiri: So sick, you mean?

Dr. Porfiri: No, not sick, but he's a queer guy, with a very evasive way of talking. It's hard to understand what he's really talking about.

Mrs. Porfiri: Confused?

Dr. Porfiri: No, not confused. He is very bright and yet—sort of unpredictable, I would say. Why don't you go on with Cynthia and Phil and I'll see you later at home. [*Points toward the waiting room.*] He, too, is a student of Oliver's!

Mrs. Porfiri: Really? No, I'll be at home and have dinner with you. We can dine with the Tenners another time! All right? I'm off! [*She leaves.*]

Dr. Porfiri: O.K. [*He sighs. Then he walks slowly toward the waiting room door, looking around as if he were searching for a way out. Finally he shrugs his shoulders and opens the door.*] Hello, Dr. Terwin!

Dr. Terwin: Hello, Dr. Porfiri! [*They sit down in chairs facing each other. There is a pause, during which Dr. Terwin carefully studies him vis-à-vis.*] You look brave. I like brave people. But I don't like to be the one to provide them with an opportunity to prove their courage. [*He pauses a little, so as to give Dr. Porfiri a chance to answer.*] But, as it is, that can't be helped, can it?

Dr. Porfiri: I am not sure that I understand you. You feel irritated?

Dr. Terwin: Not irritated, Dr. Porfiri! No, not irritated! But I notice that you don't seem especially happy to see me!

Dr. Porfiri [*with a smile*]: You expect people to feel happy whenever you appear?

Dr. Terwin: Of course not! I confess I was somewhat facetious when I said that you did not seem especially happy to see me. I meant only that you had a somewhat strained expression on your face, as if—as if you had to brace yourself—you know, a long working day and now, at 7 P.M., one more patient.

Dr. Porfiri: You might be right!

Dr. Terwin: Of course, I don't expect people to be happy just to see me. But maybe it would be nice if it happened—let's say—occasionally. [Pause] I am tired too. It seemed a very long day to me. There were not only the patients. I had to talk at a meeting—a group of social workers—quite interesting, but it's difficult for me to see their problems clearly. So it was strenuous. When I feel tired, I tend to become philosophical. I wonder whether other people react in the same way. As long as I am alert and wide awake I enjoy the details, like to see and to listen, to observe, I might say. But when I feel fatigued, I think in generalities, of generalities, and everything takes on a philosophical color. It becomes confused and self-contradictory—which is so characteristic of philosophical thoughts. No, no—I don't want to say anything against philosophy! We cannot skip over confusion. It seems an important ingredient of our thinking and its development. What is clear from the beginning isn't worth much.

Dr. Porfiri: If your theory is correct, you must be very tired indeed, as you are becoming more philosophical by the minute. But I don't think that your philosophical bent is the effect of fatigue. It rather serves a purpose. It helps you evade the real issue.

Dr. Terwin: The real issue? What's that?

Dr. Porfiri [seriously and somewhat sadly]: I can hardly believe that you don't know what I mean. I mean, of course, the things you want help for! Your philosophical speculations about the worthlessness of statements which are perfectly clear from the beginning might be very true, but in terms of your therapy—as you know as well as I—to dwell on such thoughts is simply a waste of time.

Dr. Terwin [after some hesitation]: A waste of time! As a matter of fact, I don't know as well as you. I have my doubts there. But be that as it may! You know, I made a discovery, or should I say rediscovery? I even talked to my secretary about it. Linda is her name. She is a very sensible person—originally a social worker but—one of the exceptions. You know, I would say that it belongs to those features of her which constitute her exceptionality that she had no qualms about becoming a secretary instead of continuing to do social work. Well, my rediscovery! I say *rediscovery* because I assume I must have discovered this trivial truth in my first treatment with Ingelman. Yet I can't say that I remember doing so, as this whole treatment has almost completely faded from my memory. Even the name of my therapist has only now come back—Ingelman! I am sure that if you had asked me in the previous hour who my therapist was, I would not have been able to conjure up the name. What I wanted to say is that after our previous hour, I realized what a great thing we offer our patients—*that they may say whatever they want to.* Even if we set aside the question of final results and whether we really help them or not, this opportunity to talk—to talk about what you feel like talking about—is unique. However little our patients may avail themselves of this marvelous chance, it is the most humane feature of therapy. You must think differently; or, at least, when you think of results and achievements, you feel that enjoying this unique opportunity to the fullest is a waste of time, or could possibly be a waste of time. And, as a conscientious therapist myself, somehow I have got the notion that you are a very conscientious therapist— you don't want your patient to waste time. Your brows contract a little, almost to the point of a frown. It is as if you had heard the call of duty, and, your face looking strained and somewhat sad, you dismiss humanity with a shrug and offer the warning: "You are wasting time!" [*Pause*] I admit that I respect this conscientiousness of yours—it has dignity. It certainly has. But, since it makes you look sad, it makes me feel sad too. I don't know how I would feel if you were not saddened by your submission to duty but pronounced your warning with a ringing voice and a sparkle in your eye. Maybe I would feel annoyed! Maybe I would laugh. As it is—and I can almost hear you sigh, figuratively speaking—well, here again the thought is creeping up: This will go on and on forever and ever. How awful!

Dr. Porfiri: This?

Dr. Terwin: What I mean by "this"? I'll tell you. Look how many things we have in common. We are approximately the same age and of a very similar background. We have gotten our training, partially at least, in the same place with the same teacher. We are both psychiatrists in private practice, doing psychotherapy essentially and by choice. As I did not know you before I made our first appointment, I would not have come without Oliver Redstone's mediation. But I would not have arranged for further visits, after our first interview, if I had not felt—well, that I could talk to you. Well, all these conditions making for ready mutual understanding being fulfilled in our case, all comes to naught because of the preoccupation with purpose, with rules and regulations, with wasting time and good use of time, with theory and psychological concepts—in one word, with duty!

Dr. Porfiri [*after a pause of a minute*]: You sound so—well, should I say enthusiastic—almost passionate. And yet, would you ever say such things to a patient of yours?

Dr. Terwin: Do you want me to talk to you as if you were my patient?

Dr. Porfiri: Of course not! But you can't have one truth for your patients and another one for yourself!

Dr. Terwin: True, very true—and I don't!

Dr. Porfiri: You know, it seems that you have an aversion to seeing yourself in the role of a patient.

Dr. Terwin: That's very true. I have an aversion to seeing myself in any kind of role. That is essentially what I said before, though in different words. [*There is a pause of more than a minute, and then he continues in a low voice.*] I even find it unsatisfactory to see others acting a role.

Dr. Porfiri: I am not sure that I understand you.

Dr. Terwin: Perhaps you understand but don't like to think you do?

Dr. Porfiri [*after a moment's hestitation*]: I think that is correct. I, somehow, feel that you are critical of me, but I can't put my finger on it. When I listen to you, there are moments when I feel I understand what you mean and, in a way, could agree. But then, a few seconds later, I have lost you, and I get confused.

Dr. Terwin [*after 30 seconds*]: You see, Dr. Porfiri, I feel much better now. It is, of course, not a law of nature, or of logic or anything like that. There certainly are exceptions, but by and large I think it *is* true that if things are clear from the beginning, the exchange is not worth while. Only the transition from misunderstanding and confusion to—maybe only a faint sense of approaching a vague notion of something which was possibly meant. Well, it is completely empirical, but I have come to distrust a conversation where everything is lucid and transparent and one says, "Yes, indeed," or "No, under no conditions." Well, as I said, there are probably exceptions. I am not impatient. I don't have to have everything at once. And I don't expect others to expect that either. Isn't that what our job consists of most of the time, and especially where it is not in vain? Well, we use up a lot of time—we deal with months and years. We are very generous in this respect. And it would not make sense to be impatient. I often think that time has a different significance or, maybe, a different texture, in our job from that it has in many others. Though we are paid by the hour, our achievements do not consist of just surviving or staying awake for a certain number of minutes, as it is with the night watchman. Nor do we work like the pieceworker, who wants to cram into a given time as many holes drilled or springs soldered or bolts riveted as possible. One could say that we are not fighting time, neither urging it on to pass quicker, nor trying to slow it down and make it hold more. If everything goes well—whatever that means—we are at peace with time.

Dr. Porfiri [*with some irritation in his voice*]: You say "we"!

Dr. Terwin: Well, I assume that others might see it the same way I do.

Dr. Porfiri [*with a wry expression on his face*]: Or *should* see it the same way you do? Isn't that what you want to say?

Dr. Terwin [*calmly*]: Of course, I really meant to say something about the nature of our job that—more or less—everybody must notice.

Dr. Porfiri: And if they don't—

Dr. Terwin: Oh, you disagree?

Dr. Porfiri: I did not say that!

Dr. Terwin: But you mean just that! [*Dr. Porfiri keeps silent, al-*

though it takes some effort. After more than a minute Dr. Terwin continues.] So why shouldn't you disagree? Heavens, it wouldn't be the first time that two therapists disagree in how they view their work! I can't see anything bad about that. Do you?

Dr. Porfiri [*with noticeable irritation, although he tries to keep calm*]: It seems to me you constantly manage to ignore the fact that you come to me for treatment as a patient and not for a social visit as a colleague!

Dr. Terwin: And you feel that that is wrong. Well, there you may be right. And yet—I get confused. I may see things in the wrong perspective. But don't you expect that something must be wrong with a man who comes to see you for treatment? If he were not inclined to see himself or the other guy in a somewhat distorted way, what would be there for you to treat?

Dr. Porfiri: Aren't you playing with words?

Dr. Terwin: Good—that you say that! I guess I am. I know that I am tempted to do that very, very frequently. But when I do it, I don't recognize, or don't *always* recognize, that I am doing it. And sometimes—you see—sometimes I feel—Oh, my God, how can I say it and make myself understood? I feel that I am playing with words and at the same time—or by this very thing—but how could you possibly understand me? Well, perhaps I can say it this way: Sometimes—oh, not always, but sometimes—I can't find any better expression for what I want to say than just to play with words. It is like a curse! You'll probably call it an obsession! It *is* an obsession. It makes me sad or even desperate—I mean, trying to find the right words and not finding them, and playing with words instead. I get my thoughts entangled in sentences—and they are all in knots. It's like having a long wet fishing line which is all muddled up. You can't leave it alone, but the more you try to straighten it out, the more it gets entangled. So I can't leave it alone, can't stop talking and allow things to settle themselves. I have to talk on and add words, and more and more and more words, and it goes on and on and looks like an aimless playing and leads to nothing—most of the time. And there again I have the feeling: This will go on and on forever and ever. How awful!

Dr. Porfiri: Well, I think we better stop here. The time is not quite up—but I am tired, I must say—it would not—

Dr. Terwin: Oh, that is all right! We don't have to be pedantic. I am tired myself. I'll see you—?

Dr. Porfiri: Tuesday—same hour.

Dr. Terwin: Good-bye!

Dr. Porfiri: Good-bye, Dr. Terwin! [*He does not look up when Dr. Terwin leaves. He appears disconcerted, brooding and agitated at the same time.*] Thank goodness! It's over—finally. [*He sits down and looks very dejected. Two minutes pass. The telephone rings.*] Hello! Oh, Estella! Yes, I will. I can do that—easily. No, nothing special—tired perhaps. Yes, indeed. I don't know what Oliver had in mind. He didn't care to send me a note. So I don't know what he thinks about his protégé—or what he knows of him, for that matter. But I will write him. It is really a kind of imposition. Crazy! Yes, I said crazy and I mean it—very obscure— can't make him out. It is really very inconsiderate of Redstone—maybe it *is* old age! Practically no excuse—no, no—well intentioned, sure— but there is only a limited amount of good intentions one can survive— yes, I'll have to write him anyway! No, I won't forget. I'll leave soon! See you! [*He puts the receiver down with a sigh.*]

Scene 6

Dr. Terwin's office, about two weeks later. Linda is working at her desk. The telephone rings. Linda is visibly reluctant to take off the receiver, but when it rings for the fourth time she can't hold out.

Linda: Dr. Terwin's office! No, not yet, Madam. . . . I don't know. You called earlier? It's all right, but. . . . No, no. . . . Perhaps you can try later in the afternoon. Do you want to leave a message? Well, as you prefer. . . . [*Puts down the receiver.*] That's she!

[*Dr. Terwin enters. He looks tired and preoccupied.*]

Dr. Terwin: I am late, I know. I should really refuse to take part in these conferences. There's no point in it—formalities—[*Looks at her for the first time.*] Eh—what's the matter, Linda, you look so gloomy? [*As she says nothing but seems to be searching for words, he becomes alarmed.*] Has something gone wrong? What is it? Speak up! Dr. Porfiri—?

Linda: I am afraid that something *is* wrong! Mrs. Porfiri called—I don't know how many times. She didn't give her name, but I recognized her voice. She may call again any minute.

Dr. Terwin [*frowning*]: Well, hm, that's just too bad; I can't talk to her. But, you know, she has been under stress now for a long time. Besides, I am seeing Dr. Porfiri tonight. Today is Friday, isn't it? [*Linda nods.*] O.K.—so I will see him. What more can I do? [*He sits down. The telephone rings.*]

Linda [*agitatedly*]: If it's she, I think you should talk to her! Dr. Porfiri wants to stop! [*The telephone rings again.*]

Dr. Terwin: What's that? Answer the phone and tell her that I'm not in yet but will be in in 15 minutes.

Linda [*desperately*]: You have a message from Dr. Redstone about Dr. Porfiri! [*The telephone rings.*]

Dr. Terwin [*firmly*]: Take it and tell her what I told you to!

Linda [*into the phone*]: Hello, Dr. Terwin's office! Beg pardon? Whom did you say? No, you've got the wrong number! We are *not* the dry cleaners!

Dr. Terwin: Heaven knows what we are! What was that about Dr. Porfiri's stopping? Did he cancel tonight's hour?

Linda: I should have told you first! [*She is trying to control her voice.*]

Dr. Terwin [*his hands on his forehead*]: My God, already! It would have been the seventh hour—three weeks! When did he call?

Linda: He didn't! You got me wrong. There was a message from Dr. Redstone—

Dr. Terwin: From Dr. Redstone? [*He takes the receiver off the telephone and puts it on the table.*] I want to get this straight! Not from Dr. Porfiri but from Dr. Redstone?

Linda: I am sorry; a night letter came this morning from Dr. Redstone. Here it is!

Dr. Terwin [*reading*]: "Decided to let you know. Disturbed letter from Emilio. Accuses me of not telling him in advance about you. Calls you evasive, unpredictable, conceited, crazy, hostile. Without transition says all his own fault. Apologizes, thanks for my damnable, misplaced confidence. Estella called me, desperate about Emilio's getting worse, talking daily about that 'new patient.' Wants to terminate. I am ready to take next plane if you think advisable. Sorry, Oliver." Hm, that's it?

Linda [*almost in tears*]: Oh, Dr. Terwin, I knew the odds were all against you. But I had wished so much you would succeed. [*She takes the receiver to put it back on the phone.*]

Dr. Terwin: Wait, leave it on the table; let's have it nice and quiet — for a while at least! We'll do some thinking! The night letter was sent last night. Since mail reaches Oliver's mountain retreat only once a day, at 10 in the morning, Emilio's letter must have gotten there yesterday — Thursday morning. An airmail letter takes three full days to get from here to Oliver's wilderness, so Emilio's disturbed message can't have been mailed any later than Monday morning. That fits nicely with the mood of the letter. This type of confused message one may write late at night after a miserable week end.

Linda: But what's your point?

Dr. Terwin: Now look! I saw Dr. Porfiri in my Tuesday evening hour! Well, whatever he may have felt or thought — and at times he became quite emotional — he neither looked nor acted like one who is about to withdraw! And this was two days after he wrote the alarming letter, two days in which he had time to plan appropriate action. So he *gets* irritated and furious and *says* alarming things to poor Mrs. Porfiri. What, really, could we expect? If what I am doing with him is therapy at all, it must have the effect of therapy whether he thinks of it as therapy or as a course in Esperanto! And the effect of therapy is what it always is and should be: It stirs him up, tempts him to step out of his rut; and when he does and feels the wind blowing and in his first bewilderment and panic tries to bury himself even deeper — well, that's what every patient does when therapy takes. Now, with Dr. Porfiri things have to go at a sharper pace; they simply have to.

Linda: At a sharper pace?

Dr. Terwin: If any other patient under the influence of treatment steps out of his rut and then, frightened, runs for shelter again, he can soften the impact of therapy for a while by blaming the therapist and fighting him. But Dr. Porfiri can't fight his therapist because, so far as he knows, this man is his patient, with whom he should not get involved in a fight. Here his professional self-esteem is at stake.

Linda [*still shaky*]: I am glad you see it that way, and I can understand what you meant by a sharper pace. But how can you know that this extraordinary dilemma he is in will not lead to a disastrous explosion?

Dr. Terwin: I don't know. Or rather, I know it *must* lead to an explosion. This situation cannot last long. The question is only: Will the little breeze of fresh air which made him unbutton his neurotic strait jacket be sufficient to make him accept normal treatment?

Linda: I see; but how can one take this risk?

Dr. Terwin: Only if one realizes that one would take an equal or even worse risk by refusing to risk, if you see what I mean.

Linda [*thoughtfully*]: I do.

Dr. Terwin: I have to leave for my hour! Put the receiver back and send a wire to Oliver: "Don't see advisability of visit. Tonight's appointment still uncanceled. Don't see danger increased. Love, Simon." I'm off!

Linda: Good luck! [*Dr. Terwin leaves.*] What a life!

Scene 7

Dr. Porfiri's office. Dr. Terwin is sitting in the patient's chair, while Dr. Porfiri is talking over the phone.

Dr. Porfiri [*into the phone*]: No, I can't. I will call you back at, let's see—eight sharp. [*He puts the receiver down and addresses Dr. Terwin.*] Sorry, I interrupted you!

Dr. Terwin: Did you? I can't remember having said anything. As far as I am concerned, you could have continued on the phone for the whole hour. I wasn't sure for a while whether I would come today or not. Isn't that ridiculous? When I ask myself what makes me reluctant to come here, I find that it's stage fright. Will I know my lines? Or more precisely: How can I make you listen? And I resent the effort.

Dr. Porfiri: You have the feeling that I don't listen to you?

Dr. Terwin: That's the trouble. You don't! You are so busy trying to find something you can do for me that you have no time, or rather no attention, left to listen.

Dr. Porfiri [*fairly unperturbed*]: This impression of yours that I do not listen carefully enough to what you are saying—don't you think that this is just a reflection of your own evasiveness, a projection, to use the proper word?

Dr. Terwin [*after a glance at his opponent*]: My evasiveness?

Dr. Porfiri: You—well, sometimes you talk about yourself; yet most of the time you talk about me or what I am doing with you!

Dr. Terwin: When you are at the dentist's and you say to him, "You are hurting me!," are you talking about the dentist or are you talking about yourself? See what I mean? someone might say: "I am afraid to drive home now in the rush hour!," or "The show last night was superb!," or "It's too bad you don't listen to me!" If you are primarily impressed by the grammar, you may say that the one who confesses fear of driving talks about himself, but the one who praises the show talks about the show, and I—when I complain that frequently you don't listen to me—I am talking about you. But all three of us are saying what it is that concerns us—right now, at the moment.

Dr. Porfiri [*slightly uneasy, but forcing himself to speak in a serious, matter-of-fact tone*]: I think I see what you mean. Your little lecture on the ambiguity of language or grammar might be perfectly correct. Yet the fact remains that you prefer to give a little lecture which has nothing to do with the purpose of our sessions instead of talking about your personal problems. [*With a smile which is meant to be friendly but comes out sarcastic*] I am sure if one of your patients talked to you the way you did just now, you would describe him as an intellectualizer.

Dr. Terwin [*thoughtfully*]: The purpose of our sessions—look, if I were talking to you, for whatever purpose, and I saw you suddenly turn white and shiver and slump in your chair, would you expect me to continue talking about, let's say, the nomination of Dr. X for president of our psychiatric association, or about my insomnia, or about whatever we had planned to discuss? I would jump up and ask, "What is the matter with you?" and, perhaps, take your pulse; and it would be ridiculous to do otherwise—to pursue my topic in the very moment you are fainting.

Dr. Porfiri [*with some sharpness*]: Look, Dr. Terwin, look at your parallel! That's what you are fantasying about and wishing for: namely, that I fall ill right here under your nose and you jump up and take my pulse and act as the doctor and turn me into the patient. You are fighting your role as a patient and want to reverse the positions!

Dr. Terwin: I think you have a point there, Dr. Porfiri—although, perhaps, not exactly the point you want to make. Let me say first that I don't think that I would feel any satisfaction if you fainted or suffered any kind of physical accident. It would embarrass me terribly. I am not good at physical medicine and never was. I would call the nearest GP and would be afraid I might have failed to apply the proper first-aid measure. So I don't think that I wish you to fall ill. But you perceived something which I too recognize as true. It is—no, let me say it in this way: I am not sure that I would notice it if you were only to change color. But I do notice it when you are not listening to me. And it's more than just noticing it. It jolts me and absorbs my attention. If it happens it is for me: the business at hand, the one I want to attend to. Well, you see here I think you made a good point. This sensitivity—or call it hypersensitivity if you want to—I developed in working as a therapist, or maybe it determined my becoming a therapist.

Dr. Porfiri [*puzzled*]: This sensitivity?

Dr. Terwin: Well, the fact that it pains me if the other person is not listening to my words but is only registering them, as it were—that he does not talk to me but only exposes me to information, if I may say so.

Dr. Porfiri [*incredulously*]: And that, you say, determined your becoming a therapist?

Dr. Terwin: I feel it is the essence of my being a therapist! Therefore, although I can't quite go along with your formulation, I would say you made a good point when you complained that I don't adhere to my role as a patient. As a matter of fact, I don't know what the role of the patient is. Are there things which only the therapist should say and other things reserved for the patient? From my viewpoint, that is not so! You are quite right when you assume that frequently the things I am saying to you I could also have said to a patient of mine, and vice versa. Well, the expression "vice versa" is not clear. What I mean is: Sometimes patients say things to me which I could have said to them or to other patients. For instance, it has happened that a patient has said to me: "You are not listening to me!"

Dr. Porfiri [*spontaneously, and regretting it later*]: And how did you react then?

Dr. Terwin [*with a light smile*]: Of course, not always in the same way, but sometimes I have seen that the patient was right. In one case, I remember, I had noticed the patient's beautiful tie and suddenly thought of a suit of mine which I needed for that very evening but had forgotten to fetch from the cleaners. So—

Dr. Porfiri [*interrupting almost against his will*]: And what do you think is preventing *me* from listening to you?

Dr. Terwin: I might say: Your preoccupation with therapy!

Dr. Porfiri: My what?

Dr. Terwin [*calmly*]: Your preoccupation with therapy. What I mean is: You are obviously under the urge to do something—oh— *therapeutic!*—no matter what you feel or how you feel. You are keeping yourself, should I say, protected, or at a distance from what I am saying, so that you can manage not to take it in, not as you would take in an ordinary telephone message or the question of your neighbor when he asks you whether your electricity has been cut off too, or something like that. I am sure, for instance, that in this very moment you are uneasy about whether you are doing right to be interested in my views on therapy, or rather, to permit yourself to act upon this interest and ask questions about them, instead of looking into the significance of my talking the way I do, interpreting it, using it as sample behavior as a psychologist uses the Rorschach response of his subject.

Dr. Porfiri [*he jumps up from his chair, paces around his desk and, with an effort, sits down again*]: Excuse me — Why are you talking to me in this way? No, that's not what I wanted to say! Sorry! [*He makes several attempts to say something, but unsuccessfully.*]

Dr. Terwin [*seriously*]: Are you sure? I rather got the impression that that was exactly what you felt like saying, while at the same time you seemed to feel you shouldn't!

Dr. Porfiri [*passionately*]: You know damned well I shouldn't!

Dr. Terwin: Not at all! Look, Dr. Porfiri, I think — and I have no doubt you will agree with me — it is a sad truth that rarely, very, very rarely, do people say what they feel like saying. Here we are, the both of us, in this office together, free for an hour to say what we think. We do not have to sell anything to each other, nor do we have to agree on by-laws or resolutions. We don't have to fight each other, beguile each other, persuade each other. We might not always grasp immediately the other's meaning, but we have the potential of doing so. Why waste this unique opportunity?

Dr. Porfiri [*he now has one of his knees drawn up, the elbow of his right arm on the knee, and his forehead resting in his right hand. His searching glance, under drawn brows, is on Dr. Terwin's face, with an expression as if he were in a dream and trying to awake*]: Whatever the merits or demerits of your reasoning, if I may call it that, it certainly has the effect of confusing me — surprisingly. No, that is not even the whole story. If you were only confusing me, it would not be so strange! There are many things so complicated, or complex, or maybe even paradoxical — one is uncertain about them, bewildered, and one needs time to get them organized. Nothing unusual about that. So what? I get confused, so I shut up and give myself time to think! But, look, what am I doing? [*With lowered voice*] I don't shut up, I continue talking — in spite of knowing better. I could say — I feel tempted to say: You are seducing me! And so I say it! But what is the sense of putting the blame on you? You are the patient, or supposed to be the patient, so you have the privilege of talking seductive nonsense. But I, supposedly the therapist, should be able to stand up to it. I should be able to hold my own and not to succumb, no matter what you say. [*More firmly*] There is only one way out of this situation — and you know it!

Dr. Terwin: At least, I know what you mean. However, you seem to me like one who has been brought up in a religious faith, and then one day discovers that he does not believe in God. And he is terrified! "My God," he thinks, "what could be a worse insult to God than not to believe in Him!" It is true! I can see it—you have violated your principles, but—does not what you would call the violation consist of doubting them?

Dr. Porfiri [*again in a low voice*]: My principles—?

Dr. Terwin: Well, the word is questionable. It might be more than mere principles. I think it is no accident that it occurs so rarely that people say what they mean.

Dr. Porfiri [*with an effort, looking Dr. Terwin straight in the face*]: I understand what you say, but I cannot help but feel that I should not, and that I would be better off if I didn't or couldn't! But not even that is completely true! Be that as it may—one thing is for sure! I cannot treat you!

Dr. Terwin: Be that as it may—it seems pretty immaterial in comparison with the fact that we—at least at times—have managed to say to each other what we meant! I—I think that I might do even slightly better the next time! I see there are only a few minutes left, and I would like to discuss this matter more fully. Would it be all right if I kept my next appointment—under whatever heading you wish?

Dr. Porfiri: Of course, Dr. Terwin, of course! I really should not—should not have—

Dr. Terwin: Don't worry! I feel fine! Day after tomorrow at 6—all right?

Dr. Porfiri [*with a half smile*]: All right!

6

Understanding Eva

Elizabeth Brewster

Can I hope to understand Eva Fischer? Can the subject of psychoanalysis ever analyze the analyst? Why do I want to understand her, anyway? Isn't this attempt at understanding a proof that the old obsessive concern with her still exists? Or is it an indication that now, twenty years after the psychoanalysis, it has finally succeeded, and I am able to be detached from her? During that period of two years when I was visiting her, I certainly could not see her as herself. I saw her as mother, enchantress, witch doctor, quack, goddess. I depended on her. I loved her. I hated her. But only rarely did I glimpse her as a woman with hopes, fears, failings like my own.

At first I hardly saw her at all, except as someone who might help me. She was a psychoanalyst recommended by my doctor because I was suffering from headaches and tension. Why? I was a young unmarried woman without a lover, working at a boring job, and living with my parents in the rather dull Ottawa of the mid-1950s. (An incomplete explanation, but it will do well enough.) I had recently become a Catholic, and my parents disapproved of the conversion.

"Mrs. Fischer is a Catholic," my doctor told me when I mentioned this circumstance. "She is a Jungian psychoanalyst, has studied with Jung himself, I believe. You'll find her quite a personality."

I was late for my first appointment because I got lost on the way. Intentionally or unintentionally? Eva would probably have guessed intentionally, but I think not. I got off the Bank Street streetcar too soon and took a wrong turning.

The address was an apartment in a new highrise. The voice that answered my ring and told me to come up was thick and guttural. Was this Mrs. Fischer? I rose in the elevator to the tenth floor, found myself outside a door with an elaborate knocker in the shape of a mermaid.

The door was answered when I knocked by the owner of the voice, a tall, white-haired woman in a black dress and a maid's starched white cap and apron. She indicated in her rather limited English that I should wait in the living-room, and I sat down gingerly on the edge of a brocaded sofa. My wait was not long—after all I should have been there fifteen minutes earlier. The maid returned, and led me into an inner office where Eva Fischer faced me across her desk. A woman no longer young, though I could not place what her age might be. Somewhere in her fifties, perhaps? Her hair was still dark, and she had kept her figure; but the lines on her forehead and around her mouth must have been cut by age or grief, or perhaps by both. Her cheekbones were high and prominent, and had been somewhat accentuated by rouge. She had also taken some care with the eyebrows which curved over what were still fine lustrous dark eyes. A woman who had been pretty in her day, and was still not without her attractions.

"Thank you, Else, you may go," she said to the maid, who withdrew discreetly, closing the door softly behind her.

Mrs. Fischer indicated a chair opposite her, and I sat down. "You are late, Miss Summers," she said to me rather formally and with a touch of severity.

I explained that I had lost my way. Her look expressed disbelief, although it was less severe. I found myself disliking her. I was not sure what I had expected, but I had not expected this middle-aged Teutonic woman who doubted my word and who was critical of me for being late when I knew I was always early.

However, now that she had shown her disapproval of lateness, her manner became more kindly and she set out to put me at my ease by asking those routine questions one expected in doctors' offices. Eventually she asked a question which was, for me, less routine, though I suppose it was routine enough for her. "Have you ever had help of this kind before?" she asked.

I hesitated. Did I like her well enough to tell her the truth? It wasn't a question of liking. I had to trust her, because I did not know if I could find anyone else. "Only once," I told her hesitantly, "from a psychiatrist in a hospital just after I had tried to kill myself."

To my relief, she did not look upset or even much interested. "And why did you do that, Kate? I may call you Kate?"

"Because I was fond of someone who married someone else," I said telling one part of the truth.

To my surprise, she laughed. She had a pleasant, musical infectious laugh, and I almost, in my astonishment, laughed with her.

"You must excuse me," she said. "Believe me, I know it is serious. But it is your English understatement that is funny. You are fond—only a little fond—of someone, and you try to kill yourself when he marries someone else? You must see that it is funny."

Perhaps I might like her, just a little, after all.

The interview did not last long. "You must understand," she said, "that if you come late you will have a shorter session. I have another patient coming. Next time, you come on Saturday morning, at ten AM. On time."

I had not been altogether certain that I would come for another interview, but decided after all I might as well.

Within two weeks I was writing in my diary that I felt much better, that my headaches were going away, that perhaps I might complete the treatment within a few months. I had almost forgotten my initial dislike of Mrs. Fischer. I had never known anyone who was such a good listener, who was so ready to accept all those details of childhood guilt and misery. After the first few sessions, the chair I had sat in disappeared, and I lay on the analyst's couch of all those cartoons, staring at a painting (I seem to remember a beach scene with blue water and white sand, but I am not sure) and talking to Mrs. Fischer as she sat beside me. Sometimes I was disconcerted when I looked up by chance and found her either too interested or not interested enough; usually her eyes were half-closed, and she wore what I thought of as her hooded look.

What I told her then no longer matters. It is Eva Fischer I am trying to understand, not myself. I suppose those accounts of childhood troubles must have been fairly routine for her; she must have been bored at times. No doubt she was well enough aware fairly soon in the process that the analysis would take longer than the three or four months I had so optimistically predicted. No doubt she knew I would be worse before I was better. She was not, I suppose surprised by my dependency, the period when I was clinging to her and found it hard to live between sessions. She tried to explain to me the nature of transference, that I felt for her as a child feels when it is separated from its mother, or woman when she is separated from her lover.

All children feel curious at some time about their parents. If I told her everything, I also wanted to know some things about her. Who was this Mrs. Fischer, the Mrs. F. of my diary? Where did she come from? What had her life been before she came to Canada?

I put together, piece by piece, information, as one puts together the pieces of a jigsaw puzzle. She was the widow, I learned, of a writer, an Austrian Jewish novelist whom I had never heard of, but who Mrs. F. told me had been well known in his time and place. She herself had been the daughter of a wealthy Viennese family, not Jewish. She and her husband had taken refuge from Hitler in Switzerland, and after her husband's death she had come out to Canada with her daughter, who was now grown-up and living in New York. Yes, she had been psychoanalyzed by the great Jung himself during her life in Switzerland.

I couldn't think why she would have been psychoanalyzed, except out of curiosity. Aside from that flight from Hitler, I thought her life sounded happy enough, in the small glimpses she gave me to illustrate some point she was making about my own life. There was an idyllic childhood in Vienna, with her adored parents—especially her adored father—and her older brother who had later become an actor in America. She had been a lively and talented girl, had acquired some reputation as an artist. Some of the paintings on the walls were her own, although she no longer painted. Her marriage, although to a man much older than herself, sounded happy. She had obviously adored Josef Fischer, considered him one of the great talents of the age, and clearly supposed (though she did not say so in so many words) that my reason for not knowing his work was the backwardness, the rusticity of a little city like Ottawa.

My curiosity about the Fischers could not have been as great as it later became, for I did not immediately try to hunt up Josef Fischer's books. Perhaps Mrs. Fischer discouraged me. Did she say that they were for the most part badly translated? Or was it just that I lacked the energy, in the early days of analysis, to find my way to a library that might have translations of his work? I was wrapped up in my own concerns, of course, and was chiefly interested in Mrs. Fischer's marriage as a model for some hypothetical marriage I might make myself. Might I possibly, like Eva Fischer, marry a famous author older than myself? Was marriage especially difficult for a woman with talents? I thought of myself as a writer although at present I could not seem to write. Mrs. Fischer had been a painter, was obviously a woman of intelligence. Yet she seemed to have been rather domestic, to have enjoyed looking after husband and child. I was delighted by the model of married harmony that she provided for me. Might I also manage to have the best of all worlds—be a writer myself, sympathize with the career of a brilliant and charming husband, and at the same time cook nourishing meals for my lively children? Before this time, I had been rather contemptuous of women who were interested in their houses or in their own appearance. Yet it was clear that Mrs. Fischer thought these matters were not unworthy of attention. Not to care about appearances, she seemed to suggest, might mean that one didn't respect the selfhood behind the appearance. "How can a young woman who thinks she wants to marry not bother powdering her nose?" she inquired of me one day, rather acidly. Ah, Mrs. F., Mrs. F.! I suppose she was old-fashioned. Or was she?

It was autumn when I first started going to see Mrs. F. I dreaded Christmas, when she went away to New York for a couple of weeks.

She seemed to realize my almost childish dread of her absence, and, instead of our usual session of analysis, invited me into her living-room for cake and wine. She had put up a little Christmas tree with wax candles, and gave me a present, a Mexican pendant with blue stones. I still have it, at the back of a drawer somewhere, although something has happened to the chain.

When she came back she talked of the relative she had visited, her brother, about whom she worried because he had a heart condition, and her daughter. I was surprised that she mentioned disagreeing with her daugther at times. Her family life was not quite perfect, then? I was also, as my dreams at the time showed, pleased that she did not always agree with the daughter. "Family jealousy, Katie," she said to me teasingly. "You want to be my favourite child."

I found a novel of Josef Fischer's in the nearest branch of the Public Library and read it but did not like it. I tried to explain to Mrs. Fischer why I did not like it. "It was too romantic," I said, "too Gothic. I like solid, sensible novels with real details in them."

"Your tastes are incorrigibly English," she said. "Or is it that you are jealous of Josef too as well as of my daughter?"

Perhaps she was right. I began to be afraid, to be panicky about the kind of relationship that was developing.

"Don't worry, Kate," she said soothingly. "They all feel like that, all the patients. It's not really me you're attached to. Tell me who else you've been jealous of."

The winter passed. As spring gradually and grudgingly approached, I sometimes walked to Mrs. Fischer's instead of taking the streetcar. Some days come back to me: a cold, windy March day, for instance, when there has been snow and rain. A wind blows through the trees, which are full of little particles of ice that make a strange noise, as though pellets of glass were being rubbed against one another. There is a glare of ice underfoot, grey and glossy. While I am at Mrs. Fischer's a storm of thick, soft, wet snow comes up. I walk home through it, unable to see my way across the street. The ground becomes mushy rather than icy. There is a sense of release about that soft, blinding snow, connected with the ease of tension at the back of my neck just after I have talked to Mrs. Fischer. I come home weary, ready to curl up on top of my bed and fall asleep.

Or it is early summer. An Ottawa heat wave. Mrs. F. is planning to visit Vienna, for the first time in many years, and is trying to prepare me for her absence. I sense that she is already, partly absent. What are those memories, of Vienna, of Zurich, that she returns to?

I myself go off for a solitary holiday in a small Laurentian resort. I walk daily to the village, where I sit in the small toy-like church with its clutter of candles and statuary. I stare at the crucifix, half praying, half letting my mind drift around past and future. Then I walk back to the Lodge, sit on the sundeck in a bathing suit and sunglasses, reading another book by Josef Fischer. I like this better than the one I read before, but am disappointed that I cannot see anyone in the book who resembles Eva Fischer.

When we had both returned to Ottawa again, the analysis seemed stuck in a sort of doldrums area. We circled around and around the same events in the past, the same problems. I seemed even to have the same dreams. I had a feeling of not having reached deep enough into my private world; at the same time I felt that Mrs. F. (or was it myself?) was directing me outward, to external practical problems. Should I get an apartment away from my parents so as to ease the strain at home? Should I attempt to find a job that would interest me more than the one I had?

One session, when we had seemed to be making more progress than we had for a time, we were interrupted by the paper boy wanting money. To my surprise, Mrs. Fischer scolded him very vigorously. He had been told not to interrupt her at this hour. He was a stupid young oaf. I felt that she was making too much fuss, and a critical expression must have shown on my face. "As usual, Katie," she said angrily to me, "you expect perfection. It would do you good if you lost your temper now and then at your parents or your detestable boss. I at least am not to be fitted into that kind of mould. He was not to come on a day when Else isn't here to answer him. I cannot have my work interrupted."

I agreed that I was too anxious for perfection, that I had, as Mrs.

Fischer would have sometimes said, an overdeveloped superego, or, as a priest might have said, an excess of scruples. I did seem to demand of myself that I should always be sweet, gentle, and compliant, as well as very competent; that I should keep all the commandments, even the minor ones. (Mrs. F. said that I was a Baptist Catholic.) I knew that such a demand for self-perfection could prevent me from doing anything or gaining anything. I hesitated to write a poem for fear it might be flawed or to make a friendship for fear it might be a failure. Was I applying the same sort of standard to Mrs. Fischer? Surely she had the right to lose her temper at the paper boy? Yes, but not to shout at him, I thought.

Time passed, another autumn, another winter. I moved away from my parents into a bachelor apartment with a couch, a lamp, and a card table. I made a few friends. I played at cooking and keeping house. I did a little writing. I had a new job at the Public Library.

It was there, in flipping through a reference book on twentieth-century authors, that I found an entry on Josef Fischer. Why had I not looked it up before? Had I been incurious, or had I felt that I ought not to trespass on Eva's earlier life? (By this time I called her Eva, in my mind at least. She was still Mrs. Fischer when I talked to her.) Josef Fischer was, as Mrs. Fischer had said, an author of considerable reputation with a long list of novels and biographies to his credit. What about his personal life? A few years after the first Great War, the notice said, he had been separated from his wife Selma, by whom he had had several children. After his tragic separation from her (why was it tragic?) his companion had been the painter and illustrator Eva Wiebe, by whom he had also had a daughter. They had lived in Switzerland, where he had died in 1940.

I was startled by this information. Had Eva not, after all, been married to Josef Fischer? What did that word "companion" mean? If she had been married to Josef Fischer, how could she, as a Catholic, marry a divorced man? What were these implications of "tragic" circumstances? In her picture of a happy marriage (which I felt was intended as a model for a possible life of my own) there had not seemed to be room in the background for another wife and children, perhaps deserted on Eva's account. I felt that my image of Eva had been shattered, and along with it my view of the kind of person I ought to become and the kind of life I ought to lead.

What seemed especially upsetting, when I thought of it, was that Eva had not told me the truth. I had told her everything about myself; and although I had not expected her to tell me everything in return, I had not expected her to tell me lies. Surely, though, "lies" was too strong a word? Even though she might not have been legally married to Josef Fischer, she had lived with him for many years and had borne him a daughter. Baptist Catholic though she might call me, I was not so conventional as to suppose all marriages were made in church before priests.

I was not due to see her for several days. However, after spending a disturbed night, I telephoned her, as I had rarely done. What in the world had I been reading, she asked? Yes, Josef had had an earlier, unhappy marriage, made when he was only twenty-two. Frau Selma Fischer had been a difficult, indeed an abnormal person, and the marriage had not worked. There had been problems with her and with the children, though Eva had looked after the youngest child herself. It had been a difficult life in many ways, but certainly not one to be ashamed of. She would tell me more when I came in for the next interview.

When I arrived after work on Monday for my interview, I found her looking tired and worn. She had put on a black dress and had omitted her usual make-up. She was alone; it was one of Else's days off. She arose to greet me, as she did not usually do, and took my hand in both of hers. Looking earnestly into my eyes, she said, "I wish I could know what goes on in that funny little head of yours, Kate. Why are you so upset by all this? It's my tragedy, not yours. Why do you think I should have worried you with it? Am I not entitled to a life of my own, to my own past?"

"Yes—yes, of course you are. But still it is partly my business. If I went to a surgeon to have my appendix out, his character wouldn't matter, only his hands and his skill. But you aren't just operating on my appendix. It's my mind, my soul even. I have to trust you, you see."

"Can't you still trust me? I haven't lied to you; I've just omitted to tell you some truths which I didn't think concerned you. Do you think I am an evil woman? I am only an unlucky one."

"Of course I don't think you are evil. But I thought of you as my model for a happy life. I wanted to be like you. Now I'm not sure."

"I see what you mean. People imitate their parents' marriage, and I have become a second mother to you. It was a good marriage; it had its trials, but it was a true friendship to the end, and it was not at anyone's expense, whatever Selma Fischer said. I did not ruin her marriage. She ruined it herself, before I ever met Josef."

She told me the story of herself and Selma and Josef, of Selma's half-insane jealousy both before and after the divorce, of the perpetual lawsuits with which she pestered her ex-husband. The figure of Selma which was presented seemed bizarre, extravagant. Could I believe her? Was Selma unbalanced to the point of evil, or was she only pathetic and neurotic? Eva must be telling the truth; the conviction of sincerity was in every word she said. And yet Eva's truth and Selma's truth were probably different.

Did she not have some pity for Selma, this half-crazy suicidal woman?

Of course she pitied her, she tried to understand her. But it was not just a mild neurosis, I must understand. "You are seeing her as like yourself," she said glancing at me shrewdly. "You are wrong, of course. You are sane and reasonable—maybe too sane and reasonable. You are neurotic, you have your problems, you get depressed or maybe tense; but there is nothing wrong with your reason, your power of understanding. Believe me, you are not at all like Selma. You would not, if your lover or husband left you, come half-clad howling at his door like some kind of wild animal."

I laughed. "Of course you laugh at the idea," she said. "So would I. You are more like me than like her, after all. You must not go over to her side, Kate. She turned enough people against me there in Europe.

Why should she turn you against me now because you have read a silly paragraph in a book?"

She was right, of course. I was not turned against her. But I could no longer see her as someone infinitely strong, wise, and joyous placed above the storm of circumstance. She too had been unsure of herself. She too had suffered scruples of conscience. She too had lain awake all night worrying. She too was sometimes ungenerous. She too told half-truths. She too, in short, was imperfect.

That was, I suppose, a turning-point in the analysis. I never depended on Eva to quite the same extent again, and yet at times I felt closer to her than I had before. After all, I now knew something about her. Not long after that, her brother in New York died of a sudden heart attack, and once more I saw her stricken. Which of us was helping the other, I wondered, when I saw her visibly grieving? My own troubles seemed somehow smaller than hers.

I continued seeing her for my remaining six months in Ottawa, although less frequently in the later months. Then I moved to Toronto to work. I went to see her before leaving town, a mute, embarrassed farewell session, like the farewells in railway stations. For a time in Toronto I had periods when I missed her greatly. Once or twice I came to Ottawa for a weekend and had lunch or tea with her. These occasions were pleasant; we talked to each other politely about movies or books or art exhibitions. But across a table in a restaurant we no longer seemed to be quite the same people.

Then I had a period when things went wrong for me again, and I found myself blaming Eva. Had I somehow been shortchanged in my analysis so that I was not able to cope with an emergency? On one visit to Ottawa I met her on the street but failed to recognize her until she was past and did not speak to her. (How could I fail to recognize her?) She did not see me, or did not appear to see me. Yet I still remember her face as I glimpsed it then, half smiling.

Ten years after the analysis was over I heard she was dead, had died suddenly of a heart attack on a visit to Vienna. So her widowhood was over. My own parents were dead; I was no longer a Catholic;

I had never made that ideal marriage I had imagined for myself. But I still sometimes heard Eva's voice in my ear, though I did not always agree with what it said. I no longer thought her a bad analyst because my life had not been ideally happy. Why should it be? I had gone on living. I had even gone on writing. She would have been satisfied, I thought.

Lately, after all these years, I have been looking again at Josef Fischer's novels, especially that last novel he wrote, the autobiographical one. I don't remember reading it before. Was it not in the Ottawa Public Library? Was it one of the novels that Eva told me was badly translated? It is really, I discover, quite a powerful novel, though an uneven one. It tells the story of the unhappy marriage of a famous German novelist. Bertha, the novelist's first wife, is rather like Selma as Eva had portrayed her to me. And yet she has in her youth an odd charm, an absurdity that is almost lovable until she turns into a witch and ogress. She is the character who makes the book live. And then there is Johanna, the young woman who is first the hero's mistress (does Fischer use that word, or is it Bertha's?) and then his second wife. Johanna is affectionate, gentle, courageous, loyal. She is a talented musician. I recognize her high cheekbones, her dark liquid eyes, her laugh. But can Johanna be Eva? She has no temper. She is all sweetness. She is too perfect. Did Josef Fischer not understand Eva? Did I understand Eva? Did she understand herself?

And what about Kate Summers? If I have never understood Eva, do I understand Kate.

7

The Girl Who Couldn't Stop Eating

Robert Lindner

> "Sooner murder an infant in its cradle than nurse
> unacted desires."
>
> —Wm. Blake, *Marriage of Heaven and Hell*

Laura had two faces. The one I saw that morning was hideous. Swollen like a balloon at the point of bursting, it was a caricature of a face, the eyes lost in pockets of sallow flesh and shining feverishly with a sick glow, the nose buried between bulging cheeks splattered with blemishes, the chin an oily shadow mocking human contour; and somewhere in this mass of fat a crazy-angled carmined hole was her mouth.

Her appearance astonished and disgusted me. The revulsion I felt could not be hidden. Observing it, she screamed her agonized self-loathing.

"Look at me, you son-of-a-bitch!" she cried. "Look at me and vomit! Yes—it's me—Laura. Don't you recognize me? Now you see, don't you? Now you see what I've been talking about all these weeks— while you've been sitting back there doing nothing, saying nothing.

Not even listening when I've begged and begged you for help. Look at me!"

"Lie down, please," I said, "and tell me about it."

A cracked laugh, short and rasping, came from her hidden mouth. The piglike eyes raised to some unseen auditor above, while clenched fists went up in a gesture of wrath.

"Tell him about it! Tell him about it! What the hell do you think I've been telling you about all this time!"

"Laura," I said more firmly, "stop yelling and lie down"—and I turned away from her toward the chair behind the couch. But before I could move she grabbed my arms and swung me around to face her. I felt her nails bite through my coat and dig into the skin beneath. Her grip was like a vise.

She thrust her face toward mine. Close up, it was a huge, rotting wart. Her breath was foul as she expelled it in a hoarse, passionate whisper.

"No," she said, "I'm not going to lie down. I'm going to stand here in front of you and make you look at me—make you look at me as I have to look at myself. You want me to lie down so you won't have to see me. Well, I won't do it. I'm going to stand here forever!" She shook me. "Well," she said. "Say something! Go on, tell me what you're thinking. I'm loathsome, aren't I? Disgusting. Say it! Say it!" Then suddenly her grasp loosened. Collapsing, she fell to the floor. "O, God," she whimpered, "please help me. Please . . . please. . . ."

I had never met anyone like Laura before, nor had I encountered the strange symptoms she presented. In the literature of morbidity occasional reference was made to a disorder called bulimia, or pathological craving for food; and I had of course met with numerous instances of related oral disturbances, such as perverted appetite or addiction to a specific food. As a matter of fact, one of the most amusing incidents of my career concerned a case in this category. It happened at the Federal Penitentiary in Atlanta, where I had been sent on a special assignment during the first years of the war. One day I received a note from an inmate requesting an answer to the engaging question, "Do you think I will get ptomaine poisoning from eating tomatoes on top of razor blades?" I showed this provocative communication to my colleagues in the Clinic who thought, as I did, that someone was pulling my leg. In reply, therefore, I wrote the questioner that the outcome of such a meal depended on whether the razor blades were used or new. Much to my chagrin, a few days later the X-ray technician called me into his office and exhibited two pictures on the stereoscopic viewer, inviting me to look at the "damnedest thing you ever saw." I looked. In the area of the stomach I saw a number of clearly defined, oblong shadows. "What the heck are those?" I asked. "What do they look like to you?" he responded. I looked again. "To me," I said, "they look like—well, I'll be damned! Razor blades!"

We called the inmate from the hall where he had been sitting hunched over on a bench, moaning with pain. When he saw me, he complained, "I did what you said. I only ate new blades like you told me. . . . Now look what's happened!"

"Musta been the tomatoes, then," was the technician's dry comment.

When the surgeons went to work on this man they discovered him to be a veritable walking hardware store. I was present in the operating room when they opened him up, and my eyes bulged with amazement as they carefully removed piece after piece of the junk he later told us he had been swallowing for many years. Somewhere in my private collection of psychological curiosa, I have a photograph of the debris collected from this man's interior. It shows not only numerous fragments of razor blades, but also two spoons, a coil of wire, some bottle caps, a small screw driver, a few bolts, about five screws, some nails, many bits of colored glass and a couple of twisted metallic objects no one can identify.

Laura's difficulty, however, did not involve the perversion of appetite but something far more distressing psychologically. She was subject to episodes of depression during which she would be seized by an overwhelming compulsion to gorge herself, to eat almost continuously. A victim of forces beyond her ken or control, when this strange urge came upon her she was ravenous—insatiable. Until she reached a stage of utter exhaustion, until her muscles no longer responded, until her distended insides protested with violent pain, until her strained senses succumbed to total intoxication, she would cram herself with every available kind of food and drink.

The torment Laura suffered before, during and after these fits (as she called them) is really beyond description, if not beyond belief. Articulate as she was, I could not appreciate the absolute horror, the degradation, the insensate passion of these wild episodes until, with my own eyes, I saw her in the midst of one. Her own report of the onset and course of these experiences, a report I heard many times, is as follows:

"It seems to come out of nowhere. I've tried to discover what touches it off, what leads up to it, but I can't. Suddenly, it hits me. . . . It seems I can be doing anything at the time—painting, working at the Gallery, cleaning the apartment, reading, or talking to someone. It doesn't matter where I am or what's going on. One minute I'm fine, feeling gay, busy, loving life and people. The next minute I'm on an express highway to hell.

"I think it begins with a feeling of emptiness inside. Something. I don't know what to call it, starts to ache; something right in the center of me feels as if it's opening up, spreading apart maybe. It's like a hole in my vitals appears. Then the emptiness starts to throb—at first softly like a fluttering pulse. For a little while, that's all that happens. But then the pulsing turns into a regular beat, and the beat gets stronger and stronger. The hole gets bigger. Soon I feel as if there's nothing to me but a vast, yawning space surrounded by skin that grabs convulsively at nothingness. The beating gets louder. The sensation changes from an ache to a hurt, a pounding hurt. The feeling of emptiness becomes agony. In a short while there's nothing of me, of Laura, but an immense, drumming vacuum."

I remember asking her, when she reached this point in her description, where the hunger started, at what place in the course of this weird, crescendoing compound of emptiness and pain the compulsion to eat entered.

"It's there from the first," she would say. "The moment I become aware of the hole opening inside I'm terrified. I want to fill it. I have to. So I start to eat. I eat and eat—everything, anything I can find to put in my mouth. It doesn't matter what it is, so long as it's food and can be swallowed. It's as if I'm in a race with the emptiness. As it grows, so does my hunger. But it's not really hunger, you see. It's a frenzy, a fit, something automatic and uncontrollable. I want to stop it, but I can't. If I try to, the hole gets bigger, I become idiotic with terror, I feel as if I'm going to *become* nothing, become the emptiness—get swallowed up by it. So I've got to eat."

I tried to find out, in the early days of her analysis, if there was any pattern to her eating, any design, any specificity.

"No," Laura told me. "It's just a crazy, formless thing. There's nothing I *want* to eat, nothing in the world that will satisfy me—because, you see, it's the emptiness that has to be filled. So it doesn't matter what I swallow. The main thing, the only thing, is to get it inside of me. So I stuff anything I can find into my mouth, loathing myself while I do it, and swallowing without tasting. I eat. I eat until my jaws get numb with chewing. I eat until my body swells. I swill like an animal—a pig. I get sick with eating and still I eat—fighting the sickness with swallowing, retching, vomiting—but always eating more and more. And if my supply of food runs out, I send for more. Before it comes I go mad with the growing emptiness, I shiver with fear. And when it arrives I fall on it like someone who's been starved for weeks."

I would ask her how the frenzy ended.

"Most of the time I eat myself into unconsciousness. I think I reach a state of drunkenness, or something very like it. Anyhow, I pass out. This is what usually happens. Once or twice I've been stopped by exhaustion. I couldn't open my mouth any more, couldn't lift my arms. And there've been times, too, when my body just revolted, refused to take in any more food.

"But the very worst is the aftermath. No matter how the fit ends, it's followed by a long sleep, sometimes for as much as two whole days and nights. A sleep of sick dreams that go on and on, terrible dreams I can hardly recall on awakening—thank goodness. And when I awaken I have to face myself, the mess I've made of Laura. That's even more horrible than what's gone before. I look at myself and can hardly believe the loathsome thing I see in the mirror is human, let alone me. I'm all swollen, everywhere. My body is out of shape. My face is a nightmare. I have no features. I've become a creature from hell with rottenness oozing from every pore. And I want to destroy this disgusting thing I've become."

Three months of intensive analytic work had passed before the morning Laura confonted me with her tragically distorted body and insisted I look at it. They had been stormy months for both of us, each analytic hour tearful and dramatic as Laura recited the story of her life. In the recounting she could find no relief, as many other patients do, since it was a tale of almost endless sorrow in which one dismal incident was piled upon another. Used as I am to hearing the woeful stories of abuse, neglect and unhappiness that people bring to an analyst, I was nevertheless moved by Laura's narrative and could hardly help expressing my sympathy. By this I do not mean that I verbalized the feelings she aroused in me, for the discipline of these long years of practice and the experience gained through the many errors I have made safeguard against such a gross tactical blunder; but in small ways of which I was largely unaware I communicated my compassion to her. With Laura, this turned out to be a serious mistake. Typically misreading my attitude for one of pity, hardly had the analysis begun than she set out to exploit this quality and to demand more and more of it. Paradoxically, just because I somehow betrayed sympathy for her, she charged me increasingly with a total lack of warmth, and upbraided me almost daily for my "coldness," my "stonelike impassivity," my "heartless indifference" to her suffering. Our meetings, therefore, followed a curious pattern after the first few weeks. They would begin with one of her moving chronicles, to the telling of which she brought a remarkable histrionic talent; then she would wait for some response from me: when this was not forthcoming in the manner she desired, she would attack me viciously.

I recall one such hour quite clearly, not only because of its content but also, perhaps, because it preceded by a few days the episode I described earlier; and the contrast between the way Laura looked on the day I have in mind and her appearance only a short while there-after remains vivid in my memory. For Laura between seizures was nothing like the piteous wreck she made of herself at those times. Although poor, she always dressed becomingly, with a quiet good taste that never failed to emphasize her best features. The ascetic regime she imposed on herself between bouts of abnormal eating kept her fashionably thin. Her face, set off in a frame of hair so black that it reflected deep, purple lights, was not pretty in the ordinary sense, but striking, compelling attention because of its exotic cast. It conveyed an almost Oriental flavor by the juxtaposition of exceptionally high cheekbones, heavy-lidded brown eyes, a moderately small, thin nose with widely flaring nostrils, and an ovoid mouth. On the day I wish to tell about, one could hardly imagine the ruin that was even then creeping up on her.

She began the hour with her usual complaint of fantastic night-mares populated by grotesque forms whose exact description and activities always eluded her. These dreams occurred every night, she said, and interfered with her rest. She would awaken in terror from one, often aroused by her own frightened screams, only to have another of the same kind as soon as she fell asleep again. They were weird dreams, she claimed, and left her with only vague memories in the morning of surrealistic scenes, faceless figures, and nameless obscenities just beyond the perimeters of recall. Water—endless, slow-moving stretches of it, or torrential cascades that beat upon her with the fury of whips; footsteps—the haunting, inexorable beat of a disembodied pair of shoes mercilessly following her through empty corridors, or the mad staccato of an angry mob of pursuers; and laughter—the echoing hysteria of a lone madwoman's howl of mockery, or the shrieking, derisive chorus of countless lunatics: these three elements were never absent from her nighttime gallery of horrors.

"But you can't remember anything more?" I asked.

"Nothing definite—only water again, and being chased, and the sound of laughter."

"Yet you speak of odd shapes, rooms, landscapes, action of some sort, scenes. . . . Describe them."

"I can't," she said, covering her eyes with her hands. "Please don't keep after me so. I'm telling you everything I remember. Maybe they're so terrible I have to forget them—my dreams, I mean."

"What else could you mean?" I entered quickly.

She shrugged. "I don't know. My memories, I guess."

"Any particular memory?"

"They're all terrible. . . ."

I waited for her to continue, observing meanwhile that her hands were no longer over her eyes but interlocked tightly over her forehead, the knuckles slowly whitening and the fingers flushing as she increased their pressure against each other.

"I'm thinking," she began, "about the night my father left. Have I ever told you about it?"

. . . It was raining outside. The supper dishes had just been cleared away; Laura and her brother were sitting at the dining-room table doing their homework. In the kitchen Freda, the oldest child, was washing up. Their mother had moved her wheel chair into the front bedroom, where she was listening to the radio. The apartment, a railroad flat on the edge of the factory district, was cold and damp. A chill wind from the river penetrated the windows, whistling through newspapers that had been stuffed into cracks around the frames. Laura's hands were stiff with cold. From time to time she would put her pencil down and blow on her fingers or cross her arms, inserting her hands beneath the two sweaters she wore and pressing them into her armpits. Sometimes, just for fun and out of boredom with her sixth-grade geography lesson, she would expel her breath toward the lamp in the middle of the table, pretending the cloud it made was smoke from an invisible cigarette. Across from her Little Mike, intent on forming fat letters according to the copybook models before him, seemed unaware of the cold as he labored. Laura could tell which letter of the alphabet he was practicing from watching his mouth as lips and tongue traced familiar patterns.

When the door opened, Little Mike glanced up at her. Their eyes met in a secret communication of recognition and fear as heavy footsteps came down the hall. Bending again to their lessons, they now only pretended to work. In the kitchen Freda closed the tap so that she, too, could listen.

In a moment, they heard their father's grunting hello and a mumbled reply in kind from their mother. Then there was a creak of the springs as he sat heavily on the bed, followed by the sharp noise of his big shoes falling to the floor when he kicked them off. The bedsprings groaned again as he stood up.

"Peasant," they heard their mother say over the music from the radio, "if you're not going to bed, wear your shoes. It's cold in here."

"Let me alone," he replied. "I'm not cold."

" 'I'm not cold,' " their mother mimicked. "Of course you're not cold. Why should you be? If I had a bellyful of whisky I wouldn't be cold either."

"Don't start that again, Anna," he said. "I'm tired."

"Tired," she mocked. "And from what are you tired? — Not from working, that's for sure."

"Oh, shut up, Anna," he said wearily over his shoulder as he walked through the doorway. Behind him there was the click of the dial as their mother shut off the radio, then the rasping sound of her wheel chair following him into the dining room.

Laura looked up at her father and smiled. He bent to brush his lips against the cheek she offered. The stiff hairs of his thick mustache scraped her skin and the smell of whisky made her slightly dizzy. Straightening, he ruffled Little Mike's hair with one huge hand, while with the other he pulled a chair away from the table.

"Freda!" he called as he sat down.

The older girl came to the door, smoothing her hair with both hands. "Yes, Papa," she answered.

"Get the old man something to eat, huh?" he asked.

Anna wheeled herself into the space between the table and the open kitchen door where Freda stood. "There's nothing here for you," she said. "You want to eat, come home when supper's ready. This ain't a restaurant."

Ignoring her, he spoke over her head to Freda. "Do like I said, get me some supper."

As Freda turned to obey, Anna shouted at her. "Wait! Don't listen to him!" She glared balefully at her husband, her thin face twisted with hate. When she spoke, the veins in her long neck stood out and her whole shrunken body trembled. "Bum! You come home to eat when you've spent all the money on those tramps. You think I don't know. Where've you been since yesterday? Don't you know you've got a family?"

"Anna," he said, "I told you to shut up."

"I'm not shutting up. . . . You don't care what happens to us. You don't care if we're cold or starving or what. All you think about is the lousy whores you give your money to. Your wife and children can rot for all it matters to you."

"Anna," he started to say, "the kids . . ."

"The kids," she screamed. "You think they don't know what kind of rotten father they've got? You think they don't know where you go when you don't come home?"

He slammed his palm down on the table and stood up.

"Enough!" he yelled. "I don't have to listen to that. Now keep quiet!"

He started for the kitchen. Anticipating him, Anna whirled her chair across the entrance. "Where're you going?" she asked.

"If you won't get me something to eat I'll get it myself."

"No you won't," she said. "There nothing in there for you."

"Get out of my way, Anna," he said menacingly, "I want to go in the kitchen."

"When you bring home money for food you can go in the kitchen," she said.

His face darkened and his hands clenched into fists.

"Cripple!" he spat. "Move away or I'll—"

Her laugh was short and bitter. "You'll what? Hit me? Go ahead— hit the cripple! What're you waiting for?"

Framed in the doorway they faced each other, frozen in a tableau of mutual hatred. Behind the father Laura and Little Mike sat stiffly, eyes wide and bodies rigid. In the silence that followed Anna's challenge they heard the rain slap against the windows.

Their father's hands relaxed slowly. "If you don't move out of the way," he said evenly, "I'm getting out of this house and I'm never coming back."

"So go," Anna said, leering up at him. "Who wants you here anyway?"

Like a statue, he stood still for a long minute; then he turned and walked swiftly toward the bedroom, followed by their eyes. Now the tense quiet was broken by the noises he made as he moved around the next room, and shadows, cast by his tall figure, crossed and recrossed the threshold.

On Anna's face, when she became aware of what he was doing, the look of triumph gave place to alarm. Her bony fingers clutched the wheels of her chair. Hastily, she propelled herself around the table. In the doorway, she stopped.

"Mike," she said, "what're you doing?"

There was no answer—only the sound of the bedsprings, twice, and the firm stamp of his shoes against the naked floorboards.

"Mike"—her voice was louder this time and tremulous with fright—"where're you going?—Wait!"

The wheel chair raced into the bedroom, beyond sight of the children. They listened, their chests aching with terror.

She clutched at his coat. "Mike. Wait, Mike," she cried. "Please don't go. I didn't mean it. Please. . . . Come back. Come into the kitchen. I was only fooling, Mike. Don't go."

He pulled away from her, lifting her body from the chair. Her hands broke the fall as useless legs collapsed. The outer door slammed. Then there was the slapping sound of rain again between her heavy sobs. . . .

"—He meant it," Laura said. "I guess she went too far that time. He never did come back. Once in a while he'd send a few dollars in a plain envelope. On my next birthday I got a box of salt-water taffy from Atlantic City. . . . But we never saw him again."

She fumbled with the catch on her purse and groped inside for a handkerchief. Tears were streaming from the corners of her eyes. Some caught on the lobes of her ears and hung there like brilliant pendants. Idly, I wondered if they tickled.

She dabbed at her eyes, then blew her nose noisily. Her bosom rose and fell unevenly. The room was quiet. I glanced at my watch.

"Well?" she said.

"Well what?" I asked.

"Why don't you say something?"

"What should I say?"

"You might at least express some sympathy."

"For whom?"

"For me, of course!"

"Why only you?" I asked. "What about Freda, or Little Mike, or your mother? Or even your father?"

"But I'm the one who's been hurt most by it," she said petulantly. "You know that. You should feel sorry for me."

"Is that why you told me this story . . . so that I'd feel sorry for you?"

She turned on the couch and looked at me, her face drawn in a grimace of absolute malice.

"You don't give an inch, do you?" she said.

"You don't want an inch, Laura," I responded quietly. "You want it all . . . from me, from everybody."

"What d'you mean?" she asked.

"Well, for example, the story you just told. Of course it's a dreadful one, and anyone hearing it would be moved, but—"

"—But you're not," she almost spat. "Not you. Because you're not human. You're a stone—a cold stone. You give nothing. You just sit there like a goddam' block of wood while I tear my guts out!" Her voice, loaded with odium, rose to a trembling scream. "Look at you!" she cried. "I wish you could see yourself like I see you. You and your lousy objectivity! Objectivity, my eye! Are you a man or a machine? Don't you ever *feel* anything? Do you have blood or ice water in your veins? Answer me! Goddam' you, answer me!"

I remained silent.

"You see?" she shouted. "You say nothing. Must I die to get a word out of you? What d'you want from me?"

She stood up. "All right," she said. "Don't say anything. . . . Don't give anything. I'm going. I can see you don't want me here. I'm going—and I'm not coming back." With a swirl of her skirt she rushed from the room.

Curious, I reflected, how well she enacted the story she had just told. I wondered if she knew it too?

Laura came back, of course—four times each week for the next two years. During the first year she made only few—and those very minor—advances so far as her symptoms were concerned, particularly the symptoms of depression and sporadic overeating. These persisted: indeed, for several months following the "honeymoon" period of psychoanalysis—when, as usual, there was a total remission of all symptoms and Laura, like so many patients during this pleasant time, believed herself "cured"—her distress increased. The seizures of abnormal appetite became more frequent, and the acute depressions not only occurred closer to each other in time but were of greater intensity. So, on the surface, it seemed that treatment was not helping my patient very much, even that it might be making her worse. But I knew—and so did Laura—that subtle processes had been initiated by her therapy, and that these were slowly, but secretly, advancing against her neurosis.

This is a commonplace of treatment, known only to those who have undergone the experience of psychoanalysis and those who practice the art. Externally, all appears to be the same as it was before therapy, often rather worse; but in the mental underground, unseen by any observer and inaccessible to the most probing investigation, the substructure of the personality is being affected. Insensibly but deliberately the foundations of neurosis are being weakened while, at the same time, there are being erected new and more durable supports on which, eventually, the altered personality can rest. Were this understood by the critics of psychoanalysis (or better still, by friends and relatives of analysands who understandably complain of the lack of evident progress), many current confusions about the process would disappear, and a more rational discussion of its merits as a form of therapy would be made possible.

For a year, then, Laura seemed to be standing still or losing ground. Chiefly, as in the episode I have already related, she reviewed her past and, in her sessions with me, either immediately or soon after, acted out their crucial or formative aspects. My consulting room became a stage on which she dramatized her life: my person became the target against which she directed the sad effects of her experience. In this manner she sought compensation for past frustrations, utilizing the permissive climate of therapy to obtain benefits she had missed, satisfactions that had been denied, and comforts she had lacked. Since the total effect of this pattern of emotional damming had been to cut her off from the many real satisfactions life offered, and to force her energies and talents into unproductive and even self-destructive channels, I allowed her, for that first year, almost endless opportunity for the "drainage" she required. The idea behind my attitude of complete permissiveness in therapy was to hold up to her a mirror of her behavior and to let her see not only the extravagance of the methods she used to obtain neurotic gratification, but also the essential hollowness, the futility and the infantilism of the desires she had been pursuing by such outlandish methods all of her life. Finally, the procedure was designed to illustrate, in sharpest perspective, the impossibility of securing basic, long-lasting and solid satisfactions from her accustomed modes of behavior. The latter aim, of course, set definite limits on my responsiveness to her conduct: I had to be careful to measure out to her, at the proper time and in correct amounts, the rewards she deserved when these were due her as a consequence of mature behavior toward mature goals.

Yes, this first year with Laura was a trying one, not only for her but for her analyst. I often wished she had chosen someone else to take her troubles to, and could hardly help hoping, on those many occasions when she threatened to break off treatment, that I would never see her again.

One episode from this time haunts me. I set it down here to show the strain she placed me under as much as to illustrate my technique with her and the weird dynamics of her neurosis that were uncovered by this technique.

According to my notes, what I am about to tell took place in the eleventh month of psychoanalysis. By that time the pattern of treatment had stabilized, I was in possession of most of the accessible facts of Laura's life, and the more obvious psychodynamics of her personality disorder were known to us. She, meanwhile, was in a period of relative quiet and contentment. It had been a month or more since her last attack, her job at the Gallery was going well, and she had recently formed a promising relationship with an eligible young man. It was on the theme of this affair that the first of these two crucial hours began, for Laura was deeply concerned about it and wished ardently that it might develop into something more rewarding and more lasting than her many previous romances.

"I don't want to foul this one up," she said, "but I'm afraid I'm going to. I need your help desperately."

"In what way d'you think you might foul it up?" I asked.

"Oh," she replied airily, "by being my usual bitchy self. You know—you ought to since you pointed it out; you know how possessive I get, how demanding I become. But I'd like, just for a change, not to be that way. For once, I'd like to have a love affair work out well for me."

"You mean you're thinking of matrimony?" I asked.

She laughed brightly. "Well," she said, "if you must know, I've had a few choice daydreams—fantasies, you'd probably call them—about marrying Ben. But that's not what I've got my heart set on now. What I want is love—I want to give it and I want to get it."

"If that attitude is genuine," I said, "you don't need my help in your affair."

She ground out the cigarette she was smoking against the bottom of the ash tray with short, angry jabs.

"You're horrible," she complained, "just horrible. Here I tell you something that I think shows real progress, and right away you throw cold water on it."

"What d'you think shows progress?"

"Why my recognition of giving, of course. I hope you noticed that I put it first."

"I did."

"And doesn't that mean something to you? Doesn't that show how far I've come?"

"It does," I said, "if it's genuine."

"Goddammit!" she flared. "You call *me* insatiable; *you're* the one who's never satisfied. But I'll show you yet."

She lit another cigarette and for the next few moments smoked in silence. Quite naturally my skepticism had shaken her confidence somewhat, as I had meant it to do, since I knew from experience how much she was given to these pat, semianalytical formulations that were consciously designed to impress as well as mislead me. I was just considering the wisdom of pursuing the topic she had opened and getting her somehow to explore her real goals in this new relationship when she began talking again.

"Anyhow," she said, "that's not what I wanted to talk about today. I had a dream. . . . Shall I tell you about it?"

I have found that when a patient uses this way of presenting a dream—announcing it first, then withholding until the analyst asks for it; actually dangling it like some tantalizing fruit before the analyst's eyes but insisting he reach out for it—the analyst had better listen closely. For this particular mode of dream presentation signifies the special importance of the dream, and it can be anticipated that it holds some extraordinarily meaningful clue to the patient's neurosis. Unconsciously, the patient, too, "knows" this, and by the use of the peculiar formula communicates his inarticulate but nonetheless high estimate of the dream's value. More than this, he is offering the dream, when he invites attention to it this way, as a gift to the analyst, a gift that has implications extending far beyond the dream itself and including the possibility of surrendering an entire area of neurotic functioning. His reservations about giving up a piece of his neurosis and the gratifications he has been receiving from it are betrayed by his use of the "shall I tell you about it?": he wants assurance, in advance, that the sacrifice will be worth while, that the analyst will appreciate (and love him for) it, and that he (the patient) will experience an equal amount of gratification from the newer, healthier processes which will henceforth replace the old. For this reason the analyst must be wary of reaching for the tempting fruit being offered him; to grasp at it would be to rob his patient of the painful but necessary first steps toward responsible self-hood, and to commit himself to bargains and promises he has no right to make.

Therefore, when Laura held out the gift of her dream, although I was most eager to hear it, I responded with the evasive but always handy reminder of the "basic rule": "Your instructions have always been to say what comes to you during your hours here. If you're thinking of a dream, tell it."

"Well," she said, "this is what I dreamed. . . . I was in what appeared to be a ballroom or dance hall, but I knew it was really a hospital. A man came up to me and told me to undress, take all my clothes off. He was going to give me a gynecological examination. I did as I was told but I was very frightened. While I was undressing, I noticed that he was doing something to a woman at the other end of the room. She was sitting or lying in a funny kind of contraption with all kinds of levers and gears and pulleys attached to it. I knew that I was supposed to be next, that I would have to sit in that thing while he examined me. Suddenly he called my name and I found myself running to him. The chair or table—whatever it was—was now empty, and he told me to get on it. I refused and began to cry. It started to rain—great big drops of rain. He pushed me to the floor and spread my legs for the examination. I turned over on my stomach and began to scream. I woke myself up screaming."

Following the recital Laura lay quietly on the couch, her eyes closed, her arms crossed over her bosom.

"Well," she said after a brief, expectant silence, "what does it mean?"

"Laura," I admonished, "you know better than that. Associate, and we'll find out."

"The first thing I think of is Ben," she began. "He's an intern at University, you know. I guess that's the doctor in the dream—or maybe it was you. Anyhow, whoever it was, I wouldn't let him examine me."

"Why not?"

"I've always been afraid of doctors . . . afraid they might hurt me."

"How will they hurt you?"

"I don't know. By jabbing me with a needle, I guess. That's funny. I never thought of it before. When I go to the dentist I don't mind getting a needle; but with a doctor it's different. . . ." Here I noticed how the fingers of both hands clutched her arms at the elbows while her thumbs nervously smoothed the inner surfaces of the joints. "I shudder when I think of having my veins punctured. I'm always afraid that's what a doctor will do to me."

"Has it ever been done?"

She nodded. "Once, in college, for a blood test. I passed out cold."

"What about gynecological examinations?"

"I've never had one. I can't even bear to think of someone poking around inside me." Again silence; then, "Oh," she said, "I see it now. It's sex I'm afraid of. The doctor in the dream *is* Ben. He wants me to have intercourse, but it scares me and I turn away from him. That's true. . . . The other night after the concert he came to my apartment. I made coffee for us and we sat there talking. It was wonderful—so peaceful, just the two of us. Then he started to make love to me. I loved it—until it came to having intercourse. I stopped him there: I had to; I became terrified. He probably thinks I'm a virgin—or that I don't care for him enough. But it isn't that. I do—and I want him to love me. Oh, Dr. Lindner, that's why I need your help so much now. . . ."

"But other men have made love to you," I reminded her.

"Yes," she said, sobbing now, "but I only let them as a last resort, as a way of holding on to them a little longer. And if you'll remember, I've only had the real thing a few times. Mostly I've made love to the man—satisfied him somehow. I'd do anything to keep them from getting inside me—poking into me . . . like the needle, I guess."

"But why, Laura?"

"I don't know," she cried, "I don't know. Tell me."

"I think the dream tells you," I said.

"The dream I just told you?"

"Yes. . . . There's a part of it you haven't considered. What comes to your mind when you think of the other woman in the dream, the woman the doctor was examining before you?"

"The contraption she was sitting in," Laura exclaimed. "It was like a—like a wheel chair—my mother's wheel chair! Is that right?"

"Very likely," I said.

"But why would he be examining *her*? What would that mean?"

"Well, think of what that kind of examination signifies for you."

"Sex," she said. "Intercourse—that's what it means. So that's what it is—that's what it means! Intercourse put my mother in the wheel chair. It paralyzed her. And I'm afraid that's what it will do to me. So I avoid it—because I'm scared it will do the same thing to me. . . . Where did I ever get such a crazy idea?"

—Like so many such "ideas" all of us have, this one was born in Laura long before the age when she could think for herself. It arose out of sensations of terror when she would awaken during the night, shocked from sleep by the mysterious noises her parents made in their passion, and incapable yet of assembling these sounds into a design purporting the tender uses of love. The heavy climate of hate, the living antagonism between her parents, made this impossible; so the sounds in the night—the "Mike, you're hurting me," the moans and cries, the protestations, even the laughter—impressed upon her the darker side of their sex, the brutish animality of it and the pain. And when the disease struck her mother a natural bridge of associations was formed between the secret drama that played itself out while Laura slept—or sometimes awakened her to fright—and the final horror of the body imprisoned on the chair.

I explained this to Laura, documenting my explanation with material the analysis had already brought out. For her, the interpretation worked a wonder of insight. Obvious as it may seem to us, to Laura, from whom it had been withheld by many resistances and defenses, it came as a complete surprise. Almost immediately, even before she quit the couch at the end of that hour, she felt a vast relief from the pressure of many feelings that had tormented her until that very day. The idea that sexual love was impossible for her, the idea that she was so constructed physically that the joys of love would forever be denied her, feelings of self-dissatisfaction, and numerous other thoughts and emotions collected around the central theme of sex—these vanished as if suddenly atomized.

"I feel free," Laura said as she rose from the couch when time was called. "I think this has been the most important hour of my analysis." At the door she paused and turned to me with moist, shining eyes. "I knew I could count on you," she said. "And I'm very grateful—believe me."

When she left, in the ten-minute interval between patients during which I ordinarily make notes, attend to messages or read, I reviewed the hour just ended. I, too, had a feeling of satisfaction and relief from it. And while I did not consider it to have been her most important hour—for the analyst's standards are markedly different from the patient's—nevertheless I did not underestimate its potential for the eventual solution of Laura's difficulties. I therefore looked forward to her next hour with pleasurable anticipation, thinking that the mood in which she had departed would continue and hoping she would employ it to stabilize her gains.

The session I have just described took place on a Saturday. On Monday, Laura appeared at the appointed time. The moment I saw her in the anteroom I knew something had gone wrong. She sat dejectedly, chin cupped in her hands, a light coat carelessly draped about her shoulders. When I greeted her, she raised her eyes listlessly.

"Ready for me?" she asked in a toneless voice.

I nodded and motioned her into the next room. She stood up wearily, dropping the coat on the chair, and preceded me slowly. As I closed the door behind us, she flopped on the couch sideways, her feet remaining on the floor. In the same moment she raised one arm to her head and covered her brow with the back of her hand. The other arm dangled over the side of the couch.

"I don't know why we bother," she said in the same flat voice.

I lit a cigarette and settled back in my chair to listen.

She sighed. "Aren't you going to ask me what's wrong?"

"There's no need to ask," I said. "You'll tell me in due time."

"I guess I will," she said, sighing again.

She lifted her feet from the floor, then squirmed to find a more comfortable position. Her skirt wrinkled under her and for some moments she was busy with the tugging and pulling women usually go through in their first minutes of each session. Under her breath she muttered impatient curses. At last she was settled.

"I don't have to tell you I went to bed with Ben, do I?" she asked.

"If that's what you're thinking of," I said.

"I think you must be a voyeur," she commented acidly after another pause. "That's probably the way you get your kicks."

I said nothing.

"Probably why you're an analyst, too," she continued. "Sublimating . . . isn't that the word? Playing Peeping Tom with your ears. . . ."

"Laura," I asked, "why are you being so aggressive?"

"Because I hate you," she said, "I hate your guts."

"Go on."

She shrugged. "That's all. I've got nothing more to say. I only came here today to tell you how much I despise you. I've said it and I'm finished. . . . Can I go now?" She sat up and reached for her purse.

"If that's what you want to do," I said.

"You don't care?" she asked.

"Care isn't the right word," I said. "Of course I'll be sorry to see you leave. But, as I said, if that's what you want to do . . ."

"More double talk," she sighed. "All right. The hell with it. I'm here and I may as well finish out the hour—after all, I'm paying for it." She fell back on the couch and lapsed into silence again.

"Laura," I said, "you seem very anxious to get me to reject you today. Why?"

"I told you—because I hate you."

"I understand that. But why are you trying to make *me* reject *you*?"

"Do we have to go through that again?" she asked. "Because that's my pattern—according to you. I try to push people to the point where they reject me, then I feel worthless and sorry for myself, and find a good excuse to punish myself. Isn't that it?"

"Approximately. But why are you doing it here today?"

"You must be a glutton for punishment, too," she said. "How many times must I say it?—I hate you, I loathe you, I despise you. Isn't that sufficient?"

"But why?"

"Because of what you made me do over the weekend."

"With Ben?"

"Ben!" she said contemptuously. "Of course not. What's that got to do with it? All that happened was that I went to bed with him. We slept together. It was good . . . wonderful. For the first time in my life I felt like a woman."

"Then what . . .?" I started to say.

"—Keep quiet!" she interrupted. "You wanted to know why I hate you and I'm telling you. It's got nothing to do with Ben or what happened Saturday night. It's about my mother. What we talked about last time . . . that's why I hate you so. She's haunted me all weekend. Since Saturday I can't get her out of my mind. I keep thinking about her—the awful life she had. And the way I treated her. Because you forced me to, I remembered things, terrible things I did to her . . . That's why I hate you—for making me remember." She turned on her side and looked at me over her shoulder. "And you," she continued, "you bastard . . . you did it purposely. You fixed it so I'd remember how rotten I was to her. I've spent half my life trying to forget her and that goddam' wheel chair. But no; you won't let me. You brought her back from the grave to haunt me. That's why I hate you so!"

This outburst exhausted Laura. Averting her head once more, she lay quietly for some minutes. Then she reached an arm behind her.

"Give me the Kleenex," she commanded.

I gave her the box of tissues from the table by my chair. Removing one, she dabbed at her eyes.

"Let me have a cigarette," she said, reaching behind her again.

I put my cigarettes and a box of matches in her hand. She lit up and smoked.

"It's funny," she said. "Funny how I've clung to everything I could find to keep on hating her. You see, I always blamed her for what happened. I always thought it was her fault my father left us. I made it out that she drove him away with her nagging and complaining. I've tried to hide from myself the fact that he was just no good—a lazy, chicken-chasing, selfish son-of-a-bitch. I excused him for his drinking and his neglect of us all those years. I thought, 'Why not? Why shouldn't he run around, stay out all night, have other women? After all, what good was she to him with those useless legs and dried-up body?' I pushed out of my head the way he was before . . . before she got sick. The truth is he was never any different, always a bum. Even when I was small he was no good, no good to her and no good to us. But I loved him—God! how I loved that man. I could hardly wait for him to come home. Drunk, sober—it didn't matter to me. He made a fuss over me and that's why I loved him. She said I was his favorite: I guess I was. At least he made over me more than the others.

"When I'd hear them fighting, I always blamed her. 'What's she picking on him for?' I'd think. 'Why doesn't she let him alone?' And when he went away, I thought it was her fault. Ever since then, until Saturday, I thought it was her fault. And I made her suffer for it. I did mean things to her, things I never told you about, things I tried to forget—did forget—until this weekend. I did them to punish her for kicking him out, for depriving me of his love. His love!

"Would you like to hear one of the things I did? I've thought this one over for two days. . . . Maybe if I tell you I can get rid of it."

. . . Every day on the way home from school she played the same game with herself. That was the reason she preferred to walk home alone. Because what if it happened when the other kids were around? How would she explain it to them? As far as they were concerned she didn't have a father. Even on the high-school admission blank, where it said: "Father—living or dead—check one," she had marked a big X over "dead." So what would she say if, suddenly, he stepped out of a doorway, or came around a corner, or ran over from across the street—and grabbed her and kissed her like he used to? Could she say, "Girls, this is my father?" Of course not! It was better to walk home alone, like this, pretending he was in that alley near the bottom of the hill, or standing behind the coal truck, or hiding behind the newsstand by the subway entrance . . . or that those footsteps behind her—the ones she kept hearing but there was no one there when she turned around—were his footsteps.

The game was over. It ended in the hallway of the tenement house, the same house they had lived in all of her life. If he wasn't here, in the smelly vestibule, on the sagging stairs, or standing expectantly on the first-floor landing in front of their door, the game had to end. And he wasn't: he never was. . . .

She heard the radio as she climbed the stairs, and her insides contracted in a spasm of disgust. "The same thing," she thought, "the same darned thing. Why can't it be different for once, just for once?" With her shoulder she pushed open the door. It closed behind her with a bang; but Anna, sleeping in her chair as usual, hardly stirred.

Laura put her books down on the dresser, then switched the dial of the radio to "off" with a hard, vicious twist of her fingers. Crossing the room she opened the closet, hung up her coat, and slammed the door hard, thinking, "So what if it wakes her? I hope it does!" But it didn't.

On the way to the rear of the apartment she glanced briefly at her mother. In the wheel chair Anna slumped like an abandoned rag doll. Her peroxided hair, showing gray and brown at the roots where it was parted, fell over her forehead. Her chin was on her breast, and from one corner of her mouth a trickle of spittle trailed to the collar of the shabby brown dress. The green sweater she wore was open; it hung about her thin shoulders in rumpled folds, and from its sleeves her skinny wrists and the fingers tipped with bright red nails protruded like claws of a chicken, clutching the worn arms of the chair. Passing her, Laura repressed an exclamation of contempt.

In the kitchen Laura poured herself a glass of milk and stood drinking it by the drain. When she had finished, she rinsed the glass under the tap. It fell from her hands and shattered against the floor.

"Is that you, Laura?" Anna called.

"Yeah."

"Come here. I want you to do something for me."

Laura sighed. "O.K. As soon as I clean up this mess."

She dried her hands and walked into the front room. "What is it?" she asked.

Anna motioned with her head. "Over there, on the dresser," she said. "The check from the relief came. I wrote out the store order. You can stop on your way back and give the janitor the rent."

"All right," Laura said wearily. She took her coat from the closet. At the door to the hall she paused and turned to face Anna, who was already fumbling with the radio dial. "Anything else?" she asked, playing out their bimonthly game.

Anna smiled. "Yes," she said. "I didn't put it on the store list, but if they have some of those chocolate-covered caramels I like . . ."

Laura nodded and closed the door. Music from the radio chased her downstairs.

When she returned, laden with packages, she stopped in the bedroom only momentarily to turn down the volume of the radio. "The least you can do is play it quietly," she muttered. "I could hear it a block away."

In the kitchen, still wearing her coat, she disposed of the groceries.

"Did you get everything, Laura?" Anna called.

"Yeah."

"Pay the rent?"

"Uh-huh."

"Did they have any of those caramels?"

This time Laura didn't answer. Somewhere, deep inside, the low-burning flame of hate flickered to a new height.

"Laura!" Anna called.

"What d'you want?" the girl shouted angrily.

"I asked if you got my candy."

About to reply, Laura's gaze fell to the remaining package on the porcelain-topped kitchen table. It seemed to hypnotize her, holding her eyes fast and drawing her hand toward its curled neck. Slowly her fingers untwisted the bag and plunged inside. When they emerged, they carried two squares of candy to her mouth. Without tasting, she chewed and swallowed rapidly.

Behind her Laura heard the shuffle of wheels. She turned to find Anna crossing the threshold of the bedroom. Snatching up the bag, the girl hurried into the dining room and faced her mother across the oval table.

"D'you have the candy?" Anna asked.

Laura nodded and held up the sack.

"Give it here," Anna said, extending her hand.

Laura shook her head and put the hand with the paper bag behind her back. Puzzled, Anna sent her chair around the table toward the girl, who waited until her mother came near, then moved quickly to the opposite side, placing the table between them again.

"What kind of nonsense is this?" Anna asked. In reply, Laura put another piece of candy in her mouth.

"Laura!" Anna demanded. "Give me my candy!" She gripped the wheels of her chair and spun them forward. It raced around the table after the girl, who skipped lightly before it. Three times Anna circled the table, chasing the elusive figure that regarded her with narrowed eyes. Exhausted, finally, she stopped. Across from her, Laura stuffed more candy into her mouth and chewed violently.

"Laura," Anna panted, "what's got into you? Why are you doing this?"

Laura toook the bag from behind her back and held it temptingly over the table. "If you want it so bad," she said, breathing hard, "come get it." She shook the bag triumphantly. "See," she said, "it's almost all gone. You'd better hurry."

Inside, at the very core of her being, the flame was leaping. A warm glow of exultation swept through her, filling her body with a sense of power and setting her nerves on fire. She felt like laughing, like screaming, like dancing madly. In her mouth the taste of chocolate was intoxicating.

Her mother whimpered. "Give me the candy. . . . Please, Laura."

Laura held the bag high. "Come and get it!" she screamed, and backed away slowly toward the front room.

Anna spun her chair in pursuit. By the time she reached the bedroom, Laura was at the door. She waited until her mother's chair came close, then she whirled and ran through, pulling the door behind her with a loud crash.

Leaning against the banister, Laura listened to the thud of Anna's fists against the wood and her sobs of angry frustration. The wild exhilaration mounted. Hardly conscious of her actions, she crammed the remaining candies into her mouth. Then, from deep in her body, a wave of laughter surged upward. She tried to stop it, but it broke through in a crazy tide of hilarity. The sound of this joyless mirth rebounded from the stair well and echoed from the ceiling of the narrow hallway—as it was to echo, thereafter, along with the sound of footsteps and falling rain, in her dreams. . . .

The weeks following the crucial hours I have just described were very difficult ones for Laura. As she worked through the guilt-laden memories now released from repression, her self-regard, never at any time very high, fell lower and lower. Bitterly, she told the ugly rosary of her pathetic past, not sparing herself (or me) the slightest detail. In a confessional mood, she recited all her faults of behavior—toward her family, her friends, her teachers, her associates—throughout the years. Under the influence of newly acquired but undigested insights the pattern of her sessions with me changed. No longer did she find it necessary to pour out the acid of her hate and contempt, to vilify and condemn me and the world for our lack of love for her. Now she swung the pendulum to the other side: everyone had been too nice to her, too tolerant; she didn't deserve anyone's good opinion, particularly mine.

In keeping with her new mood, Laura also changed the style of her life. She became rigidly ascetic in her dress, adopted a strict diet, gave up smoking, drinking, cosmetics, dancing and all other ordinary amusements. The decision to surrender the novel joys of sex with her lover, Ben, was hard to make, but, tight-lipped and grim with determination, she declared her intention to him and stuck by her word.

For my part, in these weeks of confession and penitential repentance I remained silent and still permissive, revealing nothing of my own thoughts or feelings. I neither commented on the "sins" Laura recounted nor the expiatory measures she employed to discharge them. Instead, as I listened, I tried to reformulate her neurosis in terms of the dynamic information available to us at that point. Naturally, I saw through the recent shift in analytic content and behavior: it was, of course, but a variant of the old design, only implemented by conscious, deliberate techniques. Fundamentally, Laura was still Laura. That she now chose to destroy herself and her relationships in a more circumspect and less obvious fashion; that the weapons she now turned upon herself were regarded—at least by the world outside the analytic chamber—in the highest terms, altered not one whit the basic fact that the core of her neurosis, despite our work, remained intact. Laura, in short, was still profoundly disturbed, still a martyr to secret desires that had not been plumbed.

She did not think so—nor did her friends. As a matter of fact, they were astonished at what they called her "progress," and word reached me that my reputation in Baltimore—an intimate city where who is going to which analyst is always a lively topic at parties—had soared to new heights. And, indeed, to the casual observer Laura seemed improved. In the curious jargon of the analytic sophisticate, she was "making an adjustment." Her rigorous diet, her severity of manner and dress, her renunciation of all fleshly joys and amusements, her sobriety and devotion to "serious" pursuits, above all her maintenance of a "good" relationship with the eligible Ben (*without sex*, it was whispered)—these were taken as tokens of far-reaching and permanent alterations in personality due to the "miracle" of psychoanalysis. Those with whom she came in contact during this time of course never bothered to peer beneath the mask of public personality she wore. They were content to take her at face value. Because she no longer disrupted their gatherings with demonstrations of her well-known "bitchiness," because she no longer thrust her problems on them or called for their help in times of distress, they felt relieved in their consciences about her. In brief, without laboring the point, so long as Laura disturbed no one else and kept her misery to herself; and so long as she represented to her associates the passive surrender to the mass ideal each one of them so desperately but fruitlessly sought, just as long were they impressed by the "new look" that Laura wore.

But we knew, Laura and I, that the battle had yet to be joined, for only we knew what went on behind the closed doors of 907 in the La-trobe Building. In this room the masks fell away: either they were dis-carded because here they could not hide the truth, or they were taken from her by the soft persuasion of continuous self-examination with insight. The first to go was the last she had assumed: the defensive mask of self-abnegation.

The time came when I found it necessary to call a halt to Laura's daily *mea culpas*, to put a stop to the marathon of confession she had entered at the beginning of her second year with me. Three factors in-fluenced my decision to force her, at last, off the new course her analy-sis had taken. The first and most important of these was my perception of the danger implicit in this program of never-ending self-denun-ciation. As she searched her memory for fresh evidence of guilt, I could see how overwhelmed she was becoming by the enormity of her past behavior. Try as she might, I knew she could never salve her con-science by the penitential acts and renunciations she invented, and I feared the outcome of a prolonged contest between contrition and atonement; it could only lead to the further debility of her ego, to a progressive lowering of self-esteem which might wind up at a point I dared not think about.

The second and hardly less important reason why I felt I had to urge Laura away from this attempt to shrive herself in the manner she chose was the simple fact of its unproductiveness for therapy. As I have already said, this psychic gambit of self-abnegation only substituted one set of neurotic symptoms for another and left the basic patholog-ical structure untouched. Moreover, it provided precisely the same kind of neurotic satisfaction she had been securing all along by her old techniques. The martyrdom she now suffered by her own hand was equivalent to the self-pity formerly induced by the rejection she had unconsciously arranged to obtain from others. And while it is true that she no longer exercised hate, hostility and aggressive contempt outwardly, it was only the direction in which these negative elements were discharged that had been altered: they remained.

Finally, my decision was also influenced by sheer fatigue and boredom with what I knew to be only an act, a disguise of behavior and attitude adopted to squeeze the last ounce of neurotic gratification from me and the entire world which, by psychic extension from love-withholding parents, she viewed as rejecting and denying. To tell the truth, I became tired of the "new" Laura, weary of her pious pretenses, and a trifle nauseated with the holier-than-thou manner she assumed. And while this was the least of my reasons for doing what I did, I hold it chiefly responsible for the almost fatal error in timing I committed when I finally acted on an otherwise carefully weighed decision to eject my patient from the analytic rut in which she was, literally, wallowing.

The session that precipitated the near catastrophe took place on a Thursday afternoon. Laura was the last patient I was to see that day, since I was taking the Congressional Limited to New York where I was scheduled to conduct a seminar that night and give a lecture on Friday. I was looking forward to the trip which, for me, represented a holiday from work and the first break in routine in many months. Something of this mood of impatience to get going and pleasurable anticipation must have been communicated to Laura, for she began her hour with a hardly disguised criticism of my manner and appearance.

"Somehow," she said after composing herself on the couch, "somehow you seem different today."

"I do?"

"Yes." She turned to look at me. "Maybe it's because of the way you're dressed. . . . That's a new suit, isn't it?"

"No," I said. "I've worn it before."

"I don't remember ever seeing it." She resumed her usual position. "Anyway, you look nice."

"Thank you."

"I like to see people look nice," she continued. "When a person gets all dressed up, it makes them feel better. I think it's because they think other people will judge them on the basis of their outer appearance—and if the outer appearance is pleasing and nice, people will think what's behind is pleasing and nice, too—and being thought of that way makes you feel better. Don't you think so?"

I was lost in the convolutions of this platitude, but its inference was pretty clear.

"What exactly are you getting at?" I asked.

She shrugged. "It's not important," she said. "Just a thought . . ." There was a moment of silence, then, "Oh!" she exclaimed. "I know why you're all dressed up. . . . Today's the day you go to New York, isn't it?"

"That's right," I said.

"That means I won't see you on Saturday, doesn't it?"

"Yes. I won't be back until Monday."

"Is the lecture on Saturday?"

"No, the lecture's tomorrow, Friday."

"—But you're going to stay over until Monday. . . . Well, I think the rest will do you good. You need it. I think everyone needs to kick up his heels once in a while, just get away, have some fun and forget everything—if he can."

The dig at my irresponsibility toward my patients, particularly Laura, and the implication that I was going to New York to participate in some kind of orgy, were not lost on me.

"I hate to miss an hour," Laura continued in the same melancholy tone she had been using since this meeting began. "Especially now. I feel I really need to come here now. There's so much to talk about."

"In that case," I said, "you should take more advantage of the time you're here. For example, you're not using this hour very well, are you?"

"Perhaps not," she said. "It's just that I feel this is the wrong time for you to be going away."

"Now look here, Laura," I said. "You've known about missing the Saturday hour for more than a week. Please don't pretend it's a surprise to you. And, besides, it's only one hour."

"I know," she sighed. "I know. But it feels like you're going away forever. . . . What if I should need you?"

"I don't think you will. . . . But if you should, you can call my home or the office here and they'll put you in touch with me."

I lit a cigarette and waited for her to go on. With the first inhalation, however, I began to cough. Laura again turned around.

"Can I get you something?" she asked. "A glass of water?"

"No, thank you," I answered.

"That cough of yours worries me," she said when the spasm had passed and I was once more quiet. "You should give up smoking. I did, you know. It's been two months since I had a cigarette. And my cough's all gone. I think that's the best of it—no more coughing. I feel fine. You should really try it."

I continued to smoke in silence, wondering where she would take this theme. Before long, I found out.

"It wasn't easy. The first two weeks were agony, but I determined not to give in. After all, I had a reason. . . ."

"To stop coughing?" I suggested, permitting myself the small satisfaction of retaliating for her deliberate provocation of the past half hour.

"Of course not!" she exclaimed. "You know very well I had good reasons for giving up smoking—and other things too."

"What were they?" I asked.

"You of all people should know," she said.

"Tell me."

"Well—it's just that I want to be a better person. If you've been listening to everything I've said these past weeks you know how I used to behave. Now I want to make amends for it, to be different, better. . . ."

"And you think giving up smoking and so on will make you a better person?"

She fell silent. Glancing over at her, I noticed the rigidity of her body. Her hands, until now held loosely on her lap, were clenched into fists. I looked at my watch and cursed myself for a fool. Only ten minutes left and a train to catch! Why had I let myself rise to the bait? Why had I permitted this to come up now, when it couldn't be handled? Was there any way out, any way to avoid the storm I had assisted her to brew? I put my trust in the gods that care for idiots and took a deep breath.

"Well?" I asked.

"Nothing I do is right," she said hollowly. "There's no use trying. I just make it worse."

"What are you talking about?"

"Myself," she said. "Myself and the mess I make of everything. I try to do what's right—but I never can. I think I'm working it all out—but I'm not. I'm just getting in deeper and deeper. It's too much for me, too much. . . ."

When the hour ended, I rose and held the door open for her.

"I'll see you Monday," I said.

Her eyes were glistening. "Have a good time," she sighed.

On the train to New York I thought about Laura and the hour just ended, reviewing it word for word and wondering just where I had made my mistake. That I had committed a serious error I had no doubt, and it hardly needed Laura's abrupt change of mood to bring this to my attention. To mobilize guilt and anxiety just prior to a recess in therapy is in itself unwise. In this instance, I had compounded the blunder by losing control over myself and responding, as I seldom do in the treatment situation, to criticism and provocation. I asked myself—had she touched some peculiarly sensitive chord in me? Am I so susceptible to faultfinding? Have I, all unaware, become especially tender on the subject of my incessant smoking? my cough? my responsibility to my patients? my appearance? Or was it, as I suspected then and am sure of now, that I had made the decision to contrive a directional change in Laura's analysis but had been incited to violate the timetable of therapy by an unexpected display of the fatuousness that had become her prevailing defense?

That evening I had dinner with friends and conducted the scheduled seminar, after which many of us gathered for a series of nightcaps and further discussion in a colleague's home. I had forgotten all about Laura by the time I returned to my hotel, and when the desk clerk gave me a message to call a certain long-distance operator in Baltimore, I thought it would concern only something personal at home or a communication from my office. I was surprised when Laura's voice came over the wire.

"Dr. Lindner?"

"Yes, Laura. What is it?"

"I've been trying to get you for hours."

"I'm sorry. Is something wrong?"

"I don't know. I just wanted to talk with you."

"What about?"

"About the way I feel. . . ."

"How do you feel?"

"Scared."

"Scared of what?"

"I don't know. Just scared, I guess. Of nothing in particular — just everything. . . . I don't like being alone."

"But you're alone most other nights, aren't you?" I asked.

"Yes . . . but somehow it's different tonight."

"Why?"

"Well, for one thing, you're not in Baltimore."

The line was silent as I waited for her to continue.

"And then," she said, "I think you're angry with me."

"Why do you think that?"

"The way I acted this afternoon. It was mean of me, I know. But I couldn't help it. Something was egging me on."

"What was it?"

"I don't know. I haven't figured it out. Something . . ."

"We'll talk about it Monday," I said.

More silence. I thought I heard noises as if she were crying.

"Do you forgive me?" she sobbed.

"We'll review the whole hour on Monday," I said, seeking a way out of this awkward situation. "Right now you'd better get to bed."

"All right," she said meekly. "I'm sorry I bothered you."

"No bother at all," I said. "Good night, Laura" — and hung up with relief.

I gave the lecture on Friday afternoon, and when it was over returned to my room for a nap before beginning my holiday with dinner in a favorite restaurant and a long-anticipated evening at the theater. In the quiet room, I bathed and lay down for a peaceful interlude of sleep. Hardly had I begun to doze when the phone rang. It was my wife, calling from Baltimore. Laura, she said, had slashed her wrists: I had better come home — quick. . . .

The doctor and I sat in the corner of the room, talking in whispers. On the bed, heavily sedated, Laura breathed noisily. Even in the dim light the pallor of her face was discernible, and I could see a faint white line edging her lips. On the blanket her hands lay limply. The white bandages at her wrists forced themselves accusingly on my attention. From time to time her hands twitched.

"I doubt that it was a serious attempt," the physician was saying, "although of course you never know. It's harder than you think, trying to get out that way. You've really got to mean it—you've got to mean it enough to saw away hard to get down where it counts. I don't think she tried very hard. The cut on the left wrist is fairly deep, but not deep enough, and the ones on the right wrist are superficial. There wasn't a hell of a lot of blood, either."

"I understand you got there awfully fast," I said.

"Pretty fast," he replied. "What happened was this: Right after she slashed herself she began screaming. A neighbor ran in and had the good sense to call me immediately. My office is in the same building, on the first floor, and I happened to be there at the time. I rushed upstairs, took a look at the cuts and saw they weren't too bad—"

"They were made with a razor blade, weren't they?" I interrupted.

"Yes," he said, and then continued, "so I slapped a couple of tourniquets on, phoned the hospital that I was sending her in, then called the ambulance. I followed it here to Sinai. In the Accident Room they cleaned her up and had her wrists sutured by the time I arrived. She was still quite excited, so I decided to put her in for a day or two. I gave her a shot of morphine and sent her upstairs."

"Who called my home?" I asked.

He shrugged. "I don't know. Before the ambulance came, her neighbor called Laura's sister and told her what happened and what I was going to do. I think the sister tried to get hold of you."

"I guess so," I said. "She knows Laura's in treatment with me."

"I don't envy you," he said. "She's a lulu."

"What did she do?"

He shrugged and motioned toward the bed with a wave of his hand. "This kind of business, for one thing. Then the way she carried on until the shot took effect."

"What did she do?"

"Oh," he said vaguely, "she kept screaming and throwing herself around. Pretty wild." He stood up. "I don't think you've got anything to worry about as far as her physical condition goes, though. She'll be fine in the morning. Maybe a little groggy, that's all."

"I'm very grateful to you," I said.

"Not at all," he said on his way from the room. "There'll be some business with the police tomorrow. If you need me, just call."

Laura had her hour on Saturday—in the hospital. During it and many subsequent sessions we worked out the reasons for her extravagant, self-destructive gesture. As the physican had observed, her act was hardly more than a dramatic demonstration without serious intent, although in the way of such things it could well have miscarried to a less fortunate conclusion. Its immediate purpose was to recall me from my holiday and to reawaken the sympathetic attention she believed herself to have prejudiced by her hostile provocativeness on Thursday. But the whole affair, we learned subsequently, had much deeper roots.

The motivation behind Laura's attempt at suicide was twofold. Unconsciously, it represented an effort to reenact, with a more satisfying outcome, the desertion of her father; and, at the same time, it served the function of providing extreme penance for so-called "sins" of behavior and thought-crimes between the ages of twelve and twenty-four. So far as the first of these strange motivations is concerned, it is understandable how Laura interpreted my brief interruption of therapy as an abandonment similar to that abrupt and permanent earlier departure of her father. This time, however, as indicated by the phone call to my hotel on the night I left, she believed herself to have been at least in part responsible for it, to have driven him (in the person of the analyst) away. To call him back, her distraught mind conceived the suicidal act, which was nothing less than a frenzied effort—planned, so it appeared, but not executed, more than a decade before—to repeat the original drama but insure a different and more cordial ending.

The mad act was also powered dynamically by the fantastic arithmetic of confession and penance that Laura, like some demented accountant, had invented to discharge her guilty memories. As I had feared when the pattern became clear to me, the mental balance sheet she was keeping with her hourly testaments of culpability and the increasing asceticism of her life could never be stabilized. Self-abnegation had to lead to a martyrdom of some kind. My effort to prevent this miscarried—not because it was misconceived, but because it was so sloppily executed. My own unconscious needs—the residual infantilisms and immaturities within me—in this case subverted judgment and betrayed me into the commission of a timing error that could have cost Laura's life.

We both profited from this terrible experience and, in the end, it proved to have been something of a boon to each of us. I, of course, would have preferred to learn my lesson otherwise. As for Laura, she made a rapid recovery and returned to the analysis much sobered by her encounter with death. Apart from all else, the episode provided her with many genuine and useful insights, not the least of which were those that led her to abandon her false asceticism and to stop playing the role of the "well-analyzed," "adjusted" paragon among her friends.

The events just described furnished us with vast quantities of material for analysis in subsequent months. Particularly as it referred directly to the situation in psychoanalysis known technically as the "transference neurosis"—or the reflection in therapy of former patterns of relationship with early, significant figures in the life of the patient— the suicidal gesture Laura made led to an even deeper investigation of her existing neurotic attitudes and behavior. And as we dealt with this topic of transference—the organic core of every therapeutic enterprise; as we followed its meandering course through our sessions together, Laura rapidly made new and substantial gains. With every increase in her understanding another rich facet of personality was disclosed, and the burden of distress she had borne for so long became lighter and lighter.

The metamorphosis of Laura was a fascinating thing to observe. I, as the human instrument of changes that were taking place in her, was immensely gratified. Nevertheless, my pleasure and pride were incomplete, for I remained annoyingly aware that we had yet to find the explanation for the single remaining symptom that had so far evaded the influence of therapy. No progress at all had been made against the strange complaint which brought her into treatment: the seizures of uncontrollable hunger, the furious eating, and their dreadful effects.

I had my own theory about this stubborn symptom and was often tempted to follow the suggestion of a certain "school" of psychoanalysis and communicate my ideas to Laura. However, because I felt—and still feel—that such technique is theoretically unjustified—a reflection of the therapist's insecurity and impatience rather than a well-reasoned approach to the problems of psychotherapy—because I felt this way, I determined to curb my eagerness to bring Laura's chief symptom into focus by testing my interpretations on her. In adherence to methods in which I have been trained, therefore, I held my tongue and waited developments. Fortunately, they were not long in appearing; and when they did arrive, in one mighty tide of insight my patient's being was purged of the mental debris that had made her existence a purgatory.

Laura was seldom late for appointments, nor had she ever missed one without canceling for good cause well in advance. On this day, therefore, when she failed to appear at the appointed time I grew somewhat anxious. As the minutes passed, my concern mounted. Finally, after a half hour had sped and there was still no sign of Laura, I asked my secretary to call her apartment. There was no answer.

During the afternoon, caught up in work with other patients, I gave only a few passing thoughts to Laura's neglect to keep her hour or to inform me she would be absent. When I reminded myself of it at the close of the day, I tried, in a casual way, to recall her previous session and examine it for some clue to this unusual delinquency. Since none came readily, I pushed the matter from my mind and prepared to leave the office.

We were in the corridor awaiting the elevator when we heard the telephone. I was minded to let it ring, but Jeanne, more compulsive in such matters than I, insisted on returning to answer. While I held the elevator, she reentered the office. A few moments later she reappeared, shrugging her shoulders in answer to my question.

"Must have been a wrong number," she said. "When I answered all I heard was a funny noise and then the line went dead."

I arrived home shortly after six o'clock and dressed to receive the guests who were coming for dinner. While in the shower, I heard the ringing of the telephone, which my wife answered. On emerging from the bathroom, I asked her who had called.

"That was the queerest thing," she said. "The party on the other end sounded like a drunk and I couldn't make out a word."

During dinner I was haunted by a sense of unease. While attending to the lively conversation going on around me, and participating in it as usual, near the edges of consciousness something nagged uncomfortably. I cannot say that I connected the two mysterious calls with Laura and her absence from the hour that day, but I am sure they contributed to the vague and fitful feelings I experienced. In any case, when the telephone again rang while we were having our coffee, I sprang from my place and rushed to answer it myself.

I lifted the receiver and said, "Hello?" Over the wire, in response, came a gurgling, throaty noise which, even in retrospect defies comparison with any sound I have ever heard. Unmistakably produced by the human voice, it had a gasping, breathless quality, yet somehow seemed animal in nature. It produced a series of meaningless syllables, urgent in tone but unidentifiable.

"Who is this?" I demanded.

There was a pause, then, laboriously, I heard the first long-drawn syllable of her name.

"Laura"! I said. "Where are you?"

Again the pause, followed by an effortful intake of breath and its expiration as if through a hollow tube: "Home . . ."

"Is something wrong?"

It seemed to come easier this time.

"Eat-ing."

"Since when?"

". . . Don't—know."

"How d'you feel?" I asked, aware of the absurdity of the question but desperately at a loss to know what else to say.

"'Aw-ful . . . No—more—food . . . Hun-gry . . .'"

My mind raced. What could I do? What was there to do?

"Help—me," she said—and I heard the click of the instrument as it fell into its cradle.

"Laura," I said. "Wait!"—But the connection had been broken and my words echoed in my own ears. Hastily, I hung up and searched through the telephone directory for her number. My fingers spun the dial. After an interval, I heard the shrill buzz of her phone. Insistently, it repeated itself, over and over. There was no answer.

I knew, then, what I had to do. Excusing myself from our guests, I got my car and drove to where Laura lived. On the way there, I thought about what some of my colleagues would say of what I was doing. No doubt they would be appalled by such a breach of ortho-doxy and speak pontifically of "counter-transference," my "anxiety" at Laura's "acting out," and other violations of strict procedure. Well, let them. To me, psychoanalysis is a vital art that demands more of its practitioners than the clever exercise of their brains. Into its practice also goes the heart, and there are occasions when genuine human feel-ings take precedence over the rituals and dogmas of the craft.

I searched the mailboxes in the vestibule for Laura's name, then ran up the stairs to the second floor. In front of her door I paused and put my ear against the metal frame to listen. I heard nothing.

I pushed the button. Somewhere inside a chime sounded. A mi-nute passed while I waited impatiently. I rang again, depressing the button forcefully time after time. Still no one came to the door. Finally, I turned the knob with one hand and pounded the panel with the flat of the other. In the silence that followed, I heard the noise of something heavy crashing to the floor, then the sibilant shuffling of feet.

I put my mouth close to the crack where door met frame.

"Laura!" I called. "Open the door!"

Listening closely, I heard what sounded like sobs and faint moaning, then a voice that slowly pronounced the words, "Go—away."

I shook the knob violently. "Open up!" I commanded. "Let me in!"

The knob turned in my hand and the door opened. I pushed against it, but a chain on the jamb caught and held. In the dim light of the hallway, against the darkness inside, something white shone. It was Laura's face, but she withdrew it quickly.

"Go—away," she said in a thick voice.

"No."

"Please!"

She leaned against the door, trying to close it again. I put my foot in the opening.

"Take that chain off," I said with all the authority I could muster. "At once!"

The chain slid away and I walked into the room. It was dark, and I could make out only vague shapes of lamps and furniture. I fumbled along the wall for the light switch. Before my fingers found it, Laura, who was hardly more than an indistinguishable blur of whiteness by my side, ran past me into the room beyond.

I discovered the switch and turned on the light. In its sudden, harsh glare I surveyed the room. The sight was shocking. Everywhere I looked there was a litter of stained papers, torn boxes, empty bottles, open cans, broken crockery and dirty dishes. On the floor and on the tables large puddles gleamed wetly. Bits of food—crumbs, gnawed bones, fish-heads, sodden chunks of unknown stuffs—were strewn all about. The place looked as if the contents of a garbage can had been emptied in it, and the stench was sickening.

I swallowed hard against a rising wave of nausea and hurried into the room where Laura had disappeared. In the shaft of light that came through an archway, I saw a rumpled bed, similarly piled with rubbish. In a corner, I made out the crouching figure of Laura.

By the entrance I found the switch and pressed it. As the light went on, Laura covered her face and shrank against the wall. I went over to her, extending my hands.

"Come," I said. "Stand up."

She shook her head violently. I bent down and lifted her to her feet. When she stood up, her fingers still hid her face. As gently as I could, I pulled them away. Then I stepped back and looked at Laura. What I saw, I will never forget.

The worst of it was her face. It was like a ceremonial mask on which some inspired maniac had depicted every corruption of the flesh. Vice was there, and gluttony; lust also, and greed. Depravity and abomination seemed to ooze from great pores that the puffed tautness of skin revealed.

I closed my eyes momentarily against this apparition of incarnate degradation. When I opened them, I saw the tears welling from holes where her eyes should have been. Hypnotized, I watched them course in thin streams down the bloated cheeks and fall on her nightgown. And then, for the first time, I saw it!

Laura was wearing a night robe of some sheer stuff that fell loosely from straps at her shoulders. Originally white, it was now soiled and stained with the evidence of her orgy. But my brain hardly registered the begrimed garment, except where it bulged below her middle in a sweeping arc, ballooning outward from her body as if she were pregnant.

I gasped with disbelief — and my hand went out automatically to touch the place where her nightgown swelled. My fingers encountered a softness that yielded to their pressure. Questioning, I raised my eyes to that caricature of a human face. It twisted into what I took for a smile. The mouth opened and closed to form a word that it labored to pronounce.

"Ba-by," Laura said.

"Baby?" I repeated. "Whose baby?"

"Laur-ra's ba-by. . . . Lo-ok."

She bent forward drunkenly and grasped her gown by the hem. Slowly she raised the garment, lifting it until her hands were high above her head. I stared at her exposed body. There, where my fingers had probed, a pillow was strapped to her skin with long bands of adhesive.

Laura let the nightgown fall. Swaying, she smoothed it where it bulged.

"See?" she said. "Looks—real—this way."

Her hands went up to cover her face again. Now great sobs shook her, and tears poured through her fingers as she cried. I led her to the bed and sat on its edge with her, trying to order the turmoil of my thoughts while she wept. Soon the crying ceased, and she bared her face again. Once more the lost mouth worked to make words.

"I—want—a—baby," she said, and fell over on the bed—asleep.

. . .

I covered Laura with a blanket and went into the other room, where I remembered seeing a telephone. There, I called a practical nurse who had worked with me previously and whom I knew would be available. Within a half hour, she arrived. I briefed her quickly: the apartment was to be cleaned and aired: when Laura awakened, the doctor who lived downstairs was to be called to examine her and advise on treatment and diet: she was to report to me regularly, and in two days she was to bring Laura to my office. Then I left.

Although the night was cold I lowered the top on my car. I drove home slowly, breathing deeply of the clean air.

Two days later, while her nurse sat in the outer room, Laura and I began to put together the final pieces in the puzzle of her neurosis. As always, she had only a vague, confused memory of events during her seizure, recollecting them hazily through a fog of total intoxication. Until I recounted the episode, she had no clear remembrance of my visit and thought she had dreamed my presence in her rooms. Of the portion that concerned her pitiful imitation of pregnancy, not the slightest memorial trace remained.

It was clear that Laura's compelling desire was to have a child, that her feelings of emptiness arose from this desire, and that her convulsions of ravenous appetite were unconsciously designed to produce its illustory satisfaction. What was not immediately apparent, however, was why this natural feminine wish underwent such extravagant distortion in Laura's case, why it had become so intense, and why it had to express itself in a manner at once monstrous, occult and self-destructive.

My patient herself provided the clue to these focal enigmas when, in reconstructing the episode I had witnessed, she made a slip of the tongue so obvious in view of the facts that it hardly required interpretation.

It was about a week after the incident I have recorded. Laura and I were reviewing it again, looking for further clues. I was intrigued by the contrivance she wore that night to simulate the appearance of a pregnant woman, and asked for details about its construction. Laura could supply none. Apparently, she said, she had fashioned it in an advanced stage of her intoxication from food.

"Was this the first time you made anything like that?" I asked.

"I don't know," she said, somewhat hesitantly. "I can't be sure. Maybe I did and destroyed the thing before I came out of the fog. It seems to me I remember finding something like you describe a couple of years ago after an attack, but I didn't know—or didn't want to know—what it was, so I just took it apart and forgot about it."

"You'd better look around the apartment carefully," I said, half joking. "Perhaps there's a spare hidden away someplace."

"I doubt it," she replied in the same mood. "I guess I have to mike a new baby every . . ." Her hand went over her mouth. "My God!" she exclaimed. "Did you hear what I just said?"

Mike was her father's name; and of course it was his baby she wanted. It was for this impossible fulfillment that Laura hungered—and now was starved no more. . . .

8

The Success

John Logan

I lived these journeys always with anticipation and with dread, letting my mind race for mooring: preparations, protections, occult cheers, hopes, plans, dialogues. I was afraid to be cast from the jaws of the elevator naked and alone and in a questionable form.

Already in the machine I thought rather desperately of the doctor as *voyeur*, interested in the tabooed places of man, and of a critic like myself as a sort of scatologist, interested in (devoted to) man's effluvia—the invisible dross of his brain and breath cast onto the pages of books. This suggestion so disgusted me that if I were not at the moment rising into the heights toward the holy oracle I would have gone off to a bar. I thought of the one just to the left of the entrance to the building. Remembered I was broke anyway. But how should one protect himself from his own ideas? I was too old to run to mamma like a child afraid of the pictures he had drawn with terrible crayons.

As I crossed the small fourteenth floor court toward the doctor's suite I saw in the marble fountain (sculpted as a boy on a dolphin) a young Jonah on a young whale, and I thought that at that age it is almost as easy for the boy to carry the fish as it is somewhat later for the huge fish to drag the man out to sea. If only one could time things so that he could devour the fish before it got him! Standing in the court before the fountain I knew I had stopped in order to delay my entrance into the doctor's office, but my mind seemed to fill with dolphin images and allusions like a school breaking and leaping in a sea. I was no longer young and had a wife and family to support, but I thought of myself now as a sad youth wafted by dolphins, given to crying with the figures in fountains, constitutionally confusing the devouring shark or whale with the gentle, riding dolphin—and the erotic fish with the Christian one. I wished that any one of those marine animals—or the monster of Tobias, or that of Hippolytus—would come clear and bear me away again.

Having at last crossed that long court I sat in the foyer with its hodge podge of French provincial and modern worked-iron furniture, its foolish books, its view of a garment warehouse where grotesque and naked dummies gestured at the windows like dying women, and its stairway to The Presence—to The Hulk in the Corner that said hello without meaning it, while listening, whirring and watching and listening. The encounter with the doctor imminent as it was, I suddenly thought that the truth about myself was simple: I was a member of the species of Catholic Neurotics—a mediocre group, like most Catholic societies. But I was fairly distinguished myself as a drinker and as a narcissist, fascinated by my own nocturnal images. I was willing to have the doctor look over my shoulder at the pools of my dreams, but it was also necessary to protect oneself. At the moment my defense against the narrowing eyes of the physician, in the process now of recognizing me, was my decision to relate my most recent dream and to keep quiet about my thoughts of the instant, the last of which was a kind of wondering why I always turned to the right instead of to the left as I lay down on the couch—was it because the doctor's stairway had spiraled to the right? (Or was it left?) The doctor himself sat hidden behind my head.

II

A moment of recollection and I was able to get started with the dream, diving into myself at the chosen angle: there were jewels, pearls

and exquisitely designed ceramic boxes every detail of which I could remember, and shining large ornate trays which I thought of as Achilles'
shields I had myself designed. And there were lucent, glass vases with
mythological legends etched on them in excruciating patterns of light
on light—Orpheus and the Thracian women, Actaeon and Diana,
and others I couldn't remember. Jung's archetypes maybe, I said
smugly. The thought of the burrs or the sand on the glass, as I supposed they used, was painful and for some reason reminded me, I said,
of a stone going through the ducts of a man's guts cutting fine, colorless
lines in which the secretive blood did not appear until sometime later.

As for pearls, I remembered that one of the secretaries at my pub-
lishers wore just such earrings, dew-drop pearls in a golden and ba-
roque set. Or stag-tooth-shaped pearls, slightly curved; wasn't a stag's
tooth slightly curved? I now realized for the first time, I said, that the
stag's teeth pearls always seem to bite the lobes of the secretary's ear—
and I always expected to see blood appear in a moment under the red
ringlets of her hair or upon the gold of the jewels. Oedipus stabbed
himself in the eyes with his mother's golden brooch, and a brooch is an
instrument of sexual attractiveness. Also the piercing earring of the
girl, I said, was like the branding iron stuck through the ears of whores
and rogues and peasant slaves in *Hamlet*. I didn't mention the histor-
ical date of the edict alluded to in the play, because although it came to
mind, I was afraid of sounding pedantic. Instead, I said I was now beginning to see the connection of the pearls dream with another I had
had the same night . . .

It occurred to me to pause and see if the doctor had anything to
say, but the doctor did not. Still I knew that even if the lips were quiet
the slits of the doctor's eyes (which I could not see) changed and
changed.

I felt shocked but went on: in this other dream, I said, one of my
incisor teeth came out in my hand, having been loosened as I pulled
many shreds of carrot from around its root. I thought to myself and did
not say that I hated this part of the dream with its connotation of rabbits, silly innocuous and cuddly kinds of rats, and I admired my own
virtue and courage as I proceeded. The connection between the two
dreams, I said, is that the tooth is a dew-drop pearl—removing the

tooth was removing the potency of a playful rabbit, whose nature it is to gnaw with his incisor teeth on carrots. Suddenly I admitted, with a welling up of feeling, my dislike of the rabbit figure in my dreams, but there it was, I said and, regaining control, I added that probably it was something from the Collective Unconscious of Jung.

The doctor was silent.

And the pearl in the ear of the girl, I went on, was the organ of the playful rabbit placed there like poison in the ear of Hamlet's father. That didn't ring right I realized, and growing angry at the doctor's silence, tried again: or the word-swords of Hamlet in his mother's ear. That was better, I thought, and at the same time noticed with a certain delight how much "word" was like "sword" and commented on it. I certainly thought the doctor should speak here, but still there was no sound; only, I knew, the doctor showed his eyes like a pair of powerful teeth.

Or if the tooth is not put in the girl's ear to kill, I went on, then, to get back to the stag — since a stag is a stud isn't it, or a stallion — the stag tooth (which I said I preferred anyway to the rabbit tooth) placed in the girl's ear meant I wanted to do something else to her, maybe to fuck her. I was always uncomfortable saying sexual words in the doctor's presence and went ahead rapidly: I often watched the girl primping in her tiny mirror, I said, and once she had caught me out of the corner of her eyes, which had narrowed. Perhaps she wanted to turn me into a stag and set her dogs on me to rend me with their teeth! The story of Diana, I said, marveling at my gift of finding relations, was one of the legends on the vase in the dream. And the Thracian women tore the poet's flesh, though not with the teeth of dogs. The dog's tooth, I now remembered, is also a violet: Laertes wanted the flesh of his sister to become violets. Suddenly I felt that I was, after all, trying to say something to myself; and I almost whispered, "The hyacinth is mournful as the mandrake is."

III

Whatever it was I wanted to do to the girl, I said, after a pause (and in fact somewhat choked), kill her or kiss her, in any case I was being punished, because the tooth or organ being removed represented a form of castration and on one occasion I explicitly thought of castration when I happened to keep a dental appointment in a guilty frame of mind — mortal sin, I said to myself — and found that a tooth I thought was going to be filled actually had to be pulled. Now, the rabbit truth, or rabbit tooth, I corrected myself quickly (and blushing), when it was pulled in the dream had caused me much pain. I had never experienced pain in a dream before, I said, and had waked up moaning and taken an aspirin. I paused.

I thought I was doing extremely well and hoped for some encouragement or some indication of my grade, so to speak. But there was still no sound from the region at the back of my head. In this general area there came to my mind as I paused an indistinct figure, which I killed — a composite man with the ears of a great rabbit and great rabbit eyes, pink as wounded flesh. I then began again without mentioning the bloody battle in which I had just been victor.

As for the pain, I said, I had been worried that the tooth that was pulled would cause me a lot of trouble afterwards, because I felt I deserved it. The dentist had quite a hard time getting the tooth out, hacked and pried it with his tools, and it wouldn't budge until — and I felt a flush as I related it — I had made an act of contrition; then it came out immediately. I said I felt that the guilt I had brought to the dentist's office — it had started with drinking, I confessed, but had already decided not to go into it unless the doctor insisted — was *assuaged*. I repeated the word, lengthening the vowels. As though the dentist had put me in a state of grace, I said. I had never had the nerve to ask the doctor whether he was Catholic, but thought to hell with it now. After I left the dentist's I said I had felt that I would never get drunk, etcetera, again, but instead would become a man. I felt, I said strongly, that I was *initiated* by the experience of the tooth pulling, having made — I couldn't help laughing — the rites of passage in a dentist's office. I had started to say "doctor's office," but checked myself in time. But, I admitted, to be made a man by a kind of castration *did* seem strange. Still there was circumcision, excision and such related practices I had read about. These were painful and shocking forms of initiation, like the rites where boys had to crawl across the blood-and-guts-spattered

naked bodies of men in order to get to the throne of the king, or the
rite—Australia was it?—where the mother squats over the youth and
grunts with mock labor before turning him over to the men. I said this
seemed particularly brutal. As for castrated heroes, spread-eagling and
crucifying were common in myths and religious stories and Jesuit mar-
tyrs like Southwell were drawn and quartered alive, a kind of extended
spread-eagling, as well as being castrated: a horse pulled on each limb,
four of them, like Thracian women, and sometimes their guts were
rolled out on sticks. I myself, I said, once had a nightmare—four of
them, I thought, one mare on each limb—in which I thought I was being fondled but instead was being stripped and my hands staked to the
ground for, I supposed, castration, but had waked up in fright without
finding out. I paused. The stakes went through the hands into the natural earth, I said, believing that the phrase "natural earth" as I uttered
it had a rather mysterious sound. Raskolnikov bowed down to kiss the
earth in expiation after his crime, but he didn't really mean it until in
the epilogue of the novel when he first convicted himself in a dream
and then, his eyes freed at last of Tobias's scales, was able to look at the
beautiful countryside around him. The dactylic rhythms of this last remark I realized were the result of artifice, and I paused for a minute to
temper my control over the fantasy, which I was afraid was beginning
to sound too much like a poem, or like a critic's gloss on a poem. In any
case, I thought, the whole thing was getting away from me a little too
uncomfortably. I made myself stop thinking, and a feeling of irritation
at the doctor's silence grew stronger as I paused over-long.

IV

The forty-five minutes were nearly gone, I figured. What was the
doctor thinking? What were the doctor's eyes and teeth doing? Was the
doctor perhaps reflecting that I was trying to treat myself, remembering the cigars in my breast pocket and the new hat on the chair,
forced forms of manhood? And perhaps resenting my ability to analyze
my own dreams? For which I paid the said doctor a rather penitential

sum?—when I could. One time in one of these silences I had point
blank asked the doctor what a certain dream of mine meant. And the
doctor had answered, "I don't know what it means." This had seemed
enigmatic at the time, the awful deceit of a god. Now, today, nothing at
all had issued from the corner, nothing since the initial and ritualistic,
"What's on your mind today," when, upon entering, I turned to the
right (or was it the left, I thought) and spread-eagled myself on the
couch. After waiting in the foyer, I thought, after passing the boy and
his beast in the weeping court, after coming to the surface in the elevator. I began immediately to relate the elevator dream I had just
remembered.

The elevator was new-fangled, I said, a complicated one, buttons,
lights flashing, levers, numbers. I couldn't operate the machine right
to get off it and just rode up and down by myself, until someone got in
with me, someone who obviously—the way only things in dreams are
obvious—knew how to run it and who was a kind of authority or official. The trouble was partly in the floor—there was a zero floor, a number which puzzled me among the others, I said, and at the same time it
seemed to be the number of the floor I was going to. I said I thought the
companion was the doctor. (So it had once turned out in a dream
about riding in a truck through dry brush country looking for the turn
to the right to the pleasant land.) Now the helper suggested we try to
find my floor, I continued, by starting at the top and stopping at each
one in turn. So we tried that but seemed to slip right past it anyway.
What a queer feeling, I said and immediately wished I had used another word. And we made the trip several times together, the lights
flashing and the new machinery grinning, or rather glittering. And the
dream ended then, I said, a bit breathless.

I went on to interpret that the floor I was trying to locate, the zero
floor, was my unconscious—unknown, strange, cold in a way, like absolute zero. I realized the weakness of this association as I produced it
but went on, rather courageously I thought: I said the dream meant I
needed the doctor's help and that I couldn't go where I wanted without
him. The doctor was trying to show me that one has to go floor by floor
or step by step to make the unconscious conscious, to drain the Zuider

Zee, in Freud's phrase, I said, or that ocean which Horatio had warned Hamlet not to go closer to for fear it would make him mad. Not angry, I said, mad. Suddenly my voice took on excitement and my arms began to flail like windmills beside the sea: of course, I said, Hamlet found himself by paying no heed to Jocasta and saying to hell with Calypso. He faced the coils of the sea, he left the ship that swallowed him, and he returned to Denmark naked and alone to be king of the court in a graveyard for a dog's day, like a boy in a court yard who masters the dogfish and sees for the first time all his mothers in their opened graves. I found my throat constricting tightly and I choked with phlegm and tears. And I heard the doctor's voice echoing quietly inside its ancient skull:

"Zero is not unkown, is it? X is unknown." And I could not answer and did not know what the oracle meant, but the voice pulled at my guts like a pliers on a tooth tugged from its socket or like the rod on a cage in the sucking elevator shaft.

The voice continued now, "Zero is *no* place. There *is* no such floor. You are saying you don't want to go anywhere and you want me to help you fool yourself. You are satisfied to ride around in the elevator with me, trying the different buttons and the new machinery of the treatment and making the lights flash. You want me to let you believe you are going someplace. You seem to think something will happen to you to change you just by coming here and bringing me your dreams."

Eggs, I thought, but did not answer. Sucking eggs. My dreams are colored, fantastic eggs I bring to calm the sacred snake. And now it rolls its egg-shaped eyes and spits at . . .

"Your dreams are for you," the doctor was saying, "not for me." I found myself answering, "But I want to give you something. I want you to like me and I know you don't."

"You want to bribe me," the doctor said, "so that you won't have to know yourself. Actually the only discomfort you are willing to suffer is the slightly unpleasant motion of a new elevator, which you would quickly come to enjoy while you waited. You used to wait for a religious miracle to happen to you. Now you are waiting for something scientific to take place. As for your thinking I don't like you—it is you who think you don't like yourself. You see me as you see yourself."

I felt the dragon's bites and knew it was only a matter of time. I was done for, but would fight. "No," I said. "No. You are always right but this time you are wrong. I *do* want to go someplace. I *am* going someplace. I know transportation dreams have to do with a man's desire for change. I have dreamt of buses, cars, trains, and now elevators. I don't know why I never dream of airplanes—I'd like to dream of them—they have so much grace and open air and light around them. They suggest ecstasy. I suppose I am afraid of ecstasy, of being blasted by it, or else I love it too much. Still an elevator is not just a bus or train. It goes up. It's a start toward an airplane, a connection between land and air transportation." My excitement rose as I saw a break in the battle I had lost—"And therefore," I said, "to dream of you helping me take the elevator means you will help me to ecstasy, to happiness, to life . . . the willingness to abandon myself to life as one unafraid of freedom and unashamed of it." (The superior person of Jung, I thought to myself, the one with the necessary moral strength.) "I want you to know me," I said, solidly ending my foray.

"You want me to know you," the doctor said, "because you don't want to know *yourself*, which should be the reason why you are here. You have a misconception of psychiatry."

God, the teeth of the snake! I thought. "But I can prove I need you," I said. "I didn't get drunk (drinking is a means to ecstasy, it occurred to me) for a month and thought I was cured, and then just before this elevator dream I was stinking." (Ecstatic and stinking, I thought. A blasted youth. Real Dionysian.)

The doctor said, "No, your getting drunk was not to prove to me that you needed me. It was to prove that you *don't*. You can leave it alone or take it, you are telling me—go for a month without it if you want or go get drunk if you want. Coming to see me makes you think you're doing something about yourself whereas it's actually providing you with the license to do as you please. You don't want to be responsible for your behavior."

"Good god why do you always make me sound so despicable!" I said, heated and feeling my throat grow tight with sobs again.

"Well, you think I'm criticizing you," the doctor said, "but I'm only explaining you to yourself. You think of me as a kind of priest suitable for adults, who can make you hang your head and who will provide you with feelings of relief for your anxieties and sops for your conscience while you continue to put things off. You want to weep because you want to remain as you are. Children weep to get what they want."

I heard and ignored the last two sentences—"Put off what?" I asked. "Put off what?" I knew the answer to this because it came up in every session and I found myself responding to my own question, "Put off the responsibility that would force me to earn a decent living for myself and my family by my talent. I have let my talents go to my head . . . I mean I have put my genius into my dreams and thoughts instead of into my work, where it might buy bread." I rather liked the rounded way in which the sentenced emerged.

The doctor said, "You do not act on the basis of what you have already learned about yourself. You continue to put off. And you do not want to learn more."

Yes, I thought. Yes. I am one of the inferior. I will never unravel the secrets. "But I want to understand the mystery of the flesh," I said sadly.

The snake hissed. "Where's the mystery?" it asked. "You don't want a psychiatrist at all. You just want somebody else in the elevator, a playfellow and a confidant. What you want is another rabbit."

I had an image of two giant, friendly rabbits, and heard their teeth click together like the eyeglasses of nearsighted lovers. The dragon's victory was now complete: using its words for teeth it had bridged the gap from its corner lair, attacking from behind and above as was its habit, and it had bit clean through every mask. The hissing was terrible!

I realized slowly that the buzzer was ringing, signalling the arrival of the next patient. My thoughts shaped into lines I did not say:

Already the next neurotic
Knocked at the gates,
Crowded his several selves
In the casement, bore his several
Hats and heads at the half open door.

Emptied of energy, unable to rise yet, though I knew it was over, I struggled for air and for the shapes of words that could be let loose into space. "It's like a figure in Kafka," I said. "I have failed and I don't know why or at what."

The doctor rose from his corner and standing between the couch and the door said: "No, not Kafka. You are like Hamlet. You prefer that anyway, I believe: your visits here are occasions for eloquent and suffering soliloquies, filled with literary allusions, edited for an audience, and actually serving as delays. You have failed at what you do not want to do. Therefore you have succeeded. I believe you might just as well go on as you are, and we'll let the matter of another appointment go for now, at least until you find some way to pay your bill. Good-bye." The doctor touched the knob of the door.

I forgot to check whether the staircase spiraled to the left or the right. My mind went instead to the fountain in the court outside, which would soon be dry for the winter, and there would be white stains on the concrete mould of the basin. I entered the elevator alone and it began its dive: a night journey under the sea, I thought, and said aloud, "But I shall not be born again. I wonder if there is such a thing as a cursed trout, doomed to be drowned."

Suddenly I remembered the doctor's reference to Hamlet, and I decided the doctor was being sarcastic. It had seemed until its mention of Kafka an illiterate snake, never speaking of books often as they came into my reveries. The elevator was docking. "I *have* succeeded," I said to myself, "shall at least avoid the dragon's eye, pale as ivory buttons that flash by the elevator door like the teeth of a whale."

9

It Never Touched Me

Ann-Marie Wells

The psychiatrist was saying something about the war, as Mrs. Lewis had known he would. That was one of the reasons she hadn't wanted to consult him when her husband had urged her to; she had known that he would be like this—stupid, bland, with comforting generalizations. "The war has affected us all," he said.

"Not me," she wanted to tell him. "Everyone but me." If there was something the matter, if she was acting neurotic, it was because she was forty, or because she had made wrong choices twenty years before, or because of certain mistakes of her parents, for which she wasn't responsible—with her, it wasn't the war. She wanted to tell him, but she didn't dare speak, for she could feel herself getting angry. And after the anger would come tears. If she began to cry, she wouldn't be able to stop, and the hour would be wasted—the precious, expensive hour that was to illuminate the mistakes her parents had made, for which she wasn't responsible.

She had been a little girl in April, 1917. She remembered oatmeal bread, and the parade in November, 1918, to celebrate the false armistice, with a burning effigy of the Kaiser. And by September, 1930, she

163

had had two little girls of her own, one six and the other almost three, and a successful husband, and a pleasant, easy, full suburban life.

She remembered all the dates that meant so much to other people. September 8, 1939. She had taken the children swimming the afternoon the Germans had marched into Poland. Afterward, they had had dinner in the restaurant pavilion overlooking the lake. It was always a treat to eat away from home, not to have to cook the meal and wash the dishes. The children were unusually good, quiet, tidy, and agreeable, leaving her attention to spare for the sunset over the water and for a rich, Byronic unhappiness about the words coming from the radio: "The lamps are going out all over Europe . . ." Appropriately enough, the sun went down into the lake in a gold-and-crimson splendor. The end of civilization. It had been a pleasant afternoon. And now, seven years after the end of civilization, she was consulting an expensive psychiatrist because she couldn't control her temper with the children and flew into rages at the most trivial provocation, or at none at all.

She remembered a spring morning in 1940 when she had unfolded the *Times* and read that the Germans had invaded Norway. And a month or so later, on Mother's Day, she and her husband and the children had driven over to see her mother-in-law. Her husband's brothers and sisters and their families were there, and all the men sat around the radio with their heads in their hands and listened to the destruction of Holland. They couldn't be persuaded to come to dinner until it was cold, although you could hear the radio perfectly well in the dining room.

She was pregnant that summer, and the people who had been so flatteringly happy about the birth of her first two children looked at her a little askance, wondering—some covertly—why she should want another child now. It wasn't until a year or two later that babies got to be fashionable again. "I suppose you expect to be congratulated on the production of cannon fodder," one of her franker friends had written. It was a drearily uncomfortable pregnancy; all that summer she moved heavily about the house and yard to the sound of doom from the radio, and the boy was born in the very middle of the Battle of Britain. He was a frail and fretful baby; they tried all sorts of formulas and still he wouldn't gain weight. She remembered thinking in October when she was desperately frightened about him, If I could choose, would I rather London should stand or this new formula agree with him? It was a game she had played with herself all her life, to test the honesty of her emotions, but this time, of course, the question was its own answer. Well, the formula had turned out all right (Similac), and London had weathered the storm, too, no thanks to her.

Mrs. Lewis was a pacifist by conviction, or had been in college. Since then, there had never been time really, to reexamine her convictions. No one cared at all whether a middle-aged mother of three was a pacifist or not. She had hoped America would not try to get in the war, and yet she felt dreadfully ashamed to be happy and comfortable.

Her husband was pleased that he was not too old to register for the first draft, though of course he did not expect to be called. The December afternoon when the Japanese bombed Pearl Harbor was not pleasant, as the September afternoon two years earlier had been. The children were romping in the living room and would not be quiet. It was one of the first times she had screamed at them. "Listen!" she said. "It's war! It's the most dreadful day of your lives. You'll remember it as long as you live!" So they stopped romping to listen a few minutes, obediently, like the well-trained children they were, and then went to the basement playroom to finish the game.

She remembered that month—how gay and excited people were; the belligerent Christmas cards, the lavish Christmas parties, with people saying, "It's *just* what we needed to *unify* the country. There *couldn't* have been a better way for us to get into it"; and everyone jealously eager to be in more danger of air raids than any of his friends.

Shortly after the first of the year, she heard that young George Darnell had been killed at Pearl Harbor, and for a little while she believed that the war had touched her. George Darnell had grown up next door to her. He was six or eight years younger, and she remembered him as a gentle, large-eyed little boy, on the high-school swimming team, worrying about whether he would get an appointment to West Point. He was afraid he couldn't pass the physical examination.

She remembered how proud the Darnell family and the neighbors had been when George got the appointment. After he was commissioned, he came to call once, very handsome in his uniform, bringing his pretty, stupid little wife. Now he was dead before his thirtieth year, because his family had taken an automobile trip the year he was fifteen and he had seen West Point and decided he wanted to go to school there.

She mentioned George's death a few times at teas and luncheons; it was so early in the war that almost no one else had lost friends or relatives, and people listened solemnly and respectfully. She really felt sad about it, too, didn't she? You couldn't help being fond of the little boy who grew up next door.

She stopped mentioning him after his wife's picture was in the paper, accepting George's medal. Apparently, someone had told the girl you should always smile for a newspaper photographer but had neglected to mention that a recent widow was a sound exception to the rule. There she was in the paper, draped in silver-fox skins, clutching a huge armload of roses, and grinning like a May queen. That was all that was left of George anywhere in the world.

The dates got mixed up after 1942, Mrs. Lewis couldn't remember when the tire shortage began, and when it was coffee or gasoline or butter or cigarettes or meat—only that all the things she had worried about were inconvenient but trivial, so that she had had to be ashamed of minding. In the grocery story, they put up posters of a savage-looking Jap, labelled "Blame *Him* for shortages," but people kept right on resenting and suspecting one another.

Then there was the loneliness of thinking things that no one else seemed to think. In her youth, she had supposed it would be splendid to have original ideas and the courage of her convictions, like Newton or Galileo or Shelley, but there was no use talking pacifism when it would only embarrass the children at school. Besides, she really didn't see that anyone had more freedom of choice than she had herself, or that the country could be doing anything but what it was doing. She took it out in having odd notions—for instance, that it was a dirty trick for MacArthur to duck out at Bataan.

"But he *had* to," people would say, horrified or impatient, when they deigned to answer at all. "He was under *orders*. He was *needed*."

O.K., she would answer stubbornly, but Washington didn't duck out at Valley Forge.

Then, there were other people's dead, letters of condolence, scrap drives, correspondents coming home and expressing their horror at the way the American people were taking the war. What did they expect her to do—howl? And her own life went on, just the same, but uncomfortable.

There had been a Japanese girl in her class in college—a childish, yellow butterfly of a girl named Fumiko. Mrs. Lewis had tried to find what had happened to her; someone said Fumiko had married a Communist and been disowned by her family, someone else that she was head of a flourishing girls' school near Tokyo. There was a girl, too, who married a Dutchman and appeared in the alumnae magazine as Mevrouw Something-or-Other, with a Dutch address. First, she had not been heard from for two years, and then she was dead of malnutrition and exposure, leaving two orphan sons. But it was impossible to think of her as anything but a fat, cheerful girl with pink cheeks and yellow, curly hair.

Donating blood was nothing at all like what Mrs. Lewis had been led to expect—just lying there on the table, opening and closing her hand, wondering if the nurse had forgotten about her, and, if so, whether she should risk making a scene or just bleed quietly to death.

Once, sitting in a doctor's crowded waiting room, looking at a slick-paper magazine, she had come upon a full page picture of two dead German children. Their mother had dressed them neatly, shot each one through the head, and laid them out on the floor of the living room, hands crossed on their breasts, because the Americans were coming. Then it was Mrs. Lewis's turn, and she laid the magazine down and went into the office with her own little boy and told the doctor that the swelling in the child's glands wouldn't go down, though he'd had his tonsils out and always took his vitamin pills and got eleven hours' sleep at night. The doctor was too busy to keep his records very accurately, and she had to remind him tactfully that her little boy was the one who couldn't take sulfathiazole—at least, it always made him break out in red spots all over and his fever would go up instead of down. All right, it was funny after the picture. But it wouldn't help to shoot her own little boy through the head and lay him out on the parlor floor—though, to judge from the daily papers, an increasing number of people seemed to think that it would. What could she do, then, that would be any less absurd than looking after his glands?

Then Germany surrendered, and the thin, shrewish girl at the grocery, who kept chocolate and bacon under the counter for other people but never for Mrs. Lewis, was saying, "It's over but it's not official, so we don't close for the day." And people smiled uncertainly as the line inched forward. On V-J Day, there were guests for dinner; she had cooked a big fish on a plank, and the conversation was divided about equally between fish and victory.

The war was over, and she could be glad. And then the boys started coming back, brown, bright-eyed, smiling, showing photographs, as if they had been on an extended hunting expedition. She had seen them in newsreels, in magazines, in dispatches, in fiction, in plays—haggard, lost, turned overnight from boys to old men, destroyed—and here they were, back again, looking as if nothing had happened, griping worse than civilians about cigarettes and shirts. Those who had hated Jews or niggers or Roosevelt still did, and some who hadn't hated anything, hated labor unions now. The reckless ones who had needed Army discipline to make men of them were still boys. It was all over, the end of civilization, the greatest drama of humanity. She had watched it from a cushioned seat in the loges, and it had left her feeling dreadfully let down.

"I may as well set you straight on that now, Doctor," Mrs. Lewis said. "Whatever's wrong with me, it isn't the war." And then she began to cry.

10

The 1930 Olympics

H. L. Mountzoures

"What else?" Dr. Larsen said. I could not see him. There was a tall window behind him. His shadow fell forward on my left, long and thin, sliding across the thick olive-green carpeting. A huge potted plant grew at my feet, and another beyond that spread like a web.

"I can't remember," I said.

"Try."

I felt like looking at his long, narrow face. At thirty dollars an hour, he should have *sounded* interested. There was a silence that cost me about half a dollar. I had been going to him for a year, and he wasn't helping me. No one was. But that was my fault. I knew that. I didn't want any help. Perhaps.

"Well," I said. "Somehow, my father and I were on this train to Providence. I don't know why Providence, or why my father. I've never been there myself, except on the way to Boston . . . Wait. Once, I did go *through* Providence with him. When I still lived home, in New Haven. It was ten years ago. I remember, because my mother died shortly after. I drove his car. There were three of us—he brought along one of his friends to talk with. I don't remember who now. The windows were closed—it was winter—and the two of them smoked a lot. I was a senior in college, on the swimming team, and I remember the cigar smoke bothered me, because I didn't smoke then and I was in good shape."

"Did you talk with your father on the train in the dream?"

"In fact, I was in perfect shape. I still felt that life was sort of meaningful, you know? We drove through on Route 1. The purpose of the trip was an interview for a Midwestern medical school—the interviewer was staying at a big Boston hotel. My father was confident I would get accepted, and he was prepared to do anything to see me through—take out a second mortgage, borrow money, anything. He probably only had a couple thousand dollars in the bank, if that. I let him down."

"Did you?"

"Well, I never wanted to be a doctor. But try to tell your father that when he came from the old country and worked hard all his life, and you'd said when you were eight or ten that you would be a doctor someday. I hated him for it then. Driving to Boston, I said to him in my mind, 'You lousy bastard, I don't want to be your lousy doctor or your lousy son.' But, like I told you before, I think it had something to do with the fact that my mother was so sick at the time."

I stopped. I almost felt like telling Dr. Larsen the truth. That my father was dead, too. That I had come to this office a year before because my father had just died and my only feeling was a slight relief. Then I had begun to find it frightening to get up, to go to work. Dr. Larsen knew the last part.

I said, "I don't want to talk about it. Not now."

"Go ahead. Try to talk about it." His voice was gentle, prodding.

I couldn't. I said, "The interview went badly. I remember the man who interviewed me was thin and pale, with black hair growing out of his nostrils. He asked me a question, and I went blank and said so. I asked him if he would be patient with me. I told him I always got rattled during interviews. His face set, and I understood. A week later, at college, I got a form letter of refusal. Right away, I withdrew my applications from all the other medical schools. It was the first real decision I ever made in my life. I was scared, but I felt happy, too. Relieved. I don't think my father ever looked at me the same way again. I think he felt I was a failure. I think he still does."

"Do *you* think you are?"

I did not answer. There was a dollar pause.

"About the train, now. The train ride."

You're all the same, I thought. With your trains and pencils and monuments and screwdrivers. "The train wasn't important," I said. "It was just a way of getting there and happened in a flash. When we got off, we weren't in Providence. We were in the country. It was beautiful, in a desolate way. There were streaks of thin yellow clouds, with reddish tints. I think the sun was setting. We were near a cove that ran out to sea. On the other side of the cove a large patch of dry fronds moved in the light. The sand was soft and white. We stood on the shore together, my father and I, looking at the water. It was a beautiful blue, and right at the shore, near razor grass and beach roses, the water was frothy, white. I looked up, and far away there was a huge city— industrial, with smokestacks, yellow smoke coming out of them, and brick buildings, dirty. Something like when you pass through the Bronx on the way to Manhattan. You know?"

"Mmm. That's interesting. How did you feel about your father right at that moment, when you were standing beside the water together looking at the city?"

"I don't remember. I didn't feel any way toward him. Nothing aggressive, I mean. We were just *there*, that's all. Together."

"Beside the water."

"Yes. And then my father said, 'Aren't you going swimming?' '*Swimming?*' I said. 'But it's winter.' He said, 'I would.' The next thing, we're in a crude wooden bathhouse. I look at my father. He has on one of those old-fashioned tank suits, black. I think he even had a mustache. He looked like someone out of one of those old Victorian photographs. I only remember the top half of the suit. I was surprised at his shoulders, at his good build. He was slim and strong."

"Why only the top half?"

"How should I know?"

"How was he standing?"

"It was like a closeup in the movies, and you could only see him from the waist up."

"Could you see yourself, or feel your own whole body then?"

"I don't remember."

"You mustn't hold back anything. If there are things you remember and don't tell me, then you're wasting both your time and mine."

He has to be hard, I thought. "Honestly, Doctor, I don't recall."

"Go on, then."

"I went to a wooden beach locker and opened it, and there was nothing in it, no bathing suit. I looked at my father, and he shook his head. He pointed above him, and across a beam his name was carved, with a date: Alberto Cottelli 1930. Then, there was a bathhouse attendant, some kind of a trainer, standing beside me in black pants, a white shirt, with a black bow tie. He said, 'They don't make them like that anymore. He was a great athlete. I trained him for the 1930 Olympics'. . . Doctor, there weren't any Olympics in 1930, were there? Were there?"

"Let me see. '36, Berlin . . . No."

"I didn't think so. I think that's the year my father came to America. His name and that date were carved in the pine beam. . . . Then my father and I were at the beach again."

"What were you wearing now?"

"I don't remember. I guess clothes weren't part of it. We were on the same piece of shore, looking at the same scene. The water was moving, rippling. And then I heard a voice. Mournful. It was calling my name: 'Jo—seph . . . Jo—ey . . .' Like music. Pleading. It was my mother's voice. I turned around. There was no one there. And then I saw, on the sand, half hidden under a thick tuft of grassy bank, a small, dark-green plastic bag. It was about a foot square, shiny, full, puffed up, gathered, tied tight at the top. 'Oh, no!' I said. My father nodded slowly, wiping his eyes."

There was a long silence. For the first time, I didn't think how much it was costing, this silence.

I could hear the doctor breathing. "A bag?" he said. I thought there was a smile in his voice.

I said, "But Doctor, don't you see? It was *her*—the voice came from *that*. And my father stood there crying."

"What else?"

"Nothing. Not there, anyway. Next thing, we're home—in the old house in New Haven. While my father and I were out, someone ransacked the whole place. Christ, everything piled up in heaps in the center of the rooms—mattresses, mirrors, pictures, tables. And in my study all my books thrown down from the shelves, the papers from my files scattered all over the room. Someone had broken in and turned the place upside down. My father said, 'We must get to the bottom of this.' And that's all. There wasn't any more."

The doctor ruffled his pad. He said, "Well, I think we have some progress. We've run over the hour now. I've taken some notes, and we'll proceed from here next week. We'll try to go into this dream in detail then, and you can help me . . . Tell me. Are you on speaking terms with your father yet?"

"In fact," I said, "I'm glad you asked. He was in the city last week, and I took him to dinner. We spoke a few sentences. Without having a fight. Neither of us mentioned my mother." I got up and prepared to leave. "There's something I want to tell you, Doctor. I think I'm beginning to like him. It probably sounds stupid, but there it is." Another lie, but I thought it would give him a feeling of a breakthrough, a benevolent feeling of helping me, one of his patients.

"Good," he said. "That's very good." He stood up quickly. As usual he had been leaning back in a black leather swivel chair, and it sprang forward like a dog. He said, "Of course, next week you may come in all confused and hostile toward him again, but don't let that worry you. As I've been trying to tell you, nothing is black and white. There are awful tremors in all our relationships. Try to see your father again this week. Force yourself to converse with him, no matter how hard it is. Be pleasant with him. Try not to argue. Then we'll see what next week brings."

We stood awkwardly for a moment. I glanced at his pale-blue, almost colorless eyes, and I felt embarrassed. The afternoon light was soft, yellow. What fools we all are, I thought. I said, "Same time, same station."

He smiled.

I thanked him and walked out of his office, then through the reception room, where there was a woman waiting whom I had not seen before. She was about fifty, wearing a lot of makeup. She sat with a magazine in her lap, pulling hard on a cigarette. I went out and got into the elevator.

On the sidewalk, I turned right. Ahead of me I saw the back of a man, full length, in a cheap, baggy, silver-gray suit—a short, heavy man, walking slowly, pleasantly, as though he were taking the air and didn't have a care in the world. His hair was salt-and-pepper, blowing softly. One of his hands swung as he walked, and it was thick and slightly gnarled. From the back, he looked and walked like my father.

My impulse was to catch up with this stranger, to tell him what I had just told the doctor in his muffled office full of green plants.

People hurried past, and the man disappeared around the corner.

I felt like crying for the first time in ten years. I walked to the building I had just come out of and stood flat against it in the shade and closed my eyes.

11

An Astrologer's Day

R. K. Narayan

Punctually at midday he opened his bag and spread out his professional equipment, which consisted of a dozen cowrie shells, a square piece of cloth with obscure mystic charts on it, a notebook and a bundle of palmyra writing. His forehead was resplendent with sacred ash and vermilion, and his eyes sparkled with a sharp abnormal gleam which was really an outcome of a continual searching look for customers, but which his simple clients took to be a prophetic light and felt comforted. The power of his eyes was considerably enhanced by their position—placed as they were between the painted forehead and the dark whiskers which streamed down his cheeks: even a half-wit's eyes would sparkle in such a setting. To crown the effect he wound a saffron-coloured turban around his head. This colour scheme never failed. People were attracted to him as bees are attracted to cosmos or dahlia stalks. He sat under the boughs of a spreading tamarind tree which flanked a path running through the Town Hall Park. It was a remarkable place in many ways: a surging crowd was always moving up and down this narrow road morning till night. A variety of trades and occupations was represented all along its way: medicine-sellers, sellers of stolen hardware and junk, magicians and, above all, an auctioneer of cheap cloth, who created enough din all day to attract the whole town. Next to him in vociferousness came a vendor of fried groundnuts, who gave his ware a fancy name each day, calling it Bombay icecream one day, and on the next Delhi Almond, and on the third Raja's Delicacy, and so on and so forth, and people flocked to him. A considerable portion of this crowd dallied before the astrologer too. The astrologer transacted his business by the light of a flare which crackled and smoked up above the groundnut heap nearby. Half the enchantment of the place was due to the fact that it did not have the benefit of municipal lighting. The place was lit up by shop lights. One or two had missing gaslights, some had naked flares stuck on poles, some were lit up by old cycle lamps and one or two, like the astrologer's, managed without lights of their own. It was a bewildering criss-cross of light rays and moving shadows. This suited the astrologer very well, for the simple reason that he had not in the least intended to be an astrologer when he began life; and he knew no more of what was going to happen to others than he knew what was going to happen to himself the next minute. He was as much a stranger to the stars as were his innocent customers. Yet he said things which pleased and astonished everyone: that was more a matter of study, practise and shrewd guesswork. All the same, it was as much an honest man's labour as any other, and he deserved the wages he carried home at the end of a day.

He had left his village without any previous thought or plan. If he had continued there he would have carried on the work of his forefathers—namely, tilling the land, living, marrying and ripening in his cornfield and ancestral home. But that was not to be. He had to leave home without telling anyone, and he could not rest till he left it behind a couple of hundred miles. To a villager it is a great deal, as if an ocean flowed between.

He had a working analysis of mankind's troubles: marriage, money and the tangles of human ties. Long practise had sharpened his perception. Within five minutes he understood what was wrong. He charged three pies per question and never opened his mouth till the other had spoken for at least ten minutes, which provided him enough stuff for a dozen answers and advices. When he told the person before him, gazing at his palm, "In many ways you are not getting the fullest results for your efforts," nine out of ten were disposed to agree with him. Or he questioned: "Is there any woman in your family, maybe even a distant relative, who is not well disposed towards you?" Or he gave an analysis of character: "Most of your troubles are due to your nature. How can you be otherwise with Saturn where he is? You have an impetuous nature and a rough exterior." This endeared him to their hearts immediately, for even the mildest of us loves to think that he has a forbidding exterior.

The nuts-vendor blew out his flare and rose to go home. This was a signal for the astrologer to bundle up too, since it left him in darkness except for a little shaft of green light which strayed in from somewhere and touched the ground before him. He picked up his cowrie shells and paraphernalia and was putting them back into his bag when the green shaft of light was blotted out; he looked up and saw a man standing before him. He sensed a possible client and said: "You look so careworn. It will do you good to sit down for a while and chat with me." The other grumbled some vague reply. The astrologer pressed his invitation; whereupon the other thrust his palm under his nose, saying: "You call yourself an astrologer?" The astrologer felt challenged and said, tilting the other's palm towards the green shaft of light: "Yours is a nature . . ." "Oh, stop that," the other said. "Tell me something worthwhile . . ."

Our friend felt piqued. "I charge only three pies per question, and what you get ought to be good enough for your money . . ." At this the other withdrew his arm, took out an anna and flung it out to him, saying, "I have some questions to ask. If I prove you are bluffing, you must return the anna to me with interest."

"If you find my answers satisfactory, will you give me five rupees?"

"No."

"Or will you give me eight annas?"

"All right, provided you give me twice as much if you are wrong," said the stranger. This pact was accepted after a little further argument. The astrologer sent up a prayer to heaven as the other lit a cheroot. The astrologer caught a glimpse of his face by the matchlight. There was a pause as cars hooted on the road, *jutka* drivers swore at their horses and the babble of the crowd agitated the semi-darkness of the park. The other sat down, sucking his cheroot, puffing out, sat there ruthlessly. The astrologer felt very uncomfortable. "Here, take your anna back. I am not used to such challenges. It is late for me to-day. . . ." He made preparations to bundle up. The other held his wrist and said, "You can't get out of it now. You dragged me in while I was passing." The astrologer shivered in his grip; and his voice shook and became faint. "Leave me today. I will speak to you tomorrow." The other thrust his palm in his face and said, "Challenge is challenge. Go on." The astrologer proceeded with his throat drying up. "There is a woman . . . "

"Stop," said the other. "I don't want all that. Shall I succeed in my present search or not? Answer this and go. Otherwise I will not let you go till you disgorge all your coins." The astrologer muttered a few incantations and replied, "All right. I will speak. But will you give me a rupee if what I say is convincing? Otherwise I will not open my mouth, and you may do what you like." After a good deal of haggling the other agreed. The astrologer said, "You were left for dead. Am I right?"

"Ah, tell me more."

"A knife has passed through you once?" said the astrologer.

"Good fellow!" He bared his chest to show the scar. "What else?"

"And then you were pushed into a well nearby in the field. You were left for dead."

"I should have been dead if some passer-by had not chanced to peep into the well," exclaimed the other, overwhelmed by enthusiasm. "When shall I get at him?" he asked, clenching his fist.

"In the next world," answered the astrologer. "He died four months ago in a far-off town. You will never see any more of him." The other groaned on hearing it. The astrologer proceeded.

"Guru Nayak—"

"You know my name!" the other said, taken aback.

"As I know all other things. Guru Nayak, listen carefully to what I have to say. Your village is two days' journey due north of this town.

Take the next train and be gone. I see once again great danger to your life if you go from home." He took out a pinch of sacred ash and held it out to him. "Rub it on your forehead and go home. Never travel southward again, and you will live to be a hundred."

"Why should I leave home again?" the other said reflectively. "I was only going away now and then to look for him and to choke out his life if I met him." He shook his head regretfully. "He has escaped my hands. I hope at least he died as he deserved." "Yes," said the astrologer. "He was crushed under a lorry." The other looked gratified to hear it.

The place was deserted by the time the astrologer picked up his articles and put them into his bag. The green shaft was also gone, leaving the place in darkness and silence. The stranger had gone off into the night, after giving the astrologer a handful of coins.

It was nearly midnight when the astrologer reached home. His wife was waiting for him at the door and demanded an explanation. He flung the coins at her and said, "Count them. One man gave all that."

"Twelve and a half annas," she said, counting. She was overjoyed. "I can buy some *jaggery* and coconut tomorrow. The child has been asking for sweets for so many days now. I will prepare some nice stuff for her."

"The swine has cheated me! He promised me a rupee," said the astrologer. She looked up at him. "You look worried. What is wrong?"

"Nothing."

After dinner, sitting on the *pyol*, he told her. "Do you know a great load is gone from me today? I thought I had the blood of a man on my hands all these years. That was the reason why I ran away from home, settled here and married you. He is alive."

She gasped. "You tried to kill!"

"Yes, in our village, when I was a silly youngster. We drank, gambled and quarrelled badly one day—why think of it now? Time to sleep," he said, yawning, and stretched himself on the *pyol*.

12

The Fairy Godfathers

John Updike

"Oh, Pumpkin," Tod would say. "Nobody likes us."

"That's not quite true," she would answer, her lips going cloudy in that way they had when she thought.

They were lovers, so the smallest gesture of hers flooded his attention, making his blood heavy. He knew exactly whom she meant. He objected, "But they're paid to."

"I think they would anyway," she answered, again after thought. She added, "Oz *loves* you."

"He doesn't love me, he just thinks that my self-hatred is slightly excessive."

"He loves you."

Oz was his psychiatrist. Rhadamanthus was hers. Tod had met Rhadamanthus but once, in the grim avocado hall outside his office. Pumpkin had gone in, as usual, flustered and harried, self-doubting and guilty, and had emerged flushed and smoothed and cheerful. Behind her, on this one occasion, loomed a shadow, but a shadow Tod could no more contemplate than he could look directly into the sun. He knew that, via her discourse, he dwelt, session after session, within this shadow, and as he took the man's unenthusiastically offered hand Tod had the strange sensation of reaching out and touching, in a sense, himself.

After her next session, Pumpkin said, "He wondered why you wouldn't look him in the eye."

"I couldn't. He's too wonderful."

"He thinks *you're* wonderful."

"The hell he does."

"He does. He loves what you're doing for me."

"I'm ruining your life."

"He thinks my life was very neurotic and I'm incredibly stupid to grieve the way I do."

"Life is grief," Tod said, tired of this conversation.

"He thinks my life was very neurotic," Pumpkin told him, "and I'm incredibly stupid to grieve."

"She repeats herself," Tod told Oz. Oz rustled in his chair and touched the fingertips of his right hand to his right temple. His every gesture, however small, won Tod's full attention. "That doesn't seem to me so very bad," the psychiatrist said, with the casual power of delivery attainable at only the highest, thinnest altitude of wisdom. It was like golf on the moon; even a chip shot sailed for miles. Oz's smile was a celestial event. "You spend so much of your own energy"—he smiled— "avoiding repeating yourself."

Tod wondered why Oz was so insistently Pumpkin's champion. Through the tangle of his patient's words, Oz seemed to see an ideal Pumpkin glowing. They looked rather alike: broad pale faces, silver hair, eyes the no-color of platinum. Unearthly personalities. Whereas Rhadamanthus, in Tod's sense of him, was subterranean in essence: there was something muddy and hearty and dark and directive about the man. Pumpkin would return from her sessions as from a cave, blinking and reborn. Whereas Tod descended from a session with Oz giddy and aerated, his blood full of bubbles, his brain intoxicated by its refreshened power to fantasize and hope. Oz was, Tod flattered himself, more purely Freudian than Rhadamanthus.

"Oz says," he would say, "I shouldn't mind your repeating yourself."

"Rhadamanthus says," was her answer, "I don't repeat myself. At least he's never noticed it."

"You trust him to hear you the first time," Tod theorized. "He's realer to you than I am. You repeat yourself with me because you doubt that I'm there."

"Where?"

"In the world your head makes. Don't be sad. Freud says I'm not really real to anybody." It was seldom out of Tod's mind that his name in German was the word for death. He had been forty before this had really sunk in.

In those days, their circumstances were reduced. He lived in a room in a city, and she would visit him. From the fourth-floor landing he would look down, having rung the buzzer of admission, and see her hand suddenly alight, like a butterfly in forest depths, on the stair railing far below. As she ascended, there was something sinister and inexorable in the way her hand gripped the bannister in steady upwards hops. After the second-floor landing, her entire arm became visible — in fur or tweeds, in cotton sleeve or bare, depending on the season and at the turn of the third landing she would gaze upward and smile, her face broad and luminous and lunar. She would be coming from a session with Rhadamanthus, and as he embraced her on the fourth-floor landing Tod could feel in the smoothness of her cheeks and the strength of her arms and the cloudy hunger of her lips the recent infusion of the wizard's blessing. She would go into her meagre room and kick off her shoes and tell him of the session.

"He was good," she would say, judiciously, as if each week she tasted a different wine.

"Did he say you should go back to Roger?"

"Of course not. He thinks that would be terribly neurotic. Why do you even ask? You're projecting. *You* want me to go back. Does Oz want me to go back, so you can go back? He hates me."

"He loves you. He says you've done wonders for my masculinity."

"So would weight-lifting."

He paused to laugh, then continued to grope after the shadow of himself that lived in the magic cave of her sessions with Rhadamanthus. He flitted about in there, he felt, as a being semi-sublime, finer even than any of the approbation Pumpkin reported. "He thinks," she would say, wearily, "one of my problems is I've gone from one extreme to the other. You sound just utterly lovely to him, in the way you treat me, your children, Lulu . . . "

The mention of Lulu did bad things to him. "I am *not* utterly lovely," he protested. "I can be quite cruel. Here, I'll show you." And he seized Pumpkin's bare foot as it reposed before him and twisted until she screamed and fell to the floor with a thump.

"I think it was her foot I chose," Tod told Oz the next Tuesday, "rather than twisting her arm or pulling her hair, say, because her feet are especially freighted for me with erotic import. The first time I was vividly conscious of wanting to, you know, *have* her, I had dropped over at their house on a Saturday afternoon to return a set of ratchet wrenches of Roger's I had borrowed, and while I was standing there in the hall she came up from the cellar in bare feet. I thought to myself. Goes into the cellar barefoot—that's great. The only other woman I knew who went barefoot everywhere was my wife. Lulu even plays tennis barefoot, and leaves little toe marks all over the clay. Then, about Pumpkin, at these meetings of the Recorder Society she would wear those dumb sort of wooden sandals that are supposed to be good for your arches, and during the rests of the tenor part I could see underneath the music sheet her little pink toes beating time for the soprano, very fast and fluttery—eighth notes. Soprano parts tend to have eighth notes. And then, the first time we spent the whole night together, coming back from the bathroom, with her still asleep and feeling sort of strange—me, I mean—here she was asleep with this wonderful one foot stuck out from beneath the blankets. She loves to have her toes sucked."

It seemed to Tod that Oz shifted uneasily in his chair, there was a creak that could be leather or a furtive noise of digestion. Tod's weekly appointment came after the lunch hour, and he had a sensation, sometimes, of being engorged by the psychiatrist, of dissolving, attacked by enzymes of analysis. Tod persisted with his pedal theme. "The winter before last, I just remembered, Lulu took the wrong Wellington boots away from the carol sing, and they turned out to be *her* boots, and they were too big for Lulu, which is surprising, since Lulu is taller. *Her* feet, I should say, Lulu's, are quite high-arched, almost like hooves, which is why they leave such marks on the tennis court. When I met her at college, the soles were so tough she could stamp out cigarettes barefoot, as a trick. The third and fourth toes aren't divided all the way down, and she used to hate to have me mention this. Or anything about her feet, for that matter. Yet she never wore shoes if she could help it, and when we'd walk on the beach she'd always admire her own prints in the sand. For the gap where the arch was." Suddenly the theme was exhausted. "What do you make of it?" Tod asked weakly.

Oz sighed. His platinum eyes seemed to be watering. Tod felt that Oz, gazing at him, saw a deep, though fathomable, well of sorrow—sorrow and narcissistic muddle. "It's a paradox," the psychiatrist said, sadly.

Lulu's attitude toward her own feet, he must mean. Tod went on, "After they swapped the right boots back, Pumpkin said to me at a party that Lulu's had pinched and I had this odd wish to defend Lulu, as if she had been insulted. Even now, I keep wanting to defend Lulu. Against you, for example, I feel you've undermined her, by giving some sort of silent approval to my leaving her. Everybody else is horrified. Everybody else likes Lulu. So do I. She's very likable."

Oz sighed in the special way that signalled the end of a session. "What's that old saying?" he asked, casually. "If the shoe fits . . . "

"What did he say?" Pumpkin asked anxiously, over the telephone. She had had a bad day, of crying children and unpayable bills. Roger was bombarding her with affidavits and depositions.

"Oz attacked Lulu," Tod told her. "He implied she was a shoe I should stop wearing."

"That's not an attack, it's a possibility," Pumpkin said. "I'm not sure you're quite sane, on the subject of Lulu."

"I'm as sane as you are on the subject of Roger."

"I'm quite sane on the subject of Roger. Rhadamanthus says I was all along, only I doubted my own perceptions."

"I've always liked Roger. He's always been very sweet to me."

"That's one of his poses."

"He loaned me his ratchet wrenches."

"You should hear him go on about those ratchet wrenches now. He calls them 'those wretched ratchet wrenches.' "

"Who do you trust more on the subject of Roger—me who's met him or Rhadamanthus who hasn't? I say he is *sweet*." Whence this irritability and unreason? Tod couldn't understand himself. Once, when Pumpkin had wavered and it seemed she might go back to her husband, he had been in agony. His heart had turned over and over in jealousy like a lump of meat in a cauldron of stew.

"Rhadamanthus," Pumpkin answered, to a question he had forgotten asking.

"He thinks you're his princess," Tod snapped. "He thinks I sully you, no doubt."

"He thinks you're *beautiful*," she said, infuriatingly.

"Who *are* these men anyway," Tod countered, "to run our lives? What do you know about *them*? Are *their* marriages so great, that they should put ours down? From the way Oz's stomach burbles I think he has an ulcer. As to your guy, I didn't like the shifty way he shambled out the door that time. He wouldn't look me in the eye. What do you two *do* in there anyway?"

Pumpkin was crying. "Go back," she said. "That's what you're saying to me you want to do. Go back to Lulu and have pinchy feet." She hung up.

But the next time he saw her, after her Thursday session with Rhadamanthus, the psychiatrist had told her that wasn't what Tod had meant at all: he meant that in truth he loved her very much, and she loved him. She felt all smooth and plumped-up on the fourth-floor landing, and inside his room she kicked off her shoes and told all that had been disclosed in the cave of knowing.

They seemed, sometimes, as they moved about the city enacting their romance, gloves on the hands of giants, embodiments of others' hopes. They had no friends. They had children, but these they had wounded. Tears glistened about them like the lights of the city seen reflected in the square pool beside the round white table of an outdoor restaurant. In the museums, tall stainless-steel constructs probed space to no clear purpose, and great striped canvases rewarded their respectful stares with a gaudy blankness. In movie houses, her hair tickled his ear as pink limbs intertwined or Sherlock Holmes stalked through the artificial mist of a Hollywood heath. They liked revivals; Esther Williams smiled triumphantly underwater, and Judy Garland, young again, hit the high note. Outside, under the glitter of the marquee, ice glistened on the brick pavements, and chandeliers warmed the bay windows of apartments whose floors and furniture they would never see. They were happy in limbo. At night, sirens wailed lullabies of disasters that kept their distance. Traffic licked the streets. Airplanes tugged snug the blanket of sky. They awoke to find it had snowed through all their dreaming, and the street was as hushed as a print by Currier & Ives—the same street where in spring magnolias bloomed first on the sunny side and then, weeks later, on the side of constant shade. They walked enchanted, scared, unknown but for the unseen counsellors whose blessings fed the night like the breathing of stars. Then the world rotated; the children stopped crying, the pace of legal actions slowed, the city lights faded behind them. They bought a house. He built bookshelves, she raised flowers. For economy's sake, they stopped seeing psychiatrists. Now when she said to him, "You're beautiful," it came solely from her, and when he answered, "So are you," it was to quell the terror that visited him, stark as daylight, plain as the mailman. For Tod was death and Pumpkin was hollow and the fair godfathers had vanished, taking with them the lovers' best selves.

13

The Ordeal of Dr. Blauberman

Lillian Ross

In Dr. Blauberman's office, on the seventeenth floor of a new Fifth Avenue apartment house facing Central Park, Ephraim Samuels was lying on the analytic couch, saying nothing. Dr. Blauberman sat near the head of the couch, where Ephraim could not see him, in a gigantic chair that tilted up at the feet and down at the back, to rest his heart and improve his general well-being. The chair was upholstered in cream-colored leather, and Dr. Blauberman, wearing a cream-colored jacket and a cream-and-red striped bow tie, blended right into it. He was a tall man, with coarse, black conspicuously barbered hair, a sharp nose, and a thin-lipped, dissatisfied mouth. He had deep lines at right angles to his mouth. His stomach, as he sat, protruded in a medium-sized paunch. He wore dark-horn-rimmed glasses. He was smoking a slim Dunhill pipe. In years gone by, at hotels and summer resorts, mothers with marriageable daughters had pointed him out to one another as "that gorgeous-looking fella." On the wall behind Dr. Blauberman's head was a Currier & Ives print of a horse-drawn sleigh full of chubby, laughing, red-cheeked, mittened, mufflered, ear-muffed, healthy men, women and children. On the wall over the couch were framed diplomas, including one from the N.Y.U. College of Medicine, class of 1939. Waiting for Ephraim to speak, Dr. Blauberman crossed and recrossed his legs. "So," he said, finally. And when this produced nothing, he said, "You show your hostility with your silence. Mmmm? Because I say I cannot go on with you as a patient. Yes?"

Dr. Blauberman glanced with discouragement and distaste at the young man on the couch. This was their next-to-last session together. Deadwood. Uncooperative. Why struggle any more to help him? It was pointless. It was demoralizing. it was leading neither of them anywhere. There were too many sick people waiting to be helped who wanted to be helped, whose suitability for psychoanalysis was better. At first, Dr. Blauberman had thought that Ephraim, with his honesty and sincerity and intelligence and what Dr. Blauberman had hoped would turn out to be a classic symptom-neurosis, was extremely suitable. And Dr. Fifield, who had sent Ephraim to him, had thought so, too. But for a whole year now—you could, of course, call the period one of *trial* analysis—using all the technique he had accumulated in years of practice, Dr. Blauberman had been striving to give Ephraim Samuels an awareness of his masochistic self-victimization, and to show him how, by changing his outlook, he could realize himself fully in his music, with his composing and with his clarinet. But there had been no change. And neither had there been a successful transference. Not really. There was no free-associating, and Dr. Blauberman suspected considerable ego regression, reinstating Ephraim's tie to his dead mother. For practically the entire year since his analysis had begun, the previous July, Ephraim had not touched the clarinet, but no analyst would blame Dr. Blauberman for *that*.

He had wanted so much to help this boy, this promising musician, and to set him on the healthy path. He'd been so glad when he got Ephraim as a patient. Ephraim had been such a welcome relief, not only from the dull housewife patients but from the medical profession—the largest category of patients in analysis, according to a recent survey made of psychoanalytic education in the United States. All those doctors, surgeons, social workers, and psychologists. Here was a "gifted" patient. There had been a good deal of discussion lately among Dr. Blauberman's colleagues about "gifted" patients. Dr. Blauberman had never had a really "gifted" patient before. Here was a *musician*. And a musician, moreover, who moved—that is, if Dr. Blauberman could *get* him to move—in the interesting worlds of chamber music and jazz, night clubs and Broadway, as well as Carnegie Hall. Dr. Blauberman was so fascinated by these worlds that, listening to Ephraim, he sometimes forgot about free association and dream interpretation. No harm in that. It was all adding up. Ephraim had even inspired Dr. Blauberman with the idea for a paper to be read at a meeting of the New York Psychoanalytic Society. Dr. Blauberman had actually thought of two appropriate titles: "The Id, the Ego, and the Clarinet" and "An Inquiry Into the Meaning of the Psychodynamics of Musical Composition and the Application of Psychoanalysis to Chamber Music and Jazz, from Bach to Brubeck."

Well. So. Mmmm. That was in the early weeks. Now it was all one big mess. Transference, that *sine qua non* of analyzability, was now kaput. True, Ephraim had formed a kind of attachment to him. And he had not always been silent, as he was now. He had talked about his relationships with various members of his family, and with various girls; had confided to Dr. Blauberman his modest estimates of his compositions and his involved plans for works he wanted to write in the future; had related all those cozy family anecdotes starring, nine times out of ten, his father, Joseph Samuels; had expressed his passionate enthusiasm for—and made clear his dependence on—his old clarinet teacher, Gustave Lefevre. But they had got nowhere. They hadn't worked a damn thing through. Dr. Blauberman had gone way beyond the call of duty for this boy, but Ephraim wanted to remain tied to his teacher, to his father, to his family. The more familiar and uninteresting it became—the very same sort of people, in fact, that Dr. Blauberman himself had managed to leave so far behind him. There was nothing he didn't know about that world, and he didn't want to be reminded of it any more than he wanted to be pushed back into it. Ephraim, it seemed, did want that very world. Naturally, the reasons were sick reasons, and all of Dr. Blauberman's ingenious ideas and devices for bringing him to act with drive and ambition and get somewhere with himself and with his music were rejected.

During his internship, in a small Jewish hospital in Brooklyn, not far from the Williamsburg section, where he grew up, Dr. Blauberman had decided he was as smart as the next guy. Maybe he couldn't get an internship in one of the large, fancy hospitals in Manhattan, but he could measure up alongside any other hospital intern in town. And he knew exactly what he wanted out of life. He wasn't going to be pushed around in medicine as a lousy general practitioner. Not for Al Blauberman a lifelong dependence on the grudged pennies of the Jewish poor. While he was still interning, he divorced the wife he had taken right after he graduated from medical school; she had been nothing but a burden to him and a handicap. She went home to her family. For a while, he received wild telephone calls from her, until he told her family in no uncertain terms that if she continued to bother him he would turn her over to the police. Then he discovered psychiatry. In the veterans' hospitals after the war, he found his experience and tested his hand. This was more like it. No house calls in the middle of the night. No hordes of sufferers pulling and pushing at him. He worked for a while at Bellevue, where he continued to absorb experience; he learned what he could from the European refugees, the devoted disciples of Freud.

"Mmmm?" he said now, around his pipe. "I cannot help you if you don't want to be helped. Yes?"

Ephraim said nothing.

Dr. Blauberman sniffed noisily. What an analyst had to fight against! Nothing came out of this young man, who could have had the whole world if he had only listened to his analyst and let himself be helped. Instead, here he was—sickly, pale, dressed like one of those young Greenwich Village tramps, with soiled, baggy trousers, cheap shoes, sweater, no necktie. The large mouth closed so stubbornly. The blue eyes, so clear, so light, their color undiminished by the dimly lit office. The matted brown hair in need of cutting. The thick, kinky, straw-colored eyebrows. Like his father's, Ephraim had boasted so many times—as though the straw-colored eyebrows were a heritage of great importance.

"Pop is the only man I know who can comb his hair with a towel," Ephraim could say. "He's got this thick hair, the same as mine, and these wild bushy eyebrows, and he never uses a comb—he just gets it fixed up with the towel. That's one thing I've never been able to do. He hates hats, but he's got this old cap he wears that he's had for years—it smells of gasoline . . . . Sometimes I wear a cap. It makes a big hit with girls."

Dr. Blauberman grunted. He himself went in for hats with fancy bands and feathers. As for that father, what he led the family to! The unhealthy sense of values. The denial of society. His children made overdependent. The retardation of Ephraim's emotional development. The lack of drive and ambition to carry the music to fulfillment. They had spent three weeks—fifteen sessions—on Lefevre alone, as Dr. Blauberman demonstrated one way and another how Ephraim was held to the teacher by immature dependence. The running back to the old man, instead of breaking into new territory on his own. And still Ephraim was stubborn. He rejected everything. Negative. Negative. Dr. Blauberman was tired of it. After all, it was only human to want a little reward for your efforts. The analyst's narcissistic gratifications were important, too. Why give and give and give and get nothing, not even a sign of recognition? It wasn't healthy. It wasn't healthy for *anybody*. You had to do what was right for yourself at all times, and in that way you did what was right for the patients. If asked, all his colleagues would agree.

Just the other night, after a meeting of the New York Psychoanalytic Society, he had stood around waiting impatiently for Harold Seltzer to finish discussing with other colleagues Norman Reider's paper on "Chess, Oedipus, and the Mater Dolorosa." Dr. Blauberman had walked home with Seltzer, who lived near Dr. Blauberman's office, where Dr. Blauberman slept on meeting nights instead of going all the way home to Scarsdale. Seltzer owned a beautiful town house on a side street. Seltzer was no fool. He knew his business. At fifty, Seltzer looked ten years younger. Sailboat Seltzer, he was called, even by pa-

tients, who knew he was crazy about sailing. Seltzer escaped from the
telephone by the simple expedient of spending long weekends and long
vacations on his boat. He always had a tan. He always looked relaxed
and happy. He was very popular with the older European analysts and
went to all their parties. He was a tremendous rumba dancer and he
knew a lot of sailing songs, which he sang in a near-professional bari-
tone voice. He also played the banjo. The Europeans considered him
the typical healthy American. He had presented half a dozen papers already at Psychoanlaytic Society meetings, on such subjects as "The Id,
the Ego, and the Sea" and "Columbus, Narcissism, and the Discovery
of America." Seltzer's name was appearing regularly in the indexes of
leading psychoanalytic journals. Dr. Blauberman's name had never
appeared there even once. Seltzer looked his patients over carefully,
and managed to select the ones who could afford to pay thirty-five dollars an hour and up, and give him the least possible inconvenience and
bother, as well as a classic and analyzable neurosis. It was important to
get patients who came to you five or even six times a week, nicely, quietly, cooperatively, without making a mess, so that from hour to hour
you knew where you were. It was important to have patients who were
comfortably analyzable from session to session. Dr. Blauberman admired the way Seltzer got the most, in every way, out of his practice.

"Listen, Sailboat, hmmm?" Dr. Blauberman had said. "I've been
doing a lot of thinking about criteria for suitability for psychoanalysis.
It's a very important question."

"Of course," Seltzer said. "So?"

"I'm thinking of doing a paper on it."

"Blauberman, you know Waldhorn? Mmmm? Waldhorn just *did*
a paper on it."

Dr. Blauberman sniffed deeply. "I'll have to read it," he said. "It's a
very important question in our work. Do you accept Fenichel's criteria
for suitability?"

"Fenichel's. And Freud's."

"How do *you* tell, Sailboat?" Dr. Blauberman said. "About
suitability? Mmmm?"

"It ain't so difficult," Seltzer said. "Stay away from the narcissistic neuroses and perverse characters, Blauberman. As you well know, Freud always said they lent themselves poorly to analysis. Yes?"

Dr. Blauberman sighed.

"Don't take it so hard, Blauberman," Seltzer said, laughing. "Hmmm?"

Laughing boy. It was easy enough for him to laugh. Him and his year-round sun tan. "What about Freud's contra-indications to suitability, enlarged by Fenichel?" Dr. Blauberman asked.

"Ha!" Seltzer said. "Lack of a reasonable and cooperative ego! Stay away from it! Never take such a case. You have to protect yourself in our work. You know what we mean by ego strength. Right away I spot rigid defenses, I won't even start with them. I should say not. Listen to me, Blauberman. Develop an attitude and stick to it firmly. Remember that Fenichel holds that the crucial factor in determining accessibility is really the dynamic relationship between resistance and the wish for recovery."

"So how do you tell who's suitable for analysis when you don't know them yet?" Dr. Blauberman asked. "Who decides?"

"*You* do, Blauberman."

"Mmmm," Dr. Blauberman said. "After a trial analysis, who is to say suitable or unsuitable? Mmmm?"

"Blauberman, *you* are, mmmm?" Seltzer said, and laughed.

What would Sailboat Seltzer have done with Ephraim, Dr. Blauberman wondered. How would he have dealt with Ephraim's unshakable involvement with his old teacher, Gustave Lefevre?

"I just love the old guy," Ephraim had said. "I'd rather spend a day playing duets with Gus than almost anything."

"So. Mmmm. Two clarinets. Just the two of you. Yes?"

"Oh, man, you just ought to hear the tone Gus gets, even now! At his age!"

Two clarinets. Dr. Blauberman patiently tried to elicit something, anything, from Ephraim on the symbolic significance of the two clarinets. Silence. Nothing. Nowhere. Impossible. If just once he could get Ephraim to react emotionally. The emotion was there, all right. No mistake about it. But Dr. Blauberman couldn't get at it. He tried charm. He tried sympathy. He tried anger. He tried sarcasm. He tried coldness. He tried silence, and usually it was Dr. Blauberman who spoke first. It was very disheartening.

Dr. Blauberman couldn't find anything particularly helpful in his reading. In the hope of getting some elucidation, he looked up an old paper that he recalled his own analyst's having once made a big fuss over—Franz S. Cohn's "Practical Approach to the Problem of Narcissistic Neuroses," written over twenty years ago. And he read, "There is dull but agitated talking, very rapid without pause, or else scarcely any talk, with long intervals of silence. There is no important difference between these types. In both, thoughts are drifting like a cork on a deep sea of narcissistic libido that presently is going to wash away the analyst." Mmmm? Ephraim Samuels wanted to wash Blauberman away? Very disheartening.

In the beginning, Dr. Blauberman reported enthusiastically to Dr. Fifield during *his* analytic hour (Vertical Position) that Ephraim had a-lot-to-give and could achieve get-well, and that he thought he'd make out satisfactorily with Ephraim—better than he had done with Dr. Fifield's boyhood friend Lester Greenthal. Lester Greenthal's progress, after eight years in analysis with Dr. Blauberman, had been very slight. Lester Greenthal now accused Dr. Blauberman of loving Spencer Fifield more than Lester Greenthal. On the other hand, Marvin Krakower, the pathologist, had made terrific progress. In less than four years, after Marvin Krakower had come to him via Spencer Fifield, the pathologist had married Sally Mandel, the girl Spencer Fifield had been going around with. "Look at Marvin Krakower," Dr. Blauberman was able to tell Spencer Fifield when Fifield was lying on the couch. "Married to Sally. Two lovely children. If you get well, you might have all that." Spencer Fifield, unfortunately, still had a long way to go—chronically intellectualizing patients were, after all, reluctant even to go through the motions of acting on their newly acquired awareness—but he, unlike the deadwood, was working *with* Dr. Blauberman.

Together, Dr. Blauberman and Dr. Fifield had kept Joan Stone, the daughter of Dr. Fifield's wealthiest patient, Hiram Stone, from eloping with the manager of a neighborhood Christian Science Reading Room. Dr. Fifield had steered her into getting engaged to Barry Rosenblatt, another pathologist Spencer Fifield knew, whose ambition—and he was absolutely unneurotic and open about it—was to marry a rich girl, somebody who would make it economically possible for him to devote his attention fully to science. It had taken plenty out of Dr. Blauberman, the analyst frequently reminded Spencer Fifield, to put Barry Rosenblatt over. That one had been exhausting.

Dr. Blauberman had, in spite of himself, a kind of wistful admiration for some of the older psychoanalysts—especially the Europeans. But they were clannish and snobbish, and tended to treat him in a patronizing manner. They made jokes about life in the suburbs. They occupied prewar-rental apartments on Central Park West—office and home on a single rental—that were filled with the dark-brown, dreary, heavy furniture they had brought with them from Europe. They talked with fervor about "our work." They could afford to make their scholarly, erudite studies in a vacuum. They always seemed to be so lighthearted, so full of humor. They had good appetites. And they were highly sociable, always giving parties. For each other. Dr. Blauberman would hear them talking about their parties at the Psychoanalytic Institute, where he put in his voluntary work with the rest of them. He wasn't invited to their parties, and they seemed to look right through him in the corridors at the Institute or at conventions and conferences. It was apparently simple enough for them to resist being drawn into their patients' neuroses. The analytic discipline they talked so much about was also, it seemed, easy for them. Dr. Blauberman didn't find it easy. Nothing was easy for him. He had to watch his own strength, his own energies, how *much* he gave. If you let them, patients would eat you up. All of you. "Let's face it," Dr. Blauberman said to himself and to his patients. "The neurotic patient is hungry. Mmmm?" And what was the point of letting yourself be eaten up? That was right neither for you nor for your patients. It was debilitating. And the frustration of getting nowhere with a patient was debilitating. After all, Dr. Blauberman was a family man. He had a wife and two children. The children were very popular in their school. His son had just been elected president of his seventh-grade class. Dr. Blauberman worked hard for his living. He wanted something to show for it. He had a lovely sixty-thousand-dollar split-level house in Scarsdale. That was something. This summer, he was going to send both children to one of the finest camps in Vermont. That was something. And he and his wife were going to Spain. That would be something. His father-in-law owned one of the largest laundry chains in the city, and Dr. Blauberman admired him very much. He never saw his own father, who still lived in the section of Brooklyn where Dr. Blauberman had grown up. He didn't bother his father and his father didn't bother him. Like all accredited psychoanalysts, Dr. Blauberman had been psychoanalyzed himself. He was *free* of his father. And of the bitterness and the meanness his father represented. That was something, too.

After disposing of Ephraim Samuels, Dr. Blauberman would be in a position to tackle the problem of what to do about Lester Greenthal. Other Fifield-recommended patients had come and gone, including a young painter who had quit after having tried and failed to commit suicide, and a young strip-teaser who had tried and succeeded. Dr. Blauberman had made his mistakes, but he had learned from them, as he often told his patients, and never made the same mistake twice. His only mistake with Ephraim Samuels had been taking him on in the first place. Still, in the early days things had looked promising.

"And this music you compose," Dr. Blauberman had said at one session. "You will give it to some conductor? Yes? Maybe to Lenny Bernstein?" Dr. Blauberman liked being on a familiar basis with celebrated people his patients talked about.

Ephraim smiled at the ceiling. "I told you, Dr. Blauberman. I'm not ambitious—not that way. Not everybody can be a great man. But I've got a little stuff that's my own. For the time being, I just like to write these little pieces to see what comes out."

"You are afraid of a rejection. Mmmm?"

"You don't follow, Dr. Blauberman. I just don't want to—"

"I follow more than you think. Why don't you go to this party you are invited to for Lenny?"

"Well, I just don't enjoy those big parties. They're too confusing."

"Are you afraid Lenny or Adolph will reject you?"

"Gosh, no. I like them. They're a lot of fun. But hanging around with them can use up all your time."

"You back away *before* you are rejected. You feel inadequate."

"If I wanted to, I could run around from one party to another, trying to make it with television producers and all that junk. But that isn't what I want."

"Lenny Bernstein is on television. Television is good enough for Lenny Bernstein to show millions of people what he can do. Television is a healthy outlet. No?"

"It depends on what you want," Ephraim said.

"Maybe there is something missing in your sense of values about what you want," Dr. Blauberman said.

"Well—" Ephraim began. Then he stopped. As though inspired, he continued, "Here's the way it is, Dr. Blauberman. Last week, I went over to my sister Leah's house for dinner. She's married to Vic, you know, and they have this four-year-old kid, Eugene, named after Eugene Victor Debs—"

"I know, I know," Dr. Blauberman said, impatient with Ephraim's way of breaking into laughter over the child's name.

"I still get a blast out of it, after all these years."

"Mmmm," Dr. Blauberman said, making noises of dissatisfaction.

"What I wanted to tell you," Ephriam went on, "my father was there, too, and Eugene comes over to him and says, 'Grampa, guess the name of a delicious Jewish drink beginning with the letter A.' "

Dr. Blauberman made further sounds of dissatisfaction. How he loathed these homey stories of the family's self-appreciation.

"So Pop says he gives up, and Eugene screams, 'Ah-malted!' " Ephraim put on an exaggerated Jewish accent. "It turns out that Vic rehearses him in the accent. Vic says he's going to put Eugene on television someday, with Pop's collie, in a new gimmick—a Jewish 'Lassie' program, with Eugene sitting on the dog, relaxed, and telling Jewish jokes. Isn't that wild?" He stopped, realizing that he was getting no response.

"You are not a child," Dr. Blauberman said. "For you, work in television would be a healthy outlet. You are afraid to engage yourself in the competitive activities in television? Even to the extent of going to a social party?"

"No. You don't get the message, Dr. Blauberman," Ephraim said, in a low voice. "You don't understand. I like to see those people once in a while, but I don't like to run with anybody. I get more pleasure out of talking to my father."

"You go only where it is safe, where you won't be rejected. Yes?"

"Oh, God!" Ephraim said, "I told you. My father is an original, unusual man. I don't know anybody else like him."

Dr. Blauberman made loud sounds of disapproval. "So. At your age. You feel safe only with Papa. You still insist on living with your father. No?"

"Well, sure. Why not? It's not just that he'd be all alone. I *like* being with him. Do you know how he escaped from Siberia? He was—"

"Don't start telling me all that heroic garbage about the Socialists." Dr. Blauberman's anger cut through Ephraim with terrible force. "You won't face the truth about your real feeling about your father. You refuse to admit your hostility to him."

"Well, I've got my beefs and all, but—"

"Why are you so lacking in drive? Why? You don't think it's because of your father? You refuse to admit there is something basically unhealthy about your home situation? *Why* do you stay with him?"

"Pop makes terrific coffee," Ephraim said softly, with a laugh.

"You're twenty-eight. At your age, you should have your own apartment."

"Well, I guess you're right, Dr. Blauberman. And, naturally, when I get married I'll have my own home. But right now I sort of like it where I am. And I can save money. It leaves me free to do my work or anything I please."

"And it gives you an excuse not to compete in the world? To risk letting people hear your music. To sell it. To make some decent money. To be a man. Mmmm?"

"Well—" Ephraim said, and stopped.

One day, Dr. Blauberman had wanted to know why Ephraim played the clarinet in the first place. "The clarinet is basically a symbol, no?" he said. "You prefer an inanimate symbol to real satisfaction. Hmmm. Yes?"

Ephraim laughed. "I like them *both*, Dr. Blauberman. But I do love the clarinet sound. No question about that. It sounds good to me. Of all the musical instruments, the clarinet is closest to nature. It's the tree itself, hollowed out. The sound is *natural*."

"So. You refuse to face the meaning of the symbolism?"

"Well—" Once more, Ephraim stopped talking.

As time went on, it became clear to Dr. Blauberman that the depression in Ephraim was growing deeper. He evidently felt dissatisfied with himself. He lost interest in the clarinet. After awhile, he told Dr. Blauberman he could not enjoy what had been the simple pleasure of sitting down to a quiet supper with his father, or of amusing his small nephews with jazzy tunes on his clarinet. Everything seemed to drop away. So many things had been stirred up into one big hodgepodge in his head. He didn't know where he was. He questioned everything he was and everything he had been doing. He complained to Dr. Blauberman that he couldn't sleep at night. Dr. Blauberman gave him prescriptions for Seconal, to help him sleep. When a single capsule didn't work, he took increasingly large dosages, and showed up at Dr. Blauberman's office still groggy from the effects of Seconal. One day, Dr. Blauberman announced that there would be no more prescriptions.

"What'll I do, Dr. Blauberman? I can't sleep without it."

"Get it from a physical doctor."

"Dr. Fifield?"

"If he chooses to give it to you."

"But if he doesn't?"

"I can't be responsible for what Dr. Fifield gives you. That is his business. Physical medicine is another department. So."

So. Ephraim went to see Spencer and said he needed Seconal or something to help him sleep. After a few months of giving Ephraim prescriptions for sleeping pills, Spencer, during his analytic hour with Dr. Blauberman, expressed interest over the large amounts of Seconal that Ephraim was consuming. "Frankly, I think he's overintellectualizing, about women and everything, and that's why he can't sleep." Spencer was fresh from the analyst's consideration of Spencer's own tendency to overintellectualize. "Although he denies it, of course, he seems to be opening up. He seems to have made a lot of progress in treatment since that first time I saw him. He had hepatitis, and that leaves you feeling depressed for weeks afterward, but there was more to it than that. Frankly, he needed help if anybody did."

"You really think he is opening up?" Dr. Blauberman said.

"Definitely! He told me he hasn't been able to bring himself to touch the clarinet for months. He says he just doesn't have the wind to blow, and when he tries to play, it makes him feel physically sick. That must show, frankly, that the deep disturbances are rising to the surface. Frankly, I'm sure you're getting somewhere with him."

Dr. Blauberman looked pleased. "So," he said, in a mock-fatherly reproach. "My siblings are talking about me."

Spencer gave a happy laugh.

"See you tomorrow, mmmm?" Dr. Blauberman said.

And a couple of weeks later Spencer again expressed concern over the sleeping pills Ephraim asked for. "This time, I questioned him about his emotional involvements. I asked him whether he brings up material for you to work with."

"Mmmm," Dr. Blauberman said.

"I asked him whether he had a real relationship with a girl," Spencer went on. He had been chewing over with the analyst his own impoverished relationships with girls. "I really pinned him down and asked him whether his physical needs were being satisfied. I told him he shouldn't be avoiding sexual involvements with emotional content. Mmmm?" he said, giving Dr. Blauberman back his own. "He became upset, very disturbed. He said, 'Who's *avoiding* anything?' Classical defense-mechanism anger."

Dr. Blauberman sighed.

"I told him psychoanalysis has been extremely helpful to me in my own work," Spencer said stiffly. "Then he asked me whether he ought to have a consultation with Dr. Hans Radelsheim. And I told him he had to bring up *that* question with you. I told him, frankly, it's not a good idea for us in sibling relationships to talk about you with each other."

"I am a psychoanalyst," Dr. Blauberman said to Ephraim at the next-to-last session as Ephraim lay, still not speaking, on the couch. "I don't know how to break you of the Seconal addiction. It is not in my field. You need to go where you can be helped in that respect now."

"Would it be a good idea to have a consultation about what I should do?" Ephraim said, finally talking. "I mean, what I've been trying to figure out is why I got into analysis in the first place. Nothing ever seemed right—now that I think about it—that I tried to do here."

"And whose fault is that?"

"Mine, I guess. But, anyway, my friend Charlie Donato—the bassoonist?—says I ought to have a consultation with this Dr. Hans Radelsheim, you know?"

"Why Radelsheim, hmmm?"

"I don't know. Just because Charlie says he's good, that he knows a lot."

"So. I *don't* know a lot?"

"Well, no. It's just that all I want is to get back to my music. I don't really have a good idea of what's happened to me this past year, and what I should do."

"I am telling you what you should do. You should go to Dr. Fifield and ask him what to do, where to go to be cured of your addiction to Seconal."

"But if I feel worse, should I go to a different *kind* of analyst?"

"If *this* analyst couldn't analyze you at this point, *no* analyst can analyze you," Dr. Blauberman said. "We found that out. At least, not in your present state. Mmmm?"

"Would it hurt just to ask this Dr. Radelsheim about me?"

"There is no reason to call Radelsheim. I have nothing to ask Radelsheim." He stood up from his chair. "See you tomorrow."

That night, at another meeting of the Psychoanalytic Society, Dr. Blauberman sat next to Sailboat Seltzer, who was sitting next to

Dr. Abe Letkin, one of the old-timers—one of the oldest practitioners of analysis in town, as a matter of fact. Letkin didn't let anybody ever forget it, either. He always irritated Dr. Blauberman, with all his *gemutlich*, good-natured, relaxed ways—the Middle European Barry Fitzgerald of psychoanalysis. Once, Dr. Blauberman telephoned Letkin about a clinic patient, and Letkin took the opportunity to make one of his speeches, lecturing Dr. Blauberman about how Freud was a saint, a poet, and a philosopher, not a scientist. When Dr. Blauberman tried to get a word in edgewise, Letkin said he had to go, and cut him off with a "Lotsa luck." Letkin's signoff was always "Lotsa luck." Some dignified way for one of the elders of psychoanalysis to speak! But, for reasons Dr. Blauberman could not understand, Letkin was admired and respected by all the big wheels in the Psychoanalytic Society. Why? All he did was make cracks about the stuffiness, the narrow-mindedness, the limitations, the godlike pretensions, the short-comings of analysts—particularly some of the younger analysts, who, according to Letkin, were constitutionally unfitted for the work they tried to do. In the discussion that followed the reading of a paper at a meeting, Letkin would get up and try to turn it into philosophical channels. Philosophical channels bored Dr. Blauberman. And it wasn't as though Letkin's views came as a surprise to his listeners. Every time he got up to talk about Freud's really *significant* qualities, his *spiritual* qualities, he would be received with affectionate groans. "Leanness," Letkin would say, with the kind of inflection Dr. Blauberman always found so embarrassing. "Leanness and asceticism constituted Freud's ego-ideal." And everybody would look at Letkin as though he were *the* father symbol. It was infuriating. Dr. Blauberman sometimes wished he had the nerve to get up and say something about it.

Before the meeting was called to order, Letkin was talking, in a conspiratorial, laughing manner, to Sailboat Seltzer. Letkin was saying what a terrible collection of paintings had been donated to the Psychoanalytic Society for its art show to raise money for the Psychoanalytic Institute. "I tell you, Sellbought, instead of throwing out these lousy paintings by name painters, they give them to *psychoanalysts* to sell. That is what they think of psychoanalysts."

And Seltzer said, putting the Letkinese on thick, "A rummage sale is a rummage sale by anybody, no?"

It happened that Dr. Blauberman and his wife had picked up an Abstract Expressionist painting by a well-known painter for only three hundred and ninety-five dollars at the art show, and it was now hanging in their living room in Scarsdale. Dr. Blauberman started to tell them about it, but Letkin was inviting Seltzer to come to a party. Letkin was saying, "Sellbought, don't forget to bring your banjo. The food will be good, and we have lotsa whiskey."

"Letkin, by me you are the A No. 1 host among analysts," Seltzer said. That Seltzer! What he wouldn't do to make himself popular with Letkin and the other old-timers!

Letkin clapped Seltzer on the back. "Let me tell you a new Myron Cohen joke I just heard from one of my patients," he said to Seltzer, extending his attention to Dr. Blauberman with one brief eyewink and then turning back to Seltzer.

"So tell me already," Seltzer said, still putting on the schmalzy act to ingratiate himself with Letkin.

"So," Letkin began. "This patient comes to the analyst and lies down on the couch, and the analyst says to him, 'You've got to stop smoking.' 'That'll help me?' the patient asks. And the analyst says, 'Yes, you're burning the couch.' "

Letkin and Seltzer killed themselves laughing. Two laughing boys.

The meeting was called to order. There was a long paper read by Kurt Eissler and entitled "Notes on the Environment of a Genius." It was about Goethe and Goethe's loving father. Just what Dr. Blauberman needed! Not only another of those esoteric studies but one about loving fathers. At the meeting before, it was Radelsheim— one of those self-appointed saints regarded with awe by so many of the other analysts—on the psychic function of artistic compulsion. Tonight, Dr. Blauberman noticed Radelsheim sitting at the other side of the room, absorbed, rapt, listening attentively to Eissler. Radelsheim and his original theories. But it was Blauberman who had to deal with the environmental setup of an Ephraim Samuels. In the discussion that followed the presentation of the paper, Eissler said that analysts possibly are not too well prepared to deal psychoanalytically with situations in which parents might have a good effect on their children rather than the opposite. That was a big help. Everybody gave one of those arrogantly humble laughs of self-understanding. The hypocrites! Tomorrow morning, most of them would be struggling, like him, against resistance reinforced from the outside.

This time, Letkin, thank God, didn't make his usual speech. He was too busy laughing it up with Seltzer. Dr. Blauberman hung around with them, listening glumly to Letkin make disrespectful cracks about Goethe.

"Eissler should have explained why Goethe didn't know how to laugh at himself," Letkin was saying. "Goethe had no humor. Tell me, Sellbought. What kind of father gives issue to a son who does not know how to laugh at himself?"

Seltzer gave a chuckle instead of an opinion. Sailboat Seltzer always played it safe.

Dr. Blauberman tried to get in on the amusement. "Eissler you couldn't call exactly a Myron Cohen, mmmm?"

Letkin gave him a cool look and said, "I thought Eissler brought out some brilliant points, Blauberman."

"On the question of neutralized energy," Seltzer said. "For Goethe, creating, Eissler pointed out, was one of the deepest instinctual processes, mmmm?"

And Letkin said, "The environment that was beneficial for Goethe could, with someone else, have led to vastly different results, possibly delinquency or psychosis? I agree with Eissler."

"Mmmm?" Dr. Blauberman said. "Mmmm." He wanted to ask Letkin what he thought about an Ephraim Samuels. What about the resistance of an Ephraim Samuels, thanks to one of those loving fathers? But the hell with it. All these people were too busy becoming saints, developing original theories, writing papers. Dr. Blauberman thought fleetingly about "The Id, the Ego, and the Clarinet." The hell with that, too. There were more important things.

The next morning, Dr. Blauberman had two very difficult sessions in a row—first with Joan Stone, who tried to pull a sudden flip-flop in her somewhat unstable feelings about Barry Rosenblatt, and then with Lester Greenthal, who decided that day to spring on Dr. Blauberman the idea that *he* should have a consultation with some other analyst. Dr. Blauberman got Lester Greenthal quieted down. After Lester Greenthal had left, Dr. Blauberman picked up his telephone and called Mr. Samuels at his place of business, a one-man auto-repair shop in Long Island City.

"Mr. Samuels?"

"Yes, *sir*." The father had a slight Eastern European accent, and his "sir" was used not as a respectful salutation but as a form of emphasis.

"Mr. Joseph Samuels?"

"Yes, *sir*."

"Dr. Blauberman here. I'm informing you of the termination on my treatment of your son . . . . Did you hear?" Dr. Blauberman asked impatiently. "I'm discharging my obligations with this telephone call. Your son's last appointment with me will be today."

"Dr. *Blau*berman?" Mr. Samuels asked nervously, uncertainly, as though he were surprised to have proof suddenly that there *was* a Dr. Blauberman. "Is Ephraim all right, Dr. Blauberman?" He enunciated his words with care.

"He's supposed to be here for his last hour this afternoon—if he shows up," Dr. Blauberman said. "I'm afraid I can't do anything any more for your son. I can't carry him any more. I've knocked myself out for him. He just refuses to work his problems out."

"But, Dr. Blau—"

"He refuses to let himself be helped. You can't help a patient who doesn't want to be helped."

"What's all it about?" Mr. Samuels sounded terrified. He couldn't get his words out in order.

"What-it-is-all-about," Dr. Blauberman said, demonstrating extreme patience, "is simply that your son is too sick to be treated by an analyst . . . . Look, I can't spend all this time talking on the telephone. I've got a lot of sick people to see."

"Ephraim thinks the world of you," Mr. Samuels said. "He hasn't taken an interest in anything else for a whole year. Does he want to stop seeing you?"

Irritability with this slow-talking, slow-thinking man began to grow in Dr. Blauberman, but he gave a laugh and said, "Does any patient want to stop seeing the *analyst?*"

The humor seemed to be lost on Mr. Samuels. "What is the matter with my son?" he was asking, in a quavery voice. "Can you tell me—"

"I've got to hang up," Dr. Blauberman interrupted. "Sorry. If you insist on discussing this, I'll give you an appointment. This afternoon? At two-fifty? Mmmmm?"

"Well—" Mr. Samuels began.

"It's the hour following your son's. Yes?"

"Yes."

"Be here, please. Two-fifty." Dr. Blauberman hung up.

How many times in the past had he tried to get Ephraim to face the reality of what Mr. Samuels was: a neurotic, frightened, dominating figure, hanging on to the past, keeping his son tied to his own self-limiting fears of society. Always, Ephraim had denied it.

Dr. Blauberman had finally said one day, "If your father is so wise, why don't you go to *him* with your problems? Why do you come to me at all?"

"But Dr. Fifield said I needed treatment," Ephraim said. "And you said I needed it, too. Pop doesn't want to interfere with the analysis or anything else I'm trying to do for myself. But I can see he's worrying about me. He can't understand why I don't play the clarinet any more or see any friends or girls. Not that he ever says anything."

"Hmmmm. So you were so well adjusted and happy, and you were realizing yourself so fully, *before* you came to analysis, mmmm?" Dr. Blauberman asked.

"Well, no. I've always had this—this—nature, sort of quiet and sad," Ephraim said. "I told you, my mother was always that way, too."

"Mmmm," Dr. Blauberman said.

"I got hit with hepatitis just as I was starting on this project of transposing for clarinet the viola and violin parts of some Bach suites. I was working day and night on them with old Gus Lefevre. Did I tell you he wrote that basic book of instruction I began with as a kid?"

"Mmmmm." If it wasn't the father he was holding on to, it was the old teacher.

"It really got me down," Ephraim said, "having to give up working with Gus. That's when Dr. Fifield told me I ought to consult you."

"So. Maybe it was a good thing you had to give up working with Gus," Dr. Blauberman said.

"Good!" Ephraim cried out in horror. "It wasn't *good*, man. You ought to see Gus. He's retired now, in his seventies, living with his wife in his little cottage deep in the woods, way out on Long Island. I used to get up at dawn to travel three hours each way on the Long Island Rail Road just for the privilege of playing duets with Gus. I used to get up before *Pop*, and he's been getting up every morning at six. For the past fifty years. And I'm a guy who likes his sleep."

"And you stayed overnight at the teacher's house?" Dr. Blauberman asked. "You looked there for another home. Yes?"

"Sure it's home!" Ephraim cried again. "You ought to hear Gus. We'd stay up until four in the morning playing Bach, with only his wife for an audience. We'd make tape recordings of two parts, and then play two other parts along with the tapes. You ought to hear that sound. Four clarinets. It was wild. Mrs. Lefevre couldn't make Gus go to bed. You ought to hear him blow. He's almost three times my age, and I could barely keep up with him."

Dr. Blauberman said, "Not two clarinets but *four*. Yes? Do you think you know what it means, the four?"

Ephraim looked puzzled, and uninterested in numbers. "Once, I brought the tapes back and played them for Pop," he went on. "You know what he said? He said, 'It's beautiful, Eephie; it does my heart good to listen.' That's the way he talks, you know? He's been so lost and miserable ever since my mother died, and yet he can get a blast out of hearing me play."

"Why four?" Dr. Blauberman said, trying to bring him back on the track. "You think you know why you like four?"

Another thing Dr. Blauberman had tried repeatedly to accomplish with Ephraim was to make him aware of the deeper significance of his careless attitude toward money. He was so satisfied to drift along, making a few dollars here and there playing clarinet at school dances or trade-union parties, at resort hotels or small clubs in the Village. It was clear to Dr. Blauberman that the lack of drive to make money came directly from Mr. Samuels. Ephraim told him about it almost boastfully.

"Pop has just never been really *interested* in money, and he's always hated what so many other men have to do in order to earn big money," Ephraim told him. "When my mother was alive, she'd say how nice it would be to have a good set of dishes or stuff like that, but her heart wasn't really in it, either. You know what Pop always told us?"

Dr. Blauberman was silent. He despised what Pop always told them.

"Pop always said, 'As long as I have these two hands, we will never go hungry. We will always make out.' And we always did make out." Ephraim held his own hands open before him, the fingers spread out. His hands were long, the fingers tapered, the skin rough and flat at the tips from years of pressing clarinet keys.

"You made out?" Dr. Blauberman said. "You think your father makes out?"

"Well, he misses my mother," Ephraim said slowly.

"If you know what I mean, Dr. Blauberman."

"No. What *do* you mean?"

"Well, he misses her deeply. And the way he says it—remembering her face still makes it impossible, after three years, for him to look fully into the face of any other woman."

"So. He holds on to you. Yes? He insists on living in the old apartment? With you?"

"He keeps his sorrow to himself," Ephraim said. "He doesn't try to put anything off on me."

"He sees other women now? He has friends? Mmmm?"

"Well, no. He never needed many people. He never did a lot of running around. My mother was the same way. He's got his dog,"

Ephraim said, his voice lifting in sudden delight. "This four-month-old collie. Silky. He's a beautiful puppy. The first dog he's had in ten years. We used to have a retriever—he died in Pop's arms at the age of *twenty*. It took Pop ten whole years before he could bring himself to get another dog. That's the way he is."

"And that's enough?" Dr. Blauberman said. "A dog?"

"The collie is this beautiful sable-and-white puppy, so affectionate and intelligent," Ephraim said. "Pop loves that puppy."

"So," Dr. Blauberman said. "Your father doesn't have a housekeeper for the apartment where you live—in—where is it, did you say?"

"Jackson Heights."

"Yes." Dr. Blauberman couldn't bring himself to pronounce the name. How he hated the thought of anyone's wanting to remain in Jackson Heights. He had the complete family picture by this time, and to him it was not exhilarating: The eldest child, Leah, married to the trade-union organizer Victor Fine, with their four-year old boy, Eugene Victor, named after Debs. The older son, Barney, married to Terry, with a fifteen-month-old baby, Jimmy. Mr. Samuels managing all his own housekeeping in the apartment he shared with Ephraim and the dog.

But Ephraim insisted on bringing the picture into sharper focus. Dr. Blauberman indulged him and listened.

"Pop gets up every morning at six o'clock sharp, without any assistance from any alarm clock. He always makes the same breakfast for himself. Freshly squeezed orange juice. It's got to be freshly squeezed. Two soft-boiled eggs. Percolated coffee, with heavy cream and four teaspoons of sugar. Four slices of white bread with sweet butter. To Pop, white bread is a delicacy. He was born in this muddy village in pre-Revolutionary Russia. When he was just a boy in his late teens, he was exiled to Siberia and escaped to America, and so white bread to him is very special, it sort of represents—"

"All right, all right, I know that," Dr. Blauberman interrupted.

"He always leaves the white bread on the kitchen table for me," Ephraim continued, in a lower voice. "He always squeezes enough orange juice for me and leaves a large glass of it for me next to the bread. He always leaves the coffeepot for me on the stove. Then he feeds Silky and sets out in this old Plymouth sedan of his for his auto-repair shop. And Silky goes along, sitting in the front seat with him, just as Blackie always used to do."

"Yes, yes." Dr. Blauberman said. "So?"

"So that's the way he is, that's all. He's got this little yard behind his shop, for Silky to wander around in. He's got this corny picture of Abraham Lincoln hanging over his desk, and right next to it a picture of Eugene Victor Debs. He's got this big picture window in the front of his shop, that he installed with his own hands. He's got this big collection of potted plants in front of the window, that he started with my mother before I was born. Our house is full of plants, and Leah's whole living room is full of them, too. She keeps telling Pop the neighbors think she's crazy."

"So. The neighbors think she is neurotic, your sister?"

As though Dr. Blauberman had made a joke, Ephraim laughed. "Silky moseys about or sleeps near the plants at the shop," he said. "Pop loves having Silky with him there. You know Pop offered the puppy to me the other day? He saw me feeling so low, I think he wanted to cheer me up or something. . . . It's crazy, but Pop treats almost everything as though it were alive. You know, he really *loves* automobiles? You know, he always refers to a car in the feminine gender?"

"Mmmm," Dr. Blauberman said.

"And what he loves to do especially, even when cars look alike or are built alike, is to discover their individual differences, as though they were alive."

"The automobile is inanimate," Dr. Blauberman said. "The clarinet is inanimate. Yes?"

At one point, Dr. Blauberman had tried to determine how the Samuels family felt about Ephraim's career. Nobody else in the family was musical. Nobody else in the family was "gifted."

"Pop loves to listen to me play," Ephraim had said. "That is, he *used* to love to listen to me play when I still played. You know, he really gets the message in jazz? He loved to hear me play Mozart, but, believe it or not, he really gets a blast out of jazz. He really swings. Once, he came down to this dump I played in, the Zero Inn, in the Village. It was wild. Pop had never seen anything like it, and he was blushing all over the place, seeing all the chicks in pants and stuff. You know the way they dress. Then I started playing with Josh Leonard, the pianist. And I was tossing a Monk thing back and forth with Josh, and then, while Josh laid down a foundation, I blew a brand-new melodic line about a mile long, and I could see Pop's face while I played. He was excited, and I could see him bouncing with the beat. Man, what a sight!"

"So. Your father holds on to you, lives through you?"

"You don't get the message, Dr. Blauberman. He just likes to listen to me play. One hot, sweltering Sunday, I felt like staying home to practice. Pop likes to read the Sunday *Times* or play with my nephews when they visit, while I practice runs or just test reeds. That's the way he is. This one hot Sunday, it was so damn hot I took off everything except my shorts and sat around barefoot, whittling down a reed. You know, he just sat there with me, watching until I got that reed down to the exact thickness I wanted. You know why? Because he was interested. And you should have seen his face when I got the damn reed done right."

"You feel separated from him? You feel you are an individual in your own right?"

"Well, Pop is a big lemonade drinker," Ephraim said. "So I got to be one, too. I guess that's a great example of how unseparated from him I am. Whenever I'm practicing, he always makes a large pitcher of cold lemonade and leaves it handy for me to get at. Then he'll retire and read a book and listen to me practice, while I try to perfect a single run or something like that. He likes to hear me do runs as much as anything else. Once, I went over to him after I had swabbed out the clarinet, and showed him my sore, bruised underlip. I did it because I knew he'd get such a blast out of it. And I said, 'It's the wound of battle. I'm winning. I'm beginning to feel like the boss.' And you know what he said? He said, 'That's nice, Eephie,' and then he was so embarrassed and short of breath he stuck his head in the refrigerator pretending to look for something to eat for supper."

"So maybe your father should go to an analyst, to wean him away from *you*, yes?"

"Oh, God!" Ephraim said with a sigh.

" 'Oh, God,' but you don't do anything with your music. You don't realize yourself in any way. You don't play. You think that is healthy?"

"The way I feel lately, I don't want to play," Ephraim said.

"You do not face the reality of your relationship with your father. You resist the transference relationship with me. How can I help you if you do not want to be helped?"

"I just want to get back to the music," Ephraim said.

"And you will play at little Socialist meetings with your music?" Dr. Blauberman said sarcastically. "You will bury yourself in obscurity? Yes?"

"I told you, Pop was a Socialist when we were kids," Ephraim said. "But even then he always argued with the Socialists, too; he said they were too narrow-minded. He's never been able to go with any single group."

"He is too good for society, mmmmm?" Dr. Blauberman said.

"He's in a class by himself," Ephraim said. "There's always been some idea or some feeling that would make him hold to himself, no matter what anybody else was saying or doing."

"He goes his own way and you want to follow?" Dr. Blauberman said. "The way of self-victimization."

Talk about environmental resistances. No analyst could work with a patient against such a neurotic, dominating father. In a way, though, he was glad he had telephoned Mr. Samuels. It was unorthodox, but it was a goddam generous, as well as smart, thing to do.

A few minutes before the beginning of Ephraim Samuels' last session, Dr. Blauberman received a telephone call from Dr. Hans Radelsheim.

"Oh, yes, I saw you at the meeting last night. I didn't have a chance to say hello. It was an interesting paper, I thought, Eissler's paper on—"

"Yes. Blauberman, I'm calling you about the boy Ephraim Samuels. You are discontinuing treatment of him?"

"Well, yes and no," Dr. Blauberman said. "As far as suitability for analysis goes—"

"But you are discontinuing? The boy says you do not wish to treat him any more."

"You know you can't get an objective picture from the patient," Dr. Blauberman said with a little muffled laugh. "This boy is very disturbed, Radelsheim, mmmm? Narcissistic neurosis. The transference relationship—"

Again Radelsheim cut him off. "These cases are very difficult. But you have dismissed him as your patient?"

The superior bastard. Who did he think he was? Dr. Blauberman said angrily, "I have a session with him this afternoon. I'm seeing the father. The father is—"

"Yes, Blauberman. Could you tell me, please—did you terminate the treatment?"

"Yes, Radelsheim. I've decided to let the boy go, for the time being."

"All right. I'll see what I can do for him."

"The boy is in subjection to his father and incapable of transferring his libido to a new sexual object," Dr Blauberman said in a rush. "In a reaction to his infantile—"

"Thanks very much. I'll see him." And Radelsheim hung up.

"Why don't you sit on the couch today?" Dr. Blauberman said when Ephraim showed up for his last session. "No need to lie down. We're not going to be bringing up any material today. Yes?" He leaned back in his chair, and started to put fresh tobacco in his pipe. Ephraim sat on a corner of the couch. He had a self-conscious, uncomfortable smile on his face. Dr. Blauberman saw resentment there, and accusation, and strain. He brushed the tobacco crumbs off his lap. Then he put a cigarette lighter to his pipe, and, after a brief struggle, gave it up in favor of a lighted match.

"Well," Ephraim said. "I guess you know I went to see Dr. Radelsheim."

"Hmmm." Dr. Blauberman, having successfully lit the pipe, puffed a lot of smoke.

"Didn't he call you?" Ephraim asked. "He said he was going to call you."

"He called, he called."

"He says he'll see me, if you're not going to treat me any more."

"If I couldn't analyze you, no analyst can analyze you," Dr. Blauberman said. "If you have so much of your own money to throw away finding out that another analyst can do nothing with you, that is up to you. Mmmm? But I have seen you for a year. I know what you should do."

"Well—" Ephraim said.

"You need to go somewhere for a rest."

"Well—" Ephraim said.

"Perhaps someday you may want to try analysis again," Dr. Blauberman said. "In that case"—Dr. Blauberman paused and gave what was meant to be a fatherly smile—"I'll be happy to talk things over with you again. Maybe in a year or so. Mmmm?"

"I don't think so," Ephraim said, blushing. "As a matter of fact, Dr. Radelsheim said—"

"I don't need to hear what Dr. Radelsheim said," Dr. Blauberman said. "I have talked to Dr. Radelsheim myself. I don't think you are in a position to understand what Dr. Radelsheim is saying."

Ephraim looked astonished. "Dr. Radelsheim was awfully nice to me," he said. "He talked to me for almost two hours."

Oh, that bastard and his big mouth! "You must realize that a person in your position will hear only what he *wants* to hear," Dr. Blauberman said. "Don't you think that I am a little better qualified to understand Dr. Radelsheim than you are? Mmmm?"

"But he didn't think I should—"

Dr. Blauberman sat forward and made impatient noises. "You went against my advice in going to see Dr. Radelsheim," he said. "I warned you that you would become confused."

Ephraim was silent for a few moments, and Dr. Blauberman relaxed in his chair and puffed.

"But he says it's important for me to get back to my music," Ephraim said. "And that's all I care about!"

"All?" Dr. Blauberman asked.

"I'm a musician, man!" Ephraim said.

"Of course," Dr. Blauberman said indulgently. "It is important at this point that you just rest, and then get back to your clarinet. And there is no need for you to go running around to any more analysts. Mmmm?"

"Well, I told Dr. Radelsheim I'd come to see him until I got going again with my music," Ephraim said. "That is, he said he would be available if I wanted him."

"There is no need to see Radelsheim any more," Dr. Blauberman said. He cleared his throat. "Your father wanted to come in to see me today. So I agreed to see him here. It's unusual procedure, but I thought you might like it."

"*Me?*"

"You talk so much about your father—you don't want him to meet your analyst?" Dr. Blauberman said.

"Are you still my analyst?"

"Of course. I will not be treating you for a while, but once you choose an analyst, there is something of the analyst that stays with you always." He smiled at the young man. "Your father should be here soon. I will be glad to meet him."

"What do you want to do, analyze *Pop?*"

Dr. Blauberman got up from his chair. "I'll just go out and see if your father is here," he said.

He opened the door of his inner office and went out to his spacious waiting room. Through the eighteen-foot unbroken spread of window facing the park, the sun was flooding into the room. It had taken years, years of hard work and effort and giving of himself to his patients, to get that room. The room had a brand-new Old American look. Thick hooked rugs, a ladder-back maple rocking chair with a calico cotton cushion tied onto the seat, a black Boston rocker, and half a dozen Currier & Ives prints on the walls. A very low lowboy held stocks of modern, shiny magazines, including *Realites*. The interior decorator had worked out every last little detail directly with him and Mrs. Blauberman until they had precisely what they wanted.

He pushed the magazines on the lowboy into two neat stacks. A vague sensation of fear touched at his stomach, as it always did when he looked around that room. Because he had such keen self-awareness, Dr. Blauberman was not surprised. He was, in fact, accustomed to this sensation. But someday that would be gone, too, and then he would be able to enjoy the room.

As he returned to the inner office and was about to close the door, he caught a glimpse of Mr. Samuels arriving, the soiled gray cap on his head. Exactly what Dr. Blauberman had expected! The dreariness of it all! Christ! And the whole damn family seemed to have come along. Leah, the young woman must be; and her husband, Victor Fine; and the other son, Barney. Victor Fine wore a blue denim work shirt with a maroon knit tie. Nobody in the family knew how to dress! Barney, the good-natured one, who worked in the Washington produce market at night, had on brown corduroy slacks and a red-and-white checked gingham sports shirt open at the collar. The family neurosis in diagram! Dr. Blauberman left the door open a crack, and watched the father sit down in the Boston rocker, unrocking. The father took out a large steel pocket watch and nodded to the others; they had made it on time.

Opening the door all the way, his pipe between his teeth, Dr. Blauberman said, "Come in."

Mr. Samuels, his son, his daughter, and his son-in-law stood up.

"*All* of you?" Dr. Blauberman's smile was forgiving. He didn't move from the doorway as he looked the group over more closely: Leah, very serious and respectful, wearing wrinkled wool dress with an unfashionable hemline; her husband's obvious belligerence; the brother's open, untroubled face; Mr. Samuels in his badly fitting suit and curling collar, with his rough hands and paint-stained fingernails.

"Ephraim?" Mr. Samuels asked. "Is Ephraim here?"

"Yes, he's here." Dr. Blauberman sighed. "In here." He led the way inside and, lowering the foot of his chair with a lever, sat down.

Ephraim looked embarrassed as his family trooped in. Mr. Samuels went over to him and put a hand on his son's shoulder. "Hello, Eephie," he said.

"Hello, Pop. What you want to come way over here for?"

Mr. Samuels shrugged.

"Well, sit down, be seated," Dr. Blauberman said, with a kind of cozy cordiality. "You"—he nodded at Victor Fine and, taking the pipe from his mouth, pointed the stem at one of his slat-back armchairs— "sit there."

Vic sat there. Mr. Samuels sat down on the couch next to Ephraim, and the two others squeezed in alongside.

"Where'd you leave Silky, anyway, Pop?" Ephraim asked.

"He's right outside, Eeph!" Vic said quickly and in an unnaturally loud voice.

"Here?" Ephraim shouted. "*Here?*"

Mr. Samuels blushed. He looked at Dr. Blauberman and smiled.

"Tied to the umbrella stand outside, Eephie," Leah said.

"Oh, my God!" Ephraim said, and started to laugh. His father gave him a proud look and then turned expectantly to the Doctor.

"Pop didn't want to leave the puppy alone in the car," Leah said to Dr. Blauberman.

"The puppy is like a little baby," Mr. Samuels said. "Would you leave a baby alone? Somebody might break into the car and take him."

"I hope it doesn't look as though we do things neurotically," Leah said.

"It's not neurotically," her husband said.

"I mean, dragging a collie like that all over the city," Leah said. "That puppy is going to grow up to be a big dog. Normally, he'd be on a farm, out in the fields, minding the sheep or something. It might look neurotically to some people. Not to me. But that's the way we might look to other people."

"Leah's the expert on all this psychological stuff," Barney said to Dr. Blauberman.

Dr. Blauberman felt like rapping a gavel for order. "This shouldn't take too long," he began crisply. "Actually, meeting with you is a highly unusual procedure, but I happened to have the free hour"—he nodded graciously to Ephraim—"and your father wanted to come in, so"—he nodded graciously to Mr. Samuels—"here we are. I didn't know I was getting a delegation. Safety in numbers, mmmm? Well, you're all here. I've heard a lot about you." He looked from Mr. Samuels to his sons, to his daughter, to his son-in-law, and then singled Leah out to direct his remarks to. "The fact is that Ephraim and

I have reached an impasse." These people wouldn't know what an impasse was, but let it go. "Our relationship just hasn't worked out. Perhaps it's my fault"—Dr. Blauberman gave a small, self-disparaging laugh—"and perhaps it's because Ephraim refuses to do his part. He's wasting his time and mine. And he's wasting your money, Mr. Samuels."

Mr. Samuels half stood up from the couch and opened his mouth to say something. Ephraim pulled him down to the couch. Dr. Blauberman was still talking. "Frankly, Ephraim is lazy, yes? But that isn't what is our concern of the moment. That's neither here nor there." He paused and chewed on the stem of his pipe. "You must be aware," he went on, concentrating his attention on Leah, "that Ephraim is a disturbed young man. He has become—you might say— addicted to a powerful barbiturate. He takes tremendous quantities of Seconal every night. He has become stalemated. Unable to move in any direction." Dr. Blauberman looked straight into Mr. Samuels' face and pointed his pipestem at him. "After today, I cannot take any further responsibility in this case. I've tried and tried to help your son, Mr. Samuels. I've tried to get him to use his gifts to make something of himself in life, but I'm sorry to say he prefers to remain—a slob." He gave a kidding little laugh.

Mr. Samuels looked wildly at Ephraim, and then around at the members of his family. Ephraim smiled his self-conscious smile. Between great agitated gasps of breath, Mr. Samuels said, "He is an angel. Don't you know that this boy is an angel?"

"Take it easy, Pop," Ephraim said.

"Ephraim and I have been through all this over and over again," Dr. Blauberman said. "Isn't that right, Ephraim? So. We're not here for a *Kaffeeklatsch* now, are we? Who has time to sit around chatting. I have a lot of sick people to see. Mmmm? Much as I'm flattered by this family committee visit." He looked at his wristwatch. The faster he got these people out of his office, the better for everybody. He hadn't gone into medicine to be surrounded by Joseph Samuels & Co. What strength it took to maintain a casual, professional manner with them when all he wanted to do was to say please, just go away and don't bother me! He wanted air. Air! People of this kind always seemed to be

asking for help or sympathy or something, and they never had anything to offer in return. They all sat there, the bunch of them, with
their irritating innocence, accusing him of God knows what. "We
won't consider this a regular hour," he said pleasantly. "You people
have paid out enough in medical bills already. Yes?" He tried to smile at
Mr. Samuels. The smile worked at the corners of his mouth and died.
"So. Ephraim will go to a little hospital for a while and get a nice long
rest. Yes?"

"Rest?" Mr. Samuels cried. "You say *rest?* In a *hospital?*"

Dr. Blauberman smiled at Leah and said calmly, "Eephie needs to
get over taking Seconal—sleeping pills. He can do that best in a hospital. A rest home, if you will." He looked ostentatiously at his watch.

"Where do you want Eephie to go?" Leah asked. Her eyes filled
with tears. She didn't even have a decent handkerchief, Dr. Blauberman noticed; she held a rolled-up ball of damp Kleenex to her face. If
he let them, this family would eat him up. Oh, how Sailboat Seltzer,
that bastard, would run!

"That I can't tell you," he said. "Eephie . . . Ephraim has his physical doctor, Dr. Fifield. Dr. Fifield will make arrangements for where
Ephraim should go. . . . Well. That's it." Dr. Blauberman started to get
out of his chair.

"No!" Mr. Samuels cried. "I say *no!* Eephie used to play the clarinet. The Doctor tells him he needs to go to a psychoanalyst, and all the
trouble starts." Mr. Samuels was shouting. With the windows open, he
was noisy enough to be heard by the doorman downstairs, or quite
possibly by Sailboat Seltzer a couple of blocks away. Christ! This emotional old man! What a mistake! He'd never make a mistake like this
one again!

"Eephie used to play—it was beautiful," Mr. Samuels said. "The
Mozart. The Concerto for Clarinet. He was playing parts of it for my
wife and me when he was twelve."

"The trouble started when Eephie goes to Dr. Fifield for his hepatitis," Barney said. "Freddy—that concert pianist on the duo-piano
team of Freddy and Eddy—sent him to Dr. Fifield."

"*That* was when the trouble started?" Dr. Blauberman said, but
his sarcasm escaped Barney.

"Yes," Barney said earnestly. "Dr. Fifield wanted to go to concerts with Eephie and stuff. And before we knew it, he was sending Eephie to a psychoanalyst—the same one he goes to himself."

"So." Dr. Blauberman said, and sniffed. This simple-minded brother was a real prize.

"Eephie used to play all the time!" Mr. Samuels shouted. "Now there's nothing!"

"He was terrific on all that chamber music," Barney said.

"Eephie sounds as good as Benny Goodman," Leah said.

"*Nobody* sounds as good as Benny Goodman," Vic said, "but if anybody sounds as good as Benny Goodman it's Eephie."

"Look—" Dr. Blauberman said. "I would do anything I could to help your boy. But I've tried. He doesn't want to cooperate. I'm afraid there's nothing I *can* do. I'm really sorry."

"You told Eephie he had to be more aggressive. Why? Why does Eephie have to be more aggressive?" Mr. Samuels went on, still shouting. "Nobody ever thought he had to be more aggressive."

"Pop never pushed us to do anything we didn't want to do," Barney said. He, too, was speaking at the top of his voice. "Pop doesn't believe in that."

Dr. Blauberman tried to remember whether he had ever called his own father "Pop," even when he was a boy, but he couldn't remember.

"I know a patient sometimes has to be set back before he can move forward," Leah said. "But we don't care about those other things—about whether or not he should be more aggressive and all that. We just like Eephie the way he is. We just want him to be happy."

"Eeph was making out," Barney said. "He belonged to the musicians' union and played for union rates. He was playing jazz in some of those Village places. He put a lot of effort into his composing."

"Ladies and gentlemen!" Dr. Blauberman said. "I can't sit around with you, arguing this way. All I'm trying to tell you, Mr. Samuels, is that—"

"What will Eephie do in a hospital?" Barney asked. "What will happen to him there?"

"He will rest," Dr. Blauberman said edgily. "I know it must come as a surprise," he said, turning to Leah. "But we must face facts. Mmmm? It will be like going to a good, comfortable, quiet hotel for a few weeks."

"I don't like the word 'hospital,'" Mr. Samuels said stubbornly.

"There's no proof anywhere that psychoanalysis is scientific," Victor said.

"I know you're a qualified doctor," Leah said. "I looked you up in the medical directory."

Thanks. Dr. Blauberman let out a thick, impatient sigh. Thanks a lot. So what did she want him to do?

"And you belong to the most reliable analytic organization. You wouldn't belong if you weren't a good doctor." She stopped.

How many of these gratuitous progress reports on himself was he supposed to sit here and listen to?

"The doctor sees inside," Leah went on. "The doctor has scientific knowledge."

Thanks an *awful* lot.

"Leah is the expert on all this stuff," Barney said to Dr. Blauberman.

"You went to C.C.N.Y. and to N.Y.U. Medical School," Leah said. "And you interned—"

"Yes, I know," Dr. Blauberman interrupted. This girl seemed to be hypnotizing herself with the recitation of his academic history. Who the hell asked her to bring all that up?

"I want to know about my son!" Mr. Samuels shouted. "I want him to be all right!"

"So you get him to fight society," Dr. Blauberman said quickly. It was all he could do not to give way to the temptation to argue with this ignorant man.

"You mean Pop is no pinochle player?" Vic said, with heavy sarcasm.

"I always liked to stay home and not run around," Mr. Samuels said, in slightly lower tones.

"I'm like that, too," Ephraim said.

"Maybe Dr. Blauberman thinks you act neurotically because who else is still a Socialist?" Leah said to her father.

"Are *you* a Socialist?" Mr. Samuels said to his daughter. "Or Barney? If Vic wants to be a Socialist, he has the right. Or me."

"You told me you voted Democratic," Victor said to his father-in-law.

"So this year *you* are the only Socialist," Mr. Samuels said.

"I didn't mean that," Leah said. "I was trying to explain something that might give Dr. Blauberman the wrong idea about us. Sometimes this family doesn't communicate," she said to Dr. Blauberman.

Dr. Blauberman gave her a friendly "So."

"We communicate more than you think we communicate," Vic said. "We really communicate, so we don't have to waste time telling each other we're communicating."

"All I'm trying to tell Dr. Blauberman," Leah said, "is that nobody else waits forty years to name his son after Eugene Victor Debs. Things like that might give him the wrong idea about us. The point is, Dr. Blauberman, we really *like* the name. Or take how I sit in the playground with the other mothers and listen to them tell about going out. They go to theatre parties. They go to affairs. We don't even attend the P.-T.A. But that doesn't mean—"

"I always say if she wants to go to the P.-T.A., let *her* go to the P.-T.A.," Victor said.

"I don't want to go to the P.-T.A.," Leah said.

"I hate the idea of sending my son Jimmy to school at all," Barney said.

"He doesn't mean it," Leah said. "He'll send Jimmy to school."

"I mean, school can kill the spirit of a kid, the way they run most schools. Pop always said it, and its true," Barney said.

"It's true," Mr. Samuels said, and the rest of the family gave strong signs of being with him all the way.

"If I may be allowed to say something—" Dr. Blauberman began.

"I want Jimmy to be free!" Barney said, as an afterthought, and again the whole family nodded with him.

And Vic had an afterthought, too, which he immediately passed along to Dr. Blauberman. "Those playground mothers!" he said, "*They* communicate. Yakkety-yakkety-yak. My-husband-made-a-million-dollars-yesterday. Yakkety-yak."

"Who's fighting society?" Mr. Samuels said. "Because I don't push Eephie to be aggressive?"

"What for?" Vic said with a scornful laugh. "For what?"

"Dr. Blauberman wants Eephie to be more successful with the clarinet," Leah said. "And Dr. Fifield, too. Dr. Fifield told him he should be getting more out of it."

"Well, my idea of what to get out if it isn't the same as Dr. Blauberman's idea," Ephraim said.

"So maybe you're supposed to have big ambitions, like going on television," Victor said.

"And is that such an unhealthy ambition?" Dr. Blauberman found himself saying, and was surprised that he had actually got a word in.

"Aha! The cat is out of the bag!" Victor said, raising his voice.

"What about having a consultation?" Barney asked. "With Dr. Radelsheim?"

"He's the European doctor Eephie heard about?" Leah said eagerly, and blew her nose.

"European doctor?" Mr. Samuels asked, turning to Ephraim.

"That bassoonist, Charlie," Barney said to Ephraim. "You know, he told you you and Dr. Blauberman ought to have a real consultation with this Dr. Hans Radelsheim?"

"I saw Dr. Radelsheim this morning," Ephraim said. "He's a nice guy."

"Nobody told me about any Dr. Radelsheim!" Mr. Samuels said. "Why didn't you tell me before?"

"Eephie just happened to mention it once," Barney said.

"Charlie was begging Eephie to go to see him," Vic said.

The family discussion was off again. Dr. Blauberman felt himself sinking under Samuelses. Air! Air!

"Charlie is the good-natured, fat one, always making jokes!" Mr. Samuels was saying, with enthusiasm, with excitement.

"The one with the fat wife with freckles on her arms, like Terry's!" Barney said. "Terry is my wife," he said to Dr. Blauberman.

"I am happy to hear that," Dr. Blauberman said.

"Is Charlie the one who played with you at the Y, the Schoenberg?" Leah asked Ephraim.

"Wasn't that wild?" Ephraim said. "And the Mozart Divertimenti."

"You were going to get him started playing jazz," Barney said. "Isn't Charlie the one you were going to make one of the first jazz bassoonists in history?" He laughed.

The whole damn family laughed. Killing themselves laughing on the Doctor's time. Christ!

"Charlie is a wild bassoonist!" Ephraim said. "He plays chamber music with Dr. Radelsheim. Dr. Radelsheim plays the oboe."

"So," Dr. Blauberman said. "The oboe plays with the bassoon, Mmmm?"

The family didn't seem to notice him. "Dr. Radelsheim plays the oboe?" Mr. Samuels was saying with delight.

"He knows a lot about music and about musicians," Ephraim said. "Charlie is crazy about him."

"Charlie!" Dr. Blauberman said. "Is Charlie a bassoonist or a doctor?"

"Thank God he's a bassoonist," Victor said.

"Be quiet!" Mr. Samuels said to Victor. "I want to know—" He turned to Dr. Blauberman. "Could you arrange for a consultation with Dr. Radelsheim?" He asked the question in a quiet, confident tone.

"There's no need for a consultation," Dr. Blauberman said. "Dr. Radelsheim called me, and I discussed Ephraim's case over the telephone. You must realize that doctors talk to each other in a way that they can't possibly discuss the case with the family of a patient. *You* understand, mmmm?" he said specifically to Leah. She nodded.

"You mean you want Eephie to be shoved into a hospital just like that?" Victor said.

"Not shoved," Dr. Blauberman said. "He signs himself in, and he signs himself out. Now, you people don't have so much money you want to throw it away running from one doctor to another, do you? I advise, for Ephraim, rest in a hospital."

"I'm not signing myself into any hospital," Ephraim said to Dr. Blauberman. "You know that. Why are you making such a big issue of it with my family?"

"No hospital," Mr. Samuels said with determination. "He doesn't need a hospital."

"What the hell is the matter with you people?" Dr. Blauberman said.

"Is that how you talk to an older man?" Vic said.

Mr. Samuels blushed. "It doesn't matter," he said. "I am Eephie's father, and I know what he needs."

His pronunciation of "father" grated on Dr. Blauberman's nerves.

"I don't know about psychoanalysis, but I know about my family, and I know about Eephie," Mr. Samuels was saying. "Eephie doesn't need a hospital."

The other members of the family nodded in agreement and looked at him with respect. They seemed to relax in unison.

"This is all theoretical, because I'm not *going* to any hospital," Ephraim said.

Dr. Blauberman dropped his pipe on the floor. He felt a surge of rage coming up in him. "I've been Ephraim's doctor for a year," he said. Now *he* was raising *his* voice. But maybe that was just what these thick-skulled people needed. Maybe that was something they could understand. "I know Ephraim! I've sat here patiently with you people, trying to give you some professional advice. If you want to disregard it, that is up to you." He paused. "All I can do is warn you."

Ephraim looked scared. "Dr. Radelsheim told me it's important for me to get back to my music," he said.

Dr. Blauberman made impatient noises. Oh, that big-mouth Radelsheim!

"Did you ask Dr. Radelsheim about the sleeping pills?" Mr. Samuels said to Ephraim.

"No, Pop," Ephraim said. "All he said was it was a shame I couldn't sleep, because musicians have to get their sleep."

Leah put her wet wad of Kleenex into her purse and smiled, first at Ephraim and then at Dr. Blauberman.

"Eephie will cut down gradually the way he takes the pills," Mr. Samuels said. "He should never have started with the pills." He no longer sounded angry. He said the last almost apologetically.

"I'll stick with Pop," Ephraim said.

"Pop," Dr. Blauberman found himself saying aloud, as if he were trying the word out. "Pop. Pop." He gave a nervous giggle. So. He wants Pop. Let Pop have him. But Dr. Blauberman felt a curious pang. The father's straw-colored, kinky eyebrows *were*, he noticed, the original model for the boy's. The way his deep lines alongside his mouth were like the lines his father had.

"We'll make out at home," Mr. Samuels said. "What would Eephie do in a hospital?"

"People live in hospitals and die in hospitals, same as anywhere else," Dr. Blauberman said wearily. He saw them all start and look toward their father. Again Dr. Blauberman felt the pang.

"I know what I am doing," Mr. Samuels said. He stood up. Everybody else in the family stood up, too. At last. They were going.

They stood quietly for a moment, looking at him in silence. Then they started out of the office. Dr. Blauberman had meant to stay in his chair, but instead he got up and trailed the family out to the waiting room, expecting them to stop, to say they would do what he had advised. He wanted them to get out of his sight, but he wanted, also, to hold on to them a little longer. "Mr. Samuels—" he said. They all stopped. They all looked around at him. He saw how like old Abe Letkin Ephraim's father was. The same posture. The same inflection. The same. His own father had the inflection, too. But his father was not the same. His father was a cold-blooded son of a bitch. Dr. Blauberman sniffed. "I've given you some serious advice about how to help your son," he said. But he was aware that all authority had gone out of his voice.

"I know, Doctor," Mr. Samuels said. "You did what you thought was right." He headed for the door and opened it. Dr. Blauberman followed him, and looked at the collie puppy tied to his umbrella stand on the thick salmon-pink carpet. Probably shedding.

Ephraim went over to the puppy and untied him. The puppy began licking his hand.

"Freud loved dogs," Leah said to Dr. Blauberman. "Freud had several chows. He really loved dogs."

"Our old dog, Blackie, who died—you should have seen him, Dr. Blauberman," Mr. Samuels said. "When he died, it broke our hearts. It takes some people a long time to get over a thing like that."

"This collie is a terrific puppy," Ephraim said.

"Touch his head, Doctor," Mr. Samuels said. "Feel how silky he is."

Dr. Blauberman stared at Mr. Samuels, and then at Ephraim, and then at the dog. For a moment, he thought of giving them a real sendoff—of saying "Lotsa luck!" But he didn't. As he swung the door shut on the family, he heard Mr. Samuels say, "Come, children. Let's go home."

14

Black Angels

Bruce Jay Friedman

Smothered by debt, his wife and child in flight, Stefano held fast to his old house in the country, a life buoy in a sea of despair. Let him but keep up the house, return to it each day; before long, his wife would come to her senses, fly back to him. Yet he dreaded the approach of spring, which meant large teams of gardeners who would charge him killing prices to keep the place in shape. Cheapest of all had been the Angeluzzi Brothers, who had gotten him off the ground with a two-hundred-and-fifty-dollar cleanup, then followed through with ninety dollars a month for maintenance, April through October, a hundred extra for the leaf-raking fall windup. Meticulous in April, the four Angeluzzis soon began to dog it; for his ninety, Stefano got only a few brisk lawn cuts and a swipe or two at his flower beds. This spring, unable to work, his life in shreds. Stefano held off on the grounds as long as he could. The grass grew to his shins until one day Swansdowne, a next-door neighbor who had won marigold contests, called on another subject, but with much lawn-mowing and fertilizing in his voice. Stefano dialed the Angeluzzis; then, on an impulse, he dropped the phone and reached for the local paper, running his finger along

Home Services. A gardener named Please Try Us caught his fancy. He
called the number, asked the deep voice at the other end to come by
soon and give him an estimate. The following night, a return call came
through.

"I have seen and checked out the place," said the voice, the tones
heavy, resonant, solid.

"What'll you take for a cleanup?" asked Stefano. "We'll start
there."

Long pause. Lip smack. Then, "Thutty dollars."

"Which address did you go to? I'm at forty-two Spring. Big old
place on the corner of Spring and Rooter."

"That's correct. For fertilizing, that'll be eight extra, making
thutty-eight."

"Awful lot of work here," said Stefano, confused, tingling with
both guilt and relief. "All right, when can you get at it?"

"Tomorrow morning. Eight o'clock."

"You're on."

Stefano watched them arrive the next day, Sunday, a quartet of
massive Negroes in two trucks and two sleek private cars. In stifling
heat, they worked in checkered shirts and heavy pants, two with fe-
doras impossibly balanced on the backs of their great shaved heads.
Stefano, a free-lance writer of technical manuals, went back to his
work, stopping now and then to check the Negroes through the
window. How could they possibly make out on thirty-eight dollars, he
wondered. Divided four ways it came to nothing. Gas alone for their
fleet of cars would kill their nine-fifty each. He'd give them forty-five
dollars to salve his conscience, but still, what about their groceries,
rent? Late in the afternoon, he ran out with beers for each. "Plenty of
leaves, eh?" he said to Cotten, largest of them, the leader, expression-
less in dainty steel-rimmed glasses.

"Take about two and a half days," said the Negro.

"I'm giving you forty-five dollars," said Stefano. "What the hell."

The job actually took three full days, two for the cleanup, a third
for the lawn and fertilizing the beds. The last day was a bad one for
Stefano. Through his window, he watched the black giants trim the

lawn, then kneel in winter clothes and lovingly collect what seemed to be each blade of grass so there'd be no mess. He wanted to run out and tell them to do less work; certainly not at those prices. Yet he loved the prices, too. He could take it all out of expense money, not even bother his regular free-lance payments. At the end of the day, he walked up to Cotten, took out his wallet and said, "I'm giving you cash. So you won't have to fool with a check." It had occurred to him that perhaps the Negroes only did cleanups, no maintenance. By doing enough of them, thousands, perhaps they could sneak by, somehow make a living. "What about maintenance?" he asked the head gardener.

The man scratched his ear, shook his head, finally said, "Can't do your place for less than eighteen dollars a month."

"You guys do some work," said Stefano, shivering with glee. "Best I've seen. I think you're too low. I'll give you twenty-two."

The Negroes came back twice a week, turned Stefano's home into a showplace, hacking down dead trees, planting new ones, filling in dead spots, keeping the earth black and loamy. Swansdowne, who usually let Stefano test-run new gardeners and then swooped down to sign them up if they were good, looked on with envy, yet called one day and said, "I would never let a colored guy touch my place."

"They're doing a great job on mine," said Stefano.

Maybe that explains it, he thought. All of the Swansdownes who won't have Negro gardeners. That's why their rates are low. Otherwise they'd starve. He felt good, a liberal. Why shouldn't he get a slight break on money?

At the end of May, Stefano paid them their twenty-two dollars and distributed four American-cheese sandwiches. The three assistants took them back to a truck where one had mayonnaise. "You guys do other kinds of work?" Stefano asked Cotten, who leaned on a hoe. "What about painting? A house?"

The gardener looked up at Stefano's colonial. "We do," he said.

"How much would you take?" The best estimate on the massive ten-roomer had been seven hundred dollars.

"Fifty-eight dollars," said the huge Negro, neutral in his steel-rims.

"I'll pay for half the paint," said Stefano.

The following day, when Stefano awakened, the four Negroes, on high, buckling ladders, had half the house done, the paint deep brown, rich and gurgling in the sun. Their gardening clothes were wildly spattered. He'd pick up the cleaning bill, thought Stefano. It was only fair.

"It looks great!" he hollered up to Cotten, swaying massively in the wind.

"She'll shape up time we get the fourth coat on."

By mid-June, the four Negroes had cleaned out Stefano's attic for three dollars, waterproofed his basement for another sixteen; an elaborate network of drainage pipes went in for twelve-fifty. One day he came home to find the floors mopped, sanded, shellacked, his cabinets scrubbed, linen closets dizzying in their cleanliness. Irritated for the first time—I didn't order this—he melted quickly when he saw the bill. A slip on the bread box read: "You owes us $2.80." Loving the breaks he was getting, Stefano threw them bonuses, plenty of sandwiches, all his old sports jackets, venetian blinds that had come out of the attic and books of fairly recent vintage on Nova Scotia tourism. Never in the thick of marriage had his place been so immaculate; cars slowed down to admire his dramatically painted home, his shrubs bursting with fertility. Enter any room; its cleanliness would tear your head off. With all these ridiculously cheap home services going for him, Stefano felt at times his luck had turned. Still, a cloak of loneliness rode his shoulders, aggravation clogged his throat. If only to hate her, he missed his wife, a young, pretty woman, circling the globe with her lover, an assistant director on daytime TV. He saw pictures of her, tumbling with lust, in staterooms, inns, the backs of small foreign cars. He missed his son, too, a boy of ten, needing braces. God only knows what shockers he was being exposed to. The pair had fled in haste, leaving behind mementos, toys lined up on shelves, dresses spilling out of chests. Aging quickly, his confidence riddled, Stefano failed in his quest for dates with young girls, speechless and uncertain on the phone. What could he do with himself. At these prices, he could keep his home spotless. But would that make everything all right. Would that haul back a disgruntled wife and son. One night, his heart weighing a ton, he returned from an "Over 28" dance to find the burly Negroes winding up their work. Sweating long into the night, they had rigged up an elaborate network of gas lamps, the better to shcw off a brilliantly laid out thicket of tea roses and dwarf fruit trees. Total cost of the lighting: five dollars and fifty cents.

"Really lovely," said Stefano, inspecting his grounds, counting out some bills. "Here," he said to the head gardener, "take another deuce. In my condition, money means nothing." The huge Negro toweled down his forehead, gathered up his equipment. "Hey," said Stefano. "Come on in for a beer. If I don't talk to someone I'll bust."

"Got to get on," said Cotten. "We got work to do."

"Come on, come on," said Stefano. "What can you do at this hour. Give a guy a break."

The Negro shook his head in doubt, then moved massively toward the house, Stefano clapping him on the back in a show of brotherhood.

Inside, Stefano went for flip-top beers. The gardener sat down in the living room, his great bulk caving deeply into the sofa. For a moment, Stefano worried about gardening clothes, Negro ones to boot, in contact with living-room furniture, then figured the hell with it, who'd complain.

"I've got the worst kind of trouble," said Stefano, leaning back on a Danish modern slat bench. "Sometimes I don't think I'm going to make it through the night. My wife's checked out on me. You probably figured that out already."

The Negro crossed his great legs, sipped his beer. The steel-rimmed glasses had a shimmer to them and Stefano could not make out his eyes.

"She took the kid with her," said Stefano. "That may be the worst part. You don't know what it's like to have a kid tearing around your house for ten years and then not to hear anything. Or maybe you do?" Stefano asked hopefully. "You probably have a lot of trouble of your own."

Silent, the Negro sat forward and shoved a cloth inside his flannel shirt to mop his chest.

"Anyway, I'll be goddamned if I know what to do. Wait around?

Pretend she's never coming back? I don't know what in the hell to do with myself. Where do I go from here?"

"How long she gone?" asked the guest, working on the back of his neck now.

"What's that got to do with it?" asked Stefano. "About four months, I guess. Just before you guys came. Oh, I see what you mean. If she hasn't come back in four months, she's probably gone for good. I might as well start building a new life. That's a good point."

The Negro put away the cloth and folded his legs again, crossing his heavy, blunted fingers, arranging them on the point of one knee.

"It just happened out of the clear blue sky," said Stefano. "Oh, why kid around. It was never any good." He told the Negro about their courtship, the false pregnancy, how he had been "forced" to get married. Then he really started in on his wife, the constant primping, the thousands of ways she had made him jealous, the in-laws to support. He let it all come out of him, like air from a tire, talking with heat and fury; until he realized he had been talking nonstop for maybe twenty minutes, half an hour. The Negro listened to him patiently, not bothering with his beer. Finally, when Stefano sank back to catch his breath, the gardener asked a question: "You think you any good?"

"What do you mean," said Stefano. "Of course I do. Oh, I get what you're driving at. If I thought I was worth anything, I wouldn't let all of this kill me. I'd just kind of brace myself, dig out and really build something fine for myself. Funny how you make just the right remark. It's really amazing. You know I've done the analysis bit. Never meant a damned thing to me. I've had nice analysts, tough ones, all kinds. But the way you just let me sound off and then asked that one thing. This is going to sound crazy, but what if we just talked this way, couple of times a week. I just sound off and then you come in with the haymaker, the way you just did. Just for fun, what would you charge me? An hour?"

"Fo' hunnid," said the Negro.

"Four hundred. That's really a laugh. You must be out of your head. What are you, crazy? Don't you know I was just kidding around?"

The Negro took a sip of the beer and rose to leave. "All right, wait a second," said Stefano. "Hold on a minute. Let's just finish up this hour, all right. Then we'll see about other times. This one doesn't count, does it?"

"It do," said the Negro, sinking into the couch and snapping out a pad and pencil.

"That's not really fair, you know," said Stefano. "To count this one. Anyway, we'll see. Maybe we'll try it for a while. That's some price. Where was I? Whew, all that money. To get back to what I was saying, this girl has been a bitch ever since the day I laid eyes on her. You made me see it tonight. In many ways, I think she's a lot like my mom . . . "

15

The Hidden Oracle

Crystal Moore

No sooner had the mashed potatoes escaped my hand and landed with bull's-eye precision smack in the middle of Dwight's forehead, than someone yelled, "Seclusion!" and I was surrounded by attendants on all sides. Then there were just four walls, a mattress on the floor, a barred window, and a door to the hallway, where Dwight sat in his armchair, blocking my way to freedom.

"Why did you do it?" he asked me.

"Because I want some sympathy is why!"

"Honey, you ain't gonna get no sympathy throwin' things at people. If you want sympathy, you got to ask for it."

Welling tears of indignation flooded my vision, drenching the fire of my pain, blurring the glimmering lights that shone in the dark through the bars of the window—lights from offices in the clinical center, from street lamps reflected on the slick, wet highway, from cars passing in the night for destinations unknown—destinations toward which I might never again strive. I pressed my burning cheek against the bars.

"Hey, watcha doin' in there?"

"Nothing, Dwight, just watching the cars pass by."

"Oh."

"Dwight?"

"Hmmm?"

"You think I'll ever get out of here?"

"I don't know, honey. That's up to you."

"Dwight?"

"Hmmm?"

I turned to him, tears streaming down my face. "I want some sympathy."

His answer came straight away. "I sympathize, Crys, honey," he said. "I sympathize."

Somewhere a patient screamed for her doctor, and the aides tried to calm her, probably strapped her to a chair or tied her up in a cold wet sheet pack.

"You're torturing me!" echoed her plaintive wail.

Dwight cracked his gum.

"You ready to come out now, Crys honey? I ain't gonna sit here all night waitin' for you to apologize."

My eyes focused on his shiny black face in the doorway, his rhythmic jaw, the silver blue trail of his cigarette smoke a silhouette against linoleum tiles of a fluorescent corridor.

"Apologize for what?" I asked.

"You know for what."

"Tell me."

"You threw something at me."

"Oh."

A freckled boy careened down the hall, his groping hands plastered to the wall, guiding his way.

"I'm blind," he said to Dwight and me as he passed the seclusion room. "It's a sign from God."

"Dwight?" I asked. "Where am I?"

But when he told me, I couldn't listen to the words—just shook my head and whispered, "No, no, not that. Not a hospital. Not crazy. Not me."

"You're lying!" I shouted at him, and running, charged through the door where Dwight was on his feet now, sounding the alarm.

But in the hall it was no better. Just miles of lime green linoleum tile stretched into the future—visions of an endless maze of institutions—my faceless existence as a no-name fugitive.

Haunting, ephemeral ghosts rushed by—some long-forgotten dream that recalled a tortured soul. They tapped me on the shoulder like a friend, but as I turned to meet them, slapped me in the face like howling, taunting winter winds. Next instant they were gone again—vague, shadowy impressions of a memory, hidden for so long I'd begun to think I'd lost them—then suddenly returning, burning lava erupting into my consciousness.

"Never get out," whispered the voices. "Crystal, you'll never get out."

And the stench filled my nostrils—old cooking, blood, sweat, urine, vomit, Lysol, deodorant soap. Linoleum tiles saturated with infinite unheeded echoes—tears of rage, cries of pain—the stench of human despair.

Dwight found me in the solarium—racked with tears, face hidden in folded arms on the piano keyboard. Dissonant chords ripped from the instrument with my every heavy torrent.

"I know it's hard for you, Crys," said his scratchy voice.

Why does he have to keep following me? I thought. "Leave me alone," I growled at him.

"But you got to face up to it, honey. That's your problem. You're not tough enough. You got to be tough in this life. Tough as nails. You go out there on the street, there ain't nobody gonna rescue you."

"I'll never get out of here, and you know it."

"That's up to you, honey. That's what I'm sayin'. You got to fight it. Ain't nobody gonna hand you things on a silver platter. You ain't Daddy's little girl no more."

"Daddy's the one who put me in here, Dwight! They don't care about me."

"Now, don't you go cuttin' up on your parents again. Sure, they care about you. I know they got their problems. Everybody does. But

worryin' about their problems ain't gonna help you solve yours."
Dwight lit a cigarette. "Besides, you know one thing for sure. When
you're in trouble, or you're real sick, who you gonna turn to for help?"
He took a drag and let it out slowly. "I'll tell you who—your parents.
Don't deny it. You might try runnin' away, goin' to some ashram or I
don't know where all, but you know where you wind up in the end?
Right back home. They're there for you, Crys, and you know it. Ain't
nobody gonna tell you different."

I was silent.

"Where you think you got those clothes you're wearin'?"

I shrugged.

"I'll tell you where. Your sister Katie went out and bought 'em for
you, after you came into the hospital. When you'd gone and given all
your clothes away to some ashram or other. You didn't have a stitch of
your own besides the shirt on your back when you came in here."

"That's not true. I had a suitcase."

"Yeah, you remember what you had in that suitcase of yours?"

I did. One floor-length hand-stitched kelly green ruffled bath-
robe with white trim, a sheer black body stocking, a razor, and a print
of Salvador Dali's "The Last Supper." But the nursing staff went
through my bag and took away the razor.

"Those things you brought in here weren't gonna do you no
good. What if Katie didn't go out and buy you all new things? What
then? You gonna sit here and tell me your family don't care what happens to you?"

"Dwight?" My voice broke.

"Yes, honey."

The tears were starting to stream down my cheeks again. "I'm
sorry I threw the mashed potatoes," I choked.

Then that big black stranger took me in his arms like I was a lost
child, let my sobs drown out onto his strong, soft shoulder. And I
thought about how he smelled of fresh cologne, how I was bedraggled,
how he didn't care I was dirty, just I was hurting.

"I know, honey, I know you didn't mean it. Now, you just go
ahead and cry if you want to," said Dwight. "You got a lot to cry
about."

The battle lines were drawn.

In one corner of the ring stood my mother—teeth bared, claws outstretched, primed for the fight. An anticipatory snarl escaped her lips. In the opposite corner was my father—darting, first building up the defensive, then backing flat against the ropes.

He's the one who belongs in here, I thought. Not me.

Dr. Will rang the bell. "It's time for family therapy to begin," he said.

Icicle bars of frozen tension, having held us at safe if tenuous distance until that moment, instantly crashed to the floor like so much shattered glass. And Mummy was on me, the unleashed cat clawing my raw flesh. Daddy followed close behind, binding my limbs with his ties, locking me into position to receive the blows.

"Hold it!" cried Dwight. "Time out. Foul play."

Dr. Will rang the bell again. Round two.

This time my mother went straight for Daddy. "His violence," she said, "is impossible to live with. You never know from one minute to the next when his temper will flare up. And then the whole house shakes with his rage. He starts slamming doors, threatening to leave, walking out."

I was egging her on—While she attacked him, I could hope for at least momentary safety. But Katie ran to my father's aid, protected him from us, mopped the blood from his brow. Dwight and Dr. Will were staying on the sidelines.

"He's never provided adequately for the girls and me," Mummy continued. "I earn over half the income, but as soon as I bring any money home, he spends it—pretends it's his money, not mine. He steals it from me."

"That's enough!" my father roared. "I fail to see that this is getting us anywhere. It's Crystal's problem we're here to discuss, not my wife's and my petty household arguments." He turned to me with effort, saying, "I know I've failed Crys as a father. I haven't given her the kind of love she needed."

The faces of my family had frozen—still, silent, shocked, unyielding.

Then slowly, began to melt again, this time with Daddy looking

at me differently. And I saw, for the first time, that the brick wall I had
always thought was my father was in fact a person—a man with a history I had never known existed, with feelings, with long hidden,
fiercely guarded secrets he had never before deigned to share. I saw, I
finally saw, that I had made my father a grief-stricken man—and that
he had forgiven me.

Washington was a southern town, never more so than on lazy
summer afternoons when fashionable ladies sat in wrought iron chairs
on shaded lawns, holding glasses of iced tea steeped in mint, conversations laced with viciousness and charm, and a mandatory veneer of el-
egance over faces flushed with heat and exasperation. By then the
wisteria were in their second blooming, having weaved a jungle
through my parents' fence, and passersby stopped their cars to photograph that shock of lavender blossoms, careful to dodge the bees that
swarmed in air so thick with the flowers' grape perfume you could cut it
with a knife.

Tucked away on the edge of Washington—anachronistic reminder of rustic timelessness, sheltered by lush maples from any trace
of modern civilization, sat my parents' house. I was home, gratefully
clasping the daintily lace gloved hands of Mummy's tea party friends,
pecking the air beside the deftly rouged cheeks, pretending that nothing had happened.

Never, I swore to myself, heady from the air of freedom and jubi-
lantly donning my facade, never will I give them one shred of an excuse
to lock me up in that vault again.

16

Mr. Prinzo's Breakthrough

Bruce Jay Friedman

Although Mr. Prinzo, a small, hairless man of forty-one, was a highly respected technical director in television and, for a bachelor, earned a fine salary, he was forced to dwell in a tiny, however nicely decorated, apartment on New York's west side, his only luxury being top cuts of meat for his airedale. The apartment was not exactly a cold water flat (hot water did gush through unexpectedly now and then) but, in truth, the best Mr. Prinzo could count on for his midnight showers was tepid. In any case, Mr. Prinzo blamed psychoanalysis for his condition. He had been seeing Dr. Tobes four times a week now for seven years, at a cost to him of $120 a week, and there was no end in sight. The two friends with whom Mr. Prinzo started in analysis both had had their breakthroughs. One, whose problem had been lack of confidence, now was able to shout epithets at bullies, and the second, once unable to relate to intelligent women, was started on an affair with a lady amino acids specialist who looked like an attractive Golda Meir. Mr. Prinzo, whose basic difficulty was cringing, could hold himself in check now and then, but still felt most comfortable when in a good cringe, and would have been the first to admit he was far from cured. On the anniversary of his seventh year of psychoanalysis, Mr. Prinzo walked through the many doors leading to Dr. Tobes' office and took a seat on the window sill. (There were no couches in the office of Dr. Tobes, who was known for his informality. Sometimes Mr. Prinzo would sprawl out on the floor during sessions and, on other occasions, just lean against walls. Pacing was allowed, too, and once or twice, on muggy days, he and Dr. Tobes had gone out on the fire escape.)

"Friends all about me are having their breakthroughs," said Mr. Prinzo, "and I don't mind telling you I'd like to have mine. It's high time."

Dr. Tobes was perched owlishly across from Mr. Prinzo, informally chewing up a pencil. It was not only that Dr. Tobes cultivated owlish expressions. He was the dead, spitting image of an owl, a tall owl if such a thing were possible, and he would have passed muster at the most authentic of museum owl exhibitions.

"Can you think of anything that might be blocking the treatment?" asked Dr. Tobes.

"Well, something must be or I wouldn't be cringing about after seven years."

"How is your cringe, incidentally?" asked Dr. Tobes.

"A little better. Oh, why lie, I still fall right into one the minute I roll out of bed and cringe my way right through the day. Look, let's face it, there are still things I can't tell you in here. Oh, I know I've gone into my dandruff fears and there isn't much more I can learn about those dreams in which I'm a stray paramecium. But I'm holding plenty back. I'll give you an example. Where are your diplomas? You think I like coming in here and not seeing a single one? If you ask me, that's being *too* informal. But that's the kind of thing I hold back. It's been bothering me for seven years. Another is your taste in furniture. You just don't go mixing Dutch Colonial and Chinese Chippendale unless you know exactly what you're doing. And why haven't you once, just once, called me by my first name instead of Mr. Prinzo? Oh, I know it's because I'm supposed to be an adult at all times, but you'd think that in seven years you'd slip just one 'Philsy' in there. And there are others, too. I might as well get it right out now that I'm a toenail muncher. It *is* a relief just to say these things. In any case, when I get back from the studio I can hardly wait to get my Argyles off before I start right in."

"Any particular foot?" asked Dr. Tobes, writing in a pad.

"I knew I'd get you writing on that one," said Mr. Prinzo. "Both, I seem to do my lefts before my rights, though."

"Why do you feel you can't tell me something like that?" said Dr. Tobes, picking up a badminton racket and studying it owlishly.

"Sometimes I wish you weren't so informal," said Mr. Prinzo. "Maybe if there'd been a couch in here I'd have been out in three instead of beginning my seventh year. *Why* can't I tell you something like that? Because I'm afraid you'll tell, that's why. Oh, I know you won't go blurting it around town, but how do I know there aren't *some* things you won't leak out? I just don't feel I can come in here and tell you anything in the world and not have you make an immediate phone call as soon as I'm out the door."

"Who do you think I'll call?" asked Dr. Tobes.

"I don't like the way you'll casually slip a question in there as though it's unimportant, when we both know it's full of dynamite. *Who* will you call? I don't know. Authorities. Hospitals . . . the police . . ."

"Well, you *are* right about one thing," said Dr. Tobes. "I should have gone into the nature of our compact a long time ago. It was silly of me."

"Silly?" said Mr. Prinzo. "I might have been out of here five years ago. It may have cost me thirty thousand. I'm sorry I said that, I wanted to think it, but she just slipped out."

"That's all right," said Dr. Tobes, with much sweetness. "You may be right. In any case, of *course* we break the compact under certain circumstances. There are a few. For example, if you told me you were going to commit suicide tonight I might call the police and tell them."

"What are the others?" asked Mr. Prinzo. "This is fun to talk about, even though it's very serious. What if I told you I'd committed a murder? You see, that's the kind of thing I could never tell you, and yet if I've got to hold back one thing, I've got to hold back tons. What I need is to be able to tell you everything, without fear, otherwise I'll be in here forty-two more years."

"How damned silly of me not to go into this," said Dr. Tobes, slightly abashed, but owlish nonetheless, sort of like an abashed owl. "Mr. Prinzo, you may rest assured that the compact we have is pure and sacred. Dr. Berndo and his boys up at Columbia call it the most inviolable compact known to the civilized world, and I tend to go along. If you confessed a murder to me, I might *urge* you to give yourself up if I felt that was best for you. But I'd certainly never inform the police on my own accord."

"Seventeen?" asked Mr. Prinzo.

"I wouldn't care if you were seventeen or forty-one when you did it."

"I don't mean that," said Mr. Prinzo. "What if I'd committed seventeen murders and gotten away with them all?"

"The thing there," said Dr. Tobes, "is whether I thought you were going to try for another. One that might endanger *your* life. I might call the law then. That's the key to it, don't you see. *Your* life. *Your* welfare. Whatever's best for you, *my* patient. That's the rule Berndo and all of us go right down the line with."

"If I could only believe that. Oh, the things I might come out with! If I could only believe you wouldn't tell."

By the end of the hour, Mr. Prinzo had gone back over an early apple fight with his older sister (one in which he'd aimed McIntosh cores at her capacious bosoms), and had then cautiously broken new ground by telling Dr. Tobes that on seven separate occasions he'd falsely upped his studio petty cash vouchers and furthermore, felt compelled to do it again. "Now that certainly isn't the kind of thing you'll report. I know that," said Mr. Prinzo, with only the faintest hint of doubt in his voice. To which Dr. Tobes smiled owlishly as if to say, "Well, really now."

"If I could only be sure," said Mr. Prinzo, taking his leave of the doctor.

Hours later, after a long nap at home, Mr. Prinzo cringed out of his apartment building and took a cab to Riverdale in the Bronx.

"I grew up in the same neighborhood as Vincent 'Mad Dog' Coll," said the cab driver, "and might have ended up the same way had I not mended my ways early in the game."

"I don't want to do any talking on this ride," said Mr. Prinzo. "I just want to get there and do something."

In Riverdale, Mr. Prinzo got out of the cab in a neighborhood that screamed of luxury and had little difficulty finding the ground floor duplex apartment he was looking for. He knocked on the door and when a woman's voice asked who it was, said, "I've got magazines. No I haven't. Look, will you let me in? I've got something crazy to say."

A pretty, busy-looking brunette woman with glasses opened the door. She wore a flowered formal print dress of the type favored by women who serve on committees. It made her seem ten years older than she was and fought to conceal all evidence of the sturdy bosoms that lurked beneath her bodice.

"I don't know you," the woman said, "and I've got invitation lists to get out."

Mr. Prinzo cringed past her into the apartment, sinking deep into the carpeting, and said, "I don't know how long I want to be here. It's a crazy thing. Look, here's why I'm here. When you moved in, the apartment was already two years old. You didn't know the first tenant, but it was my mom and she died here. It's crazy, but I just wanted to be in here for a little while and just walk around the place where my mom spent her last years. I may do some crying."

The woman blinked her eyes beneath the hornrims, not quite sure what to make of what she had heard, and then said, "It is crazy, but it may be the sweetest thing I've ever heard in my whole life." With that, she took Mr. Prinzo's head to her bosom and he made uncontrollable snuffling sounds in there. "How many sons do that for their moms?" she said, stroking his head, her voice catching a bit. "I've got a committee at seven," the woman said. "Our theme for the evening is 'Should We Be Tolerant Toward Intolerance, Too?' but you just stay right here and bury yourself in the atmosphere as much as you like while I'm getting ready. Then maybe you can come back some other time." She left Mr. Prinzo for about ten minutes, and when she came out with her coat on he was standing in the kitchen looking at the sink.

"Mom did her dishes there," said Mr. Prinzo.

"I wish I'd known," said the woman. "I'd never have had it redone in mosaic tile. Look, can I drop you downtown? Then maybe you can come back some other time for a longer session."

"I don't think I'll want to come back," said Mr. Prinzo, snuffling and going to her bosom again. "Not after that sink."

Outside, in the blackness, the woman led Mr. Prinzo to a stationwagon and they drove silently for a while. "If more sons would do that for their moms," said the woman, "we'd have less juvenile crime, more understanding, and a better America."

"That's a lot of committee crap," said Mr. Prinzo suddenly. Then he shouted, "I wanted you to be full-blooded, rich and gurgling with life, a liberated woman given to hurling herself into frenzied modern dances. Then I might not have gone ahead. Pull over to that deserted Carvel ice cream stand."

The woman obeyed and as she stopped the car in the deserted lot, asked, "Did your mother work here, too?"

"There was no mom," said Mr. Prinzo, whipping out a small implement used for lifting the lids off junior baby dessert jars. "Goddammit, I meant to bring steak knives," he said. "This isn't going to be any good." With a shrug, he turned out the car lights and, lifting the baby jar opener, fell upon the horrified woman whose last words were: "It's 6:45. I've only got fifteen minutes to make committee."

A little later, Mr. Prinzo lifted her lifeless form behind the counter of the deserted Carvel stand and propped her up against an old sundae machine. He stood erect, flexed his arms and said, "Violence inhabits the meek, too." Then he drove the stationwagon back to the duplex and took a cab to his apartment.

The following day, at his regular session with Dr. Tobes, Mr. Prinzo took his place on the window sill and said, "I was going to go into some fresh new traumas I've come up with, but why do it when I've only got one thing on my mind. I've done one."

"One what?" asked Dr. Tobes.

"I've committed one. A murder. Only you're not going to like the one I did. It was the only way I could really test the compact. If you don't tell about this one then I know I can tell you anything. I got your wife."

Dr. Tobes said, "What do you mean you got her? Do you know my wife?"

"I got her. I sort of murdered her. Why am I saying 'sort of'? I really did. I was going to anyway, but then when I saw what she was, I *really* was going to, and I did. What the hell kind of woman was that for you to be married to?"

Dr. Tobes picked up the phone and dialed a number. "Hello, Suze, this is Gar. Did Jean stay over at your place last night, after Intolerance? She didn't *come* to Intolerance? Thanks."

Dr. Tobes put down the phone and said, "Jesus, what did you have to do that for? I'm going to turn around here for a minute." He spun his chair around and put his head in his hands and for several minutes his shoulders trembled and shook. Then he turned back and said, "All right now, look, you've got to go to the police. That's the first thing."

"I knew it," said Mr. Prinzo. "I mean didn't I just know it. Didn't I know that was the first thing you were going to say. Why should I have been in any doubt? You talked about the sacredness of our compact, sure, but then when the chips are down for one second . . . "

"It's for your own good," said Dr. Tobes. "Here, I'll ring them right up for you."

"Crapola," said Mr. Prinzo. "Look, I committed that murder for only one reason—to see just how confidential all of this is. I'm not committing any more. And it isn't going to do me any good to go to jail for seventy years. I have a lot of life and good times ahead of me. The only reason you want me to turn myself in is because it was *your* wife. If it was anybody else's, name anyone, and you wouldn't be reaching for the phone."

"You may be right," said Dr. Tobes. "All right, you've got your whole hour left. Do you want to do some dreams? How do you feel?"

"I'll feel a hell of a lot better when you help me get rid of the body."

"I'm not getting rid of any bodies," said Dr. Tobes. "That's not in it."

"It is so and you know it," said Mr. Prinzo. "Anything that'll make me feel better. You said that's the key to it all. It'll make me feel better to get her someplace where she won't be found."

"I've never been in anything like this," said Dr. Tobes. "Jesus, my wife is gone. Hang on a second, I've got to do a little more crying. I'll turn around."

Outside, in the car. Dr. Tobes drove with fury, his eyes a blur of tears. "It isn't doing me any good to see you crying," said Mr. Prinzo beside him. "I don't want to see any doctor doing that."

"All right, I'll try to blot them down," said Dr. Tobes. "But Jesus!"

"And take it easy on the driving. That certainly isn't making me feel better."

Dr. Tobes eased up on the accelerator and Mr. Prinzo said, "Each time I had a date, Sis and Mom would crowd me into a corner and make me feel ashamed. Sis once hid the cards under the piano and I found them accidentally, just fumbling around under there. As my hand accidentally touched the card box, I got a definite sexual thrill."

"This is not a session," said Dr. Tobes. "Jesus, you just got my wife. We're not in any session now."

"I didn't get a full hour in your office," said Mr. Prinzo, "and I don't see why I can't finish 'er up now. You're getting me upset."

"All right, all right," said Dr. Tobes. "Calm down. All right, see if you can pick up the thought again. You'll have to forgive me."

"I want you to be perfect," said Mr. Prinzo. "If you're not, it gets me all rattled."

The sun had gone down when they arrived at the Carvel ice cream stand. "I wonder why I picked an ice cream stand?" asked Mr. Prinzo. "Do you think that's worth analyzing?"

"I can't concentrate on any of that," said Dr. Tobes. "I'm going to see my wife. There'll be quite a bit of crying."

"Do try to be strong," said Mr. Prinzo. "If you get flustered, I'll be upset, and you're not allowed to let me be that way."

"I'll try and hold back," said Dr. Tobes, "but you're not getting any guarantee."

They put the body in a duffel bag Dr. Tobes kept in his trunk and started back to the car with it. "When I met her she was a *Redbook* reader and do you know that recently I was unable to get my *Virginia Quarterly* away from her? Oh, Jesus, Mr. Prinzo, what have you done?"

"I can't stand it when you're stern with me," said Mr. Prinzo. "Do you realize how hard it'll be for me to tell you things now? YOU MUSTN'T BE STERN."

"I didn't mean to. All right, try to relax."

The pair hefted the duffel into the back seat of Dr. Tobes' sedan. "I don't have anything complicated that we're to do now," said Mr. Prinzo. "I just know a very high place near the beach where we can drop 'er down and I'm sure nobody ever goes there, at least on the bottom part. I'm going to go away and this will at least give me time."

The place was on the North Shore of Long Island where Mr. Prinzo had monied relatives. They drove there through the night and Mr. Prinzo said, "You look so different out of doors. How come you don't wear a toupee?"

"Now who is it you *really* want to wear a toupee?"

"Me," said Mr. Prinzo. "Amazing how you get me every time. You're such an amazing possessor of wisdom. That's why I couldn't see you married to, what's her name, I guess we can call her Duffel Bag Dolores now, eh? That was in bad taste. Look, I hope you'll always let me know when I step out of line, when I offend you in any way."

"I'll let you know all right," said Dr. Tobes.

"Now you're putting me on my guard. You mustn't be stern with me."

They came to a high, barren, cool place where the noise of the surf suddenly beat against the car windows. Mr. Prinzo had Dr. Tobes pull over onto the sand and then, carrying their duffel bag, they climbed a formation of wet rocks until the beach was far below; except for some lights across Long Island Sound, they were completely enveloped by blackness. "I'm not crying," said Dr. Tobes, "but let me give her a last little squeeze." Mr. Prinzo giggled and Dr. Tobes said, "There's not a damned thing wrong in that."

When they had tossed the duffel off into the blackness, Mr. Prinzo said, "I'd like to go down below and get my feet wet, as long as we're out here. One thing that has come through in these last seven years is that I'm to just sally forth and grab my pleasures where I may."

Dr. Tobes followed him wordlessly, and below in the sand they removed their shoes and socks. A woman drifted by in a bikini, pensively kicking up sand with her toes, and Mr. Prinzo said, "It's Laurie Prinzo, my sister-in-law."

"I often come here late and wander through the surf," the woman said. "I saw it done in a James Mason movie. Your brother is what makes me so crazy. He really is a big spender. Try to get him to spend a nickel on something that *he* didn't dream up. Oh, he's got it all right. But try to get him to spend a nickel of it. He's really the last of the big spenders."

"This is Gar Tobes," said Mr. Prinzo. "We're just out here doing something. How come you didn't ask me what?"

"I always feel you get to know somebody better when you meet them out in the surf. You see a side of them you never saw before. I've got to get back. I don't know. I may suddenly develop a craving for the Late Show."

She walked off and Mr. Prinzo said, "I hope you weren't offended by my calling you Gar, Dr. Tobes. I felt sort of giddy doing it, the first time in seven years. It was like sex. What did you think of Laurie?"

"She's lovely. I don't say there's anything wrong in my looking at other women now. It's just that emotionally I'm unable to. It's unrealistic of me, but I can't help it. Oh, Jesus, it's starting to hit me now. I'm going to do a little more crying now. I'll try to wrap it up as quickly as I can. And of *course* I realize it isn't good for you to see me doing that. I'm upset, all right, though, I may go back into analysis for a few sessions, myself, now."

In the car, Mr. Prinzo said, "I'm staying at your place tonight."

"I want to be alone and get things straightened out," said Dr. Tobes.

"Now you *are* upsetting me. You probably don't even like me, really. Could you psychoanalyze me if you didn't like me?"

"Yes, I could," said Dr. Tobes. "I'm not saying I dislike you, only that I could treat you if I did."

"How about Joe McCarthy? Wait a minute. Even I can see through that question. I'm trying to find out your political views. Don't even answer. I've got to stay over with you, though. So far, all of this has been okay, but I don't know what's going to happen. What if I get one of my crazy dreams, one in which I'm in a terrible jail feeling so guilty I could just die. Nosiree, I want you right there."

"I'm not sure that any of this is analytically sound," said Dr. Tobes, heading the car in the direction of his duplex.

Dr. Tobes sat grave and ashen-faced, all through the night, in a French Provincial parlor chair, while Mr. Prinzo slept in the guest room. In the morning, Mr. Prinzo got up and said, "I feel sort of short-changed. No dream at all. I expected a beaut tonight, after all those things yesterday, and I thought it would have been great having you here so I could dash right in with all the details. I don't like to see you looking tired. Why the hell didn't you go to sleep? Look, there's a boat sailing for Barbados at five this afternoon and I want to be on it, everything arranged. It takes about three days usually to make arrangements, but I want you to hit them over the head with your doctor credentials and get me on there."

"Look, Mr. Prinzo," said Dr. Tobes. "Surely you must realize there are limits to all this. I don't want to do this for you. Surely you must realize I'm a human being with natural feelings of remorse and revenge. I don't *want* to do these things for you."

"There are no limits. You know damned well there aren't. I'm your patient and the only thing in the world that counts is how I feel. You've got to stick to that because if you don't you'll never be able to hold your head up and practice another hour of psychoanalysis. Here's this week's $120 in cash."

"I'm shaky after no sleep," said Dr. Tobes, sipping some coffee and pocketing the money.

"Well, don't be shaky," said Mr. Prinzo. "That isn't going to do me any good."

Mr. Prinzo lounged about the apartment in his pajamas all morning, and when the doctor got back, he said, "I don't like your books. You've got plenty but many of them are just fillers. What are you doing with *Favorite Canada Campsites?* That's the kind of book you shouldn't have in there."

"Why do you feel threatened when you see books you don't ap-

prove of? Did you ever ask yourself that? We're not in session now. I got
your tickets all right. A patient of mine is a travel agent. They're for
five this afternoon, but you'll have to be inoculated in Barbados if you
want to come back here. Good-by. I don't feel well at all. It's beginning
to sink in about my wife, and I don't care if it's emotional or what, it's a
very real feeling of loss that I feel."

"Don't good-by me," said Mr. Prinzo. "You're coming right down
to the boat with me. How do you think I would feel if I went off friend-
less and alone with no one saying good-by? My last impressions of the
States would be a place where I was without buddies and people didn't
come to say good-by. That wouldn't do me a helluva lot of good. Oh,
no, you don't. You're coming right down with me."

"I want to sit in a chair now," said Dr. Tobes. "I want to cry. I need
a good catharsis and then I'll be better."

"You're coming with me. You know you have to. And I hate seeing you this way. If you think it's helping my treatment, this whole
business of the way you're carrying on, you're crazy."

On a last minute impulse, Mr. Prinzo went out to a local Ber-
muda shop and bought some clamdigger pants and orange gaucho
shirts.

The ride to the boat took roughly three quarters of an hour, and
the two men agreed it would constitute a session, Dr. Tobes taking his
notes at red lights. As they pulled into the parking lot at the boat dock,
Dr. Tobes said, "We have to close the hour now," and Mr. Prinzo said,
"You always nip me off right in the middle of critical things."

Mr. Prinzo had borrowed Dr. Tobes' suitcase, and the doctor
helped him carry it toward the boat. Stopping at the foot of the gangplank, Mr. Prinzo said, "Now in one of your letters I want you to tell me
if there's a good analyst in Barbados."

"One of my letters?" said Dr. Tobes. "You'll get none from me. I'm
not writing you any letters."

"Oh, yes, you are," said Mr. Prinzo angrily. "Three a week, with
picture postal cards interspersed. No one but you knows where I'm going and how do you think I'm going to feel getting no letters from
home?"

"I'll send you the letters," said Dr. Tobes. "I don't know about the cards."

Mr. Prinzo went about half way up the gangplank and then said, "Now start waving."

"I'm not waving," said Dr. Tobes, his voice cracking. "I'm not waving to you."

"Wave," said Mr. Prinzo. "I'll feel good. I've got to be waved off."

Dr. Tobes slowly lifted his arm, and this time an avalanche of tears broke through and flooded his face. "There," he said, choking, "I'm a heartbroken man, but I'm waving."

"Good," said Mr. Prinzo. "That's good. I guess we're going now." He lifted his head and sucked in the air. "I feel fine," he said. "Say, have you noticed? I'm standing up straight now. I'm out of my cringe."

"Yes," said Dr. Tobes, and suddenly the tears stopped and his eyes brightened. "You *are* out of your cringe." With that, he whirled around, shouted, "You're cured! You've had your breakthrough," grabbed the sleeve of a dock patrolman and, as the two of them flew up the gangplank to Mr. Prinzo, shouted again, "And you're not my patient any more."

17

Psychiatric Services

Joyce Carol Oates

" . . . not *depression*, then?"

"I wouldn't define it that way, no. That's listless, indifferent, isn't it, that's all-life-drained-out, like some of my own patients. . . . No, it's a confusion of all the genres, I've sifted through everything I know, I use my mind on myself but I can't come to any diagnosis. . . ."

"Whom do you fantasize killing?"

"I can't come to any diagnosis."

" . . . what fantasies do you have?"

" . . . I don't have time for fantasies."

"What fantasies might you have, if you had time?"

"Haha, that's a very good line. . . . Well, we all have had fantasies, haven't we, of murdering people? . . . other people? That must go back into my childhood, it must go back, oh, Jesus, twenty years . . . doesn't everyone have these fantasies?"

"I don't think everyone does, necessarily."

"Didn't *you?*"

"I'm a woman."

" . . . What bothers me is the suicide fantasies, which are new."

"What means do you use?"

"Not the programmed."

"What is it, a thought, an emotion . . . ? A cluster of thoughts . . . ? Is it something that hasn't yet coalesced?"

"I'm sure it has, when I've been asleep, but when I wake up I can't remember. . . . When I'm on duty over there I wake up and can't remember anything about myself, anything private . . . If I'm being paged I hear the name, a code name, *Saul Zimmerman*, but they could be paging anyone, they could be reading off numbers; all I know is that I respond . . . getting like a fireman: the way I suppose firemen must respond. All body."

"What means would you use?"

"Hypodermic? No. I'm too young . . . it was a rumor, Edward Aikley killed himself, did you know that? . . . must have been a hypo, if anything. No, it's something stronger . . . violent . . . *visual* somehow . . . not with pills, like the poor crazy poisoned kids they bring us. . . . No, God. Do you know of Dr. Aikley?"

"No. . . . When did you begin your residency at County General?"

" . . . It isn't procedure, is it, to notify them? . . . My supervisor, uh, you're not going to notify him, are you?"

"Who is he?"

"Feucht, and he knows about some of this, I mean I've talked with him a little, he's fairly nice . . . he's interesting . . . says I'm tired."

"But you disagree with him?"

"Agree, disagree, what does it matter? You know how it is . . . who's your supervisor? . . . agree, disagree, it makes no difference whatsoever. The disturbing thing is that I'm not as tired as I should be. Everyone else is worn out, but I keep going . . . especially in the last few weeks, when I think of *it*. I mean a kind of doubleness comes over me . . . right there in the emergency ward, doing all the things, a kind of double sense, double vision . . . uh, I would define it as a mental-visual hallucination, but the word hallucination is too strong . . . hey, don't write that down! . . . No, it's too strong; there's nothing visual about it. You didn't write it down? Okay, I'll tell you: I feel very . . . I feel very powerful at those times, when I think of *it*, because it's, uh, the secret

. . . that nobody else knows. The mess is there! . . . 900 people a day we get . . . most of them are black, of course . . . how is it over here? . . . of course, you get more students; black or white, they're better patients. But Christ, the mess . . . So it occurs to me that *I* know the way out, the way they're all groping for but can't discover . . . *they don't know enough.* So in a crazy way . . . don't write that down, please, in a peculiar way, not serious, not intellectually *serious*, in a peculiar way I feel superior to them and even to the staff . . . even to my supervisor. . . . I think of *it.* The means wouldn't matter. Messes carried in here are instructional . . . I never got such specific instruction at Northwestern, where I went to medical school . . . I mean, it's so clear how and why the poor bastard blew it: some of them shoot themselves in the forehead at such an angle that the bullet ploughs up through the skull, or they try for the heart but shatter the collar bone . . . *they don't know enough.* And the ones who take poison take too much or too little. . . . So I feel very, I would say very superior . . . and I feel very masculine . . . so I don't get tired the way my friends do, which is good for my ego, I feel very masculine and I feel young again."

"How old are you?"

"Twenty-eight."

"Yeh, fine. Okay. A scrupulous detailed report, nice handwriting. But I read between the lines and am not impressed: an exhibitionist."

"But he did seem nervous. . . . He talked rapidly, he kept making small jokes and grimaces and asides . . . he looked as if he hadn't slept for a while. I asked him if he had been taking anything and he said a little Librium, but it didn't seem to help and—"

"Who's his supervisor?"

"He didn't say."

"So? So ask him."

"I . . . he. . . . He was out in the corridor waiting with everyone else . . . dressed in old clothes, he hadn't shaved, looked sullen and frightened . . . no one would have guessed who he was, I mean that he was a resident. If they had guessed, someone else would have grabbed

him, but as it was I got him. . . . I had the impression he was disappointed to draw me."

"Why, because you're a woman?"

"Yes, of course."

"Ha! The little whiner, the bastard, he wants sympathy and
someone to talk to, of course he prefers a woman . . . you'll discover it
to be a life-pattern in certain personalities. . . . How tall is he?"

"Medium height."

"Innocuous. All of it is innocuous."

"He's twenty-eight."

"I can see that here. . . . Okay, fine. Now who's this, what is this?
Deller?"

"Yes, you remember, she was the—"

"I don't remember. Stop trembling."

" . . . black woman, in the school system here . . . teaches fourth
grade. . . . "

"Jenny, does your behaviour with your patients resemble your behaviour with me?"

"I. . . . I don't know."

"Do you sit there on the edge of your seat, are your lips bluish
with fear? . . . do you lower your head like that just very very slightly—
no, don't move!—so that you can gaze at them through your lashes?
Don't be offended, Jenny, why shouldn't you show yourself to your
best advantage, however?"

"Dr. Culloch, I . . . "

"You're an attractive woman, why shouldn't you live your life to
the fullest? . . . However, there's no need to be so nervous with me;
what are the rumors, eh? . . . what have you heard about me, eh?"

"I wish you wouldn't laugh at me, Dr. Culloch."

"Who's laughing? . . . this is chuckling, sighing, this is a sympathetic noise from across the desk. But you! If you're angry, go red instead of white in the face . . . much healthier. Nothing wrong with
healthy anger."

"I'm not angry . . . "

"Nothing wrong with healthy anger."

"I know, but I'm not angry, Dr. Culloch."

"*Aren't you?*"

"No. No."

"What is all that passion, then?—all that trembling?"

"Dr. Culloch, I wish you wouldn't do this—"

"Are you happy here?"

"Oh yes. Yes."

"We treat women better here, better than the boondocks where you interned; this is a livelier place in every way, do you agree? . . . So you're happy. So stay happy."

"Yes, Dr. Culloch."

" . . . no, you're not disturbing me. . . . What time is it?"

" . . . You were asleep, weren't you. I lose track of the time myself . . . it's probably around two or three . . . my watch is untrustworthy and I can't see any clocks from here. . . . I'm sorry for waking you up, did I wake you up?"

"It's all right. It doesn't matter."

" . . . been wanting to call you all evening, but I didn't get a break until now. I'm on the fourteenth floor, staff lounge, do you know the layout here?"

"No."

" . . . The thing is, I feel awfully shaky and embarrassed, I mean about the official nature of it. . . . You aren't going to report back to Feucht, are you?"

"Who? . . . No."

"Okay. Jesus, I'm sorry to wake you; I'll hang up now."

"No, wait—"

"And the reason I didn't show up for the second appointment, I didn't even remember it until a few hours later—a friend of mine was sick, I had to take over for him off and on—I wanted to call you and explain but so much time went by I figured what the hell, you'd forgotten. . . . I'll hang up now."

"No. How are you? Do you feel better?"

" . . . I would say so, yes. Sometimes I feel very happy. That sensation of power I mentioned . . . it's rather encouraging at times. I realize this is absurd, I realize how crazy it sounds . . . God, I hope nobody's tapping this telephone! . . . I know I should hang up. . . . The reason I called you is, I feel a little strange. There's this sensation of power, of happiness, like I used to have as a boy occasionally, and when I was in high school, playing football, occasionally I'd have it also . . . a surge of joy, a pulsation of joy. . . . "

"Euphoria?"

"Euphoria. Do you know what it's like? . . . Being carried along by the pulse of it, of *it*, whatever *it* is. . . . So much excitement, so much life and death outside me, carrying me along with it, along with the flow of it. One of my patients died on me, hemorrhaged all over me, I just kept talking to him and didn't allow either of us to get excited. . . . So I thought I would call you. I've been thinking about you, but I haven't diagnosed my thinking. I'm sorry to have missed the appointment. . . . Could I come see you?"

"Now?"

"Yes."

"Of course not. No. What do you want?"

"Dr. Feucht tells me there's nothing wrong—I'm exaggerating. He says new residents always exaggerate, dramatize. Maybe that's all it is . . . maybe it's nothing real. . . . I can't come see you then?"

" . . . in love with you, eh? Don't be coy!"

"Dr. Culloch, please—"

"A long nocturnal conversation—special considerations—is this what they taught you in Baltimore, Jenny? The John F. Kennedy Clinic, did they teach you such things there?"

"He missed his appointment and sounded very excited over the phone . . . I don't know how he got my number, there must be so many *Hamiltons* in the city. . . ."

"He isn't seriously disturbed; he's pleading for your special attention, your love. . . . You'll learn to recognize these symptoms and not to be flattered by them."

"I'm sorry, Dr. Culloch, but I—"

"Being professional is the acquisition of a single skill: not to let them flatter you into thinking you're—what? Eh? *God*, eh?—Or *Venus*?"

"But . . . but Dr. Zimmerman . . . Saul. . . . Why did you bring that here? Why . . . What are you going to do with that?"

"Don't be frightened!"

"Saul—"

"The last three or four days I've been awake straight through, by my own choice. I don't want to be a zombie, I want more control . . . Don't be so alarmed, I just brought it to show you: it's rather handsome, isn't it? I'm not going to hurt you. I wouldn't hurt *you*. From where you sit, it probably looks like a toy gun, maybe; it's amazing how lifelike the toy guns are, and how toy-like the real ones are . . . makes your head spin. There's a difference in price though."

"Is that a real gun?"

" . . . insulting . . . castrating . . . No, you're very nice, the first time I saw you out in the hall I thought *She's nice, any nut would have a chance with her* . . . remind me of a cousin of mine, haven't seen for years, slight little girl with freckles, pale skin. . . . It's an insult, to ask a person whether he's carrying a toy gun, don't you know that? Don't insult me. Under the circumstances I must strike you as strange enough, but not so strange that I can't give you professional advice . . . don't insult them when they're armed . . . I'm just joking. I'm really just joking . . . The only women at County General are the nurses. I don't think they like me."

" . . . You'd better give that to me, you know. To me. You'd better . . ."

"Certainly not. Why should I give it to you?"

"I think it would be a good idea if . . . if you gave it to me."

"Why? It's my own discovery. It's my secret. I want to share it with you in a way, but I don't intend to give it to you."

"But you can't be serious! . . . Why did you bring it here, wrapped up like that—what is that, a towel?—why did you bring it here, if you don't really want to give it to me? You—you really want to give it to me—don't you? Wouldn't that be better?—You've put me in such a terrible position—I'm sure I should report you—it—you've made me an accessory to—"

"To what? I have a permit for it."

"A permit? You have . . . ?"

" . . . walked into the police station down the block from the hospital, bought a permit, went to a gun store, bought the gun. . . . They're expensive but I didn't buy much ammunition . . . You know I'm just fooling around with this, don't you? . . . just fooling around. I certainly don't intend to use it, on myself or anyone."

"That's right. That's right. . . . Obviously, you brought it here this afternoon to give to me, didn't you? . . . to give to me?"

"It's the smallest size. They have enormous ones . . . with longer barrels so that you can take better aim . . . something so small, so the man told me, has a poor aim, the bullet is likely to veer off in any direction. I don't know anything about guns. Not even rifles. I'm from Winnetka. I didn't have a father interested in hunting. It's amazing, all the things I don't know . . . don't have experience of. Now it's too late."

"Saul, why don't you let me keep the gun for you? Please?"

"I do have a permit for it. . . . However, not for carrying it on my person; I don't have a permit to carry a concealed weapon. So maybe I'd better give it to you after all. . . . But can I have it back when I'm well?"

"You're not sick."

"Yes, but when I'm well can I have it back? . . . I can pawn it at the same place I bought it; the man might remember me."

"Yes, of course you can have it back . . . I'll keep it in my desk drawer here . . . I can lock it, this desk is assigned to me for the year . . . no one can open it except me . . . I promise . . . I promise that . . . "

" . . . only afraid that if I surrender it I'll lose this feeling I have most of the time . . . it helps me get through the night shift especially . . . With one part of my mind I realize that it's absurd, that the whole thing is absurd . . . I did my stint in psychiatrics too, and I must say I hated it . . . really hated it . . . my supervisor was a bastard, and that wasn't just my private opinion either. I realize it's absurd that I'm talking to you because you don't know anything more than I do, maybe less, you're sitting there terrified . . . but if I give *it* up I might lapse into being terrified . . . and . . . I've always been so healthy, that's the goddam irony. I *am* healthy. Kids dropped out of school, blew their minds entirely, wound up in the expensive asylums along the lake, but not me, not *me*, and my father would go crazy himself if he knew I was having therapy three times a week with *you*. . . . He could do so much more for me! . . . I can hear his voice saying those words, his whining voice. . . . The one thing I'm ashamed of and must apologize for is frightening you, Dr. Hamilton."

" . . . I'm not frightened . . ."

" . . . Feucht is away for a conference, Hawaii, he says it's ordinary nerves and exaggeration, I know he's right . . . but where does he get the strength from? . . . Aikley, they said he killed himself, did you hear that? . . . no, you didn't know him . . . what it is, is, something to circle around, a fixed place, . . . a thought . . . the thinking of it, the possibility of *it* . . . what is it, transcendence? . . . At the same time I'm an adolescent, obnoxious bastard, to come over here and frighten a pretty young woman like you."

" . . . aren't you going to give me the gun? . . . to put in the desk drawer?"

" . . . maybe I only want revenge, maybe it's simplistic revenge against the usual people . . . the usual innocent people: my father, my mother. Sometimes I think that if it were possible for me to wipe out my own father, my personal father, I might get to something more primary . . . but . . . uh . . . it's difficult to talk about these things, I really don't know how to talk about them. I don't have the vocabulary. . . . must tell you, a kid in emergency hallucinating . . . shrieking and laughing and really blown . . . *very happy* . . . hadn't a good vein left in him . . . All I want is to wipe out a few memories and start again from zero but the memories accumulate faster than I can even notice them, faster faster faster. . . . all the time. But how do you wipe the memories away without blowing away the brain?"

" . . . This is the drawer, see? . . . and I have the key for it, here. Here."

"Okay."

"Thank you. Thank you."

" . . . sorry to be so . . . "

"Thank you very much, Saul, thank you . . . now, you see? . . . Dr. Zimmerman? . . . you see, I'm locking it up, it's your property and I can even, I can even give you a receipt for it . . . yes, I'll be happy to . . . I'll . . . "

"Are you all right? . . . not going to faint?"

"I—"

"Are you going to faint? Jesus!"

"No, I'm all right—I'm all right—"

"You sure?"

"I've never fainted in my life."

" . . . sorry to be disturbing you again . . . you weren't asleep, were you? . . . answered the phone on the first ring, you weren't asleep, were you?"

"No. What do you want, Saul?"

" . . . just to apologize, I feel I've made such a fool of myself . . . and it isn't fair to involve you . . . you're younger than I am, aren't you? . . . you have lots of other patients assigned to you, God, I hope they're not as troublesome as I . . . because you know, don't you, Jenny, *you know* . . . I'm really harmless; I'm just temporarily troubled about something. It isn't uncommon."

"I understand. I'm not angry, I'm not frightened . . . well, I admit that I was a little frightened at the hospital today . . . I shouldn't have been so easily upset . . . but the gun itself, seeing it, the gun shocked me . . . it was so real."

"Yes! It was so *real*. So that struck you too?"

"Oh yes it struck me . . . it struck me too."

"Where do you live, Jenny? The operator doesn't give out that kind of information, she says . . . you're not listed in the new directory, are you, you're new to the city just like me . . . Could I come over or is it too late?"

"It's too late, it's very late, Saul."

"What time is it?"

" . . . very late. Please. Why don't you visit me at the hospital tomorrow, wouldn't that be soon enough?"

"I realize I'm disturbing you but I had the sense . . . the sensation . . . that you aren't married . . . ? I mean, there's no husband there with you, is there?"

"I'll see you tomorrow. I'll squeeze you in somehow . . . somehow . . . or . . . or, please Saul, please, we could talk in the first-floor cafeteria, at the back, I'll wait for you there at noon . . . we can talk there . . . please."

"Look: you demanded I give you the gun. And I did. I obeyed you. *Good boy* you probably thought, *good boy, look how he obeys.* Now you lose interest in me . . . What do you care what I've been going through?"

"I care very much . . . "

" . . . I noticed a fly crawling out of some guy's nostril over here, some very old black guy in a coma for five days . . . filling up with maggots, he was, wasn't even dead, they're jammed in here and so stinking sick . . . and the pathologist making jokes about it . . . I wondered if *he* was the one I had wanted to kill and got very upset, to think I'd lost the gun . . . "

" . . . *What?*"

"What?"

"What about that man?"

" . . . cardiac seizure, he wasn't that old . . . fifty-five, sixty . . . it's hard to tell, they're so wrecked when they come in . . . We're busy over here . . . What kind of a tone did you take with me? . . . You sound *annoyed*."

"What about that man?—I don't believe—"

"What, are you annoyed that I woke you up? Hey look: we're in this together. I trusted you, didn't I, and you promised me, didn't you, and there's a professional bond between us . . . I'm not just another patient off the streets, off the campus, there's a professional bond between us, so don't take that tone with me. I order people around too: all the time, in fact. I order women around all the time. And they obey me. You bet they obey me! So don't you take that annoyed tone with me."

"Saul, I'm not annoyed—but I think you must be—must be imagining—must be exaggerating—"

" . . . the purpose of this call was, I think it was . . . uh . . . to apologize for frightening you earlier today. And to ask you to keep it private, all right? The business about the gun. I mean, don't include it on your report, will you, you needn't tell him everything. . . . Don't be annoyed with me, please, I think I'll be through it soon . . . out the other side, soon . . . I'll be rotated to obstetrics in seventeen days which should be better news . . . unless some freaky things happen there too . . . it's a different clientele here, you know, from what I was accustomed to. . . . Hey look: don't be annoyed with me, you're my friend, don't be annoyed that I almost caused you to faint today."

"I didn't faint . . . I didn't come near to fainting."

" . . . well, if . . . "

"I've never fainted in my life."

"You *what*?—Oh, you romantic girl! You *baby!*"

" . . . What? I don't understand. Did I do something wrong, Dr. Culloch?"

"Wrong? Wrong? *Everything you have done is wrong*. Oh, it would be comic if not so alarming, that you came to us knowing so little—so meagerly trained—Had you only textbook theory, you could have handled that problem more professionally! And with the background you have, before the Baltimore clinic you were where? Nome, Alaska?—an adventuresome young woman, not a lily, a wilting fawning creature—and a year at that girls' detention home or farm or whatever in Illinois—*didn't you learn anything?* To be sure manipulated by a cunning paranoid schizophrenic—to have him laughing up his sleeve at you—"

"But—"

"But! Yes, *but*. But but but.—You did exactly the wrong thing in taking that gun away from him. *Don't you know anything?*"

" . . . I did the wrong thing, to take it away . . . ?"

"Absolutely. Now, you explain to *me* why it was wrong."

"It was wrong?"

" . . . why it was idiotic, imbecilic."

" . . . but . . . It was wrong because . . . it must have been wrong because . . . because . . . I affirmed his suicidal tendencies? Is that it, Dr. Culloch? . . . I affirmed his suicidal tendencies . . . I took him seriously . . . therefore . . . "

"Go on."

" . . . therefore . . . I indicated that he didn't have rational control and responsibility for his own actions . . . yes, I see . . . I think I see now . . . it was a mistake because I showed him that in fact I didn't trust him: I took him at his word, that he would commit suicide."

"Not only that, my dear, let's have some fun with you . . . eh? Under cover of being the Virgin Mary and mothering him out of your own godliness, you in fact used it as a cover, the entire session, to act out your own willfulness and envy of men . . . Eh? What do you say? Ah, blushing, blushing! . . . And well you might blush, eh? . . . So you turn him loose, the pathetic little bastard, a castrated young man turned loose . . . and you have the gun, eh? . . . locked up safely, eh? . . . so you gloat about it and can't wait to rush in here to let me know the latest details, eh? Fortunate for you that Max Culloch has been around a long time . . . a very very long time . . . and knows these little scenarios backwards and forwards."

"Dr. Culloch—are you joking?"

"Joking? I?"

"Sometimes you—you tease us so—"

"If you silly little geese giggle, can I help it? I have a certain reputation for my wit, I do admit it, and a reputation—wholly unearned, I tell you in all modesty—as—what?—eh?—being rather young for my age, eh?—is that what they gossip about?—but you won't gossip with them, Jenny, will you? Of this year's crop you are *very* much the outstanding resident; I tell you that frankly . . . Only because you struck me originally as being so superior can I forgive you for this asinine blunder: affirming a paranoid schizophrenic in his suicidal delusions."

"I did wrong . . . I did wrong, then, in taking the gun from him?"

"Don't squeak at me in that little-mouse voice, you're a woman of passion and needn't make eyes at me and look through your hair . . . and don't sit like that, as if you're ashamed of your body, why be ashamed? . . . you're attractive, you know it, your physical being is most attractive and *it* senses that power whether you do or not, Dr. Hamilton . . . right? I'm decades older than you, my dear, I'm seventy-three years old and I know so much, so very much, that it's sometimes laughable even to deal with ordinary people. . . . It's become a burden to me, my own reputation, a genius, my own fame is a burden to me because it obliges me to take so seriously and so politely the opinions of my ignorant colleagues . . . when I'd like simply to pull switches, shut them up, get things done as they must be done. At least you young people don't argue with me: you know better. . . . so. Let us review this fascinating lesson, Jenny. What did you do wrong?"

"I did wrong to take the gun from him and to affirm his suicidal inclinations. And . . . and he had a permit for the gun, too . . . at least to own a gun . . . It wasn't illegal, his owning the gun . . . And so I was exerting power over him. . . ."

"Gross maternal power, yes. The prettier and smaller you girls are, the more demonic! . . . Your secret wish right this moment, Jenny, is—is what? eh? You'd like to slap old Dr. Culloch, wouldn't you?"

"Not at all—"

"Someday we'll let you; why be so restrained? . . . But at the moment, I think it wisest for you to undo the harm you've done to that poor boy. You'd better telephone him and ask him to come over and take the gun back."

" . . . ask him to take it back?"

" . . . or is he your lover, and you would rather not call *him*?"

"He isn't my lover!"

" . . . who is, then? Or have you many?"

"I haven't any lovers! I have my work. . . ."

"Yet you're attracted to him aren't you? I can literally smell it—I can smell it—the bizarre forms that love-play can take—"

"I'm not attracted to him, I feel sorry for him—I—I'm not attracted to him. I have my work . . . I work very hard . . . I don't have time for . . . "

"*I* am your work."

" . . . Yes."

"Yes what?"

"Yes, that's so."

"Everything is processed through me. Everything in this department . . . Do you dream about me?"

"Yes, of course."

"And what form do I take?"

"What form? . . . The form . . .the form you have now."

"No younger?"

"I . . . I don't know . . . Dr. Culloch, this is so upsetting to me, it's so confusing and embarrassing . . . I never know when you're joking and when you're serious."

"I am always joking and always serious. You may quote me."

" . . . I've become so mixed up during this conversation, I can't remember what . . . what we were talking about. . . . "

" . . . not that I'm Max Culloch of even eight years ago . . . Yeh, pot-bellied, going bald, with this scratchy scraggly beard . . . but . . . *but*. You understand, eh? Many a young rival has faded out of the dreamwork entirely when old Max appears. It's nature. . . . The one thing I don't like, Jenny, is the possibility of your arranging this entire scenario with the aim of manipulating Max. . . . I wouldn't like that at all. *Did you?*"

"Did I . . . ?"

"Play with the boy, take the gun, rush into my office this morning just to tantalize me with your power? . . . force me to discipline you? . . . No, I rather doubt it; you're cunning, but not *that* cunning. No. I'm inclined to think it was a simple error, one of inexperience rather than basic ignorance, and that it shouldn't be held against you. It's only nature, that you would like to manipulate me. But you haven't a clue, my child, as to the means."

" . . I . . . I . . . Yes, that's right. You're right."

"Of course I'm right."

" . . . nothing was intentional, nothing at all. When I saw the gun I followed my instincts . . . my intuition . . . I forgot to analyze the situation in terms of its consequences . . . when I saw the gun I thought *No, I don't want him to die, no, I like him, I don't want*—So I acted without thinking."

"And did you faint in his arms, my dear?"

"Of course not."

"Love-play on both sides. Totally unconscious, totally charming. Do you see it now, rationally?"

"I . . . I didn't see it at the time, but now . . . now . . . you're probably right."

"Probably?"

"You're right."

"And so?"

" . . . and . . . ?"

"And so what will you do next?"

"I . . . I will telephone him and admit my error."

"And?"

" . . . tell him I misjudged him . . . that he can pick the gun up any time he wants it . . . I'll tell him that my supervisor has . . . "

"No, no. No sloughing off of authority!"

" . . . tell him . . . tell him that I trust him . . . and . . . it was an emotional error on my side . . . inexperience . . . fear . . . I trust him and . . . and I know he'll be safe with the gun . . ."

"Go on, go on! You'll have to speak to him more convincingly than that. And smile—yes, a little—yes, not too much—try to avoid that bright manic grin, Jenny, it looks grotesque on a woman with your small facial features . . . The boy is an idealist like everyone, and like everyone he must learn . . . as I learned and you will, eh? . . . or will you? . . . he's an idealist and stupid that way but not so stupid that he wouldn't be able to see through that ghastly smile of yours. I have the impression, Jenny, that you don't believe me: that you're resisting me. Are you trying to antagonize me?"

"No, of course not! I'm . . . I'm just very nervous. I didn't sleep at all last night. I'm very nervous and . . ."

"Chatter, chatter! . . . So you've given your young friend his gun back . . . you've made things right between you again . . . yeh, fine, fine. Now what?"

"Now . . . ?"

"Now what do you say? Will you say anything further?"

" . . . I will say that . . . that he'll be rotated out of the service he's in, and he'll be eventually out of the hospital . . . maybe he'll have a private practice in the area . . . his hometown is north of here, along the lake . . . and . . . and . . . and he'll escape, he'll forget . . . I can't remember what I was saying."

"What a goose! . . . At any rate, what do you think *he* will say? When you give him his masculinity back?"

"He'll say . . ."

"Think hard!"

"He'll say . . . probably . . . He'll probably say *Thank you.*"

"*Thank you?*"

" . . . *Thank you.*"

18

The Patient

Barbara Lawrence

To Alexander's surprise, Dr. Kahmstetter did not pay much attention to the problem of his nose. He was more interested, it seemed, in the kind of people Alexander knew.

Alexander began by describing the Ones. These were the gapers, he said. He found them staring at his nose on buses and trains, their faces signs of aberration. They did not bother him particularly. Did not bother him at all, in fact. If they were his only problem, he would not have come to a doctor. Even the Twos were not exactly what he would call a problem—more disturbing than the Ones, to be sure, since their covert, embarrassed observation carried with it a certain sensitivity. But it was nothing that he could not deal with. Had dealt with quite successfully for years. No, it was neither the Ones nor the Twos. It was the Threes who had finally made his position unendurable.

"The Threes?" said Dr. Kahmstetter.

"The Threes," Alexander explained, "realize that my nose is growing larger, but they never even look at it. They look at *me*."

"Well?" said the Doctor.

"Well," Alexander told him in an anguished voice, "I am so amazed at their kindness that when I am with them I tremble and behave in such a peculiar way that they cannot possibly enjoy my company. You see," he continued, suddenly avoiding the Doctor's eyes, "I know now that I must solve the problem of my nose or I shall never win the love of the Threes."

"And in the meantime who are your friends?" Dr. Kahmstetter asked him.

"People I detest." Alexander sighed. "The Fours. They pretend to have all the qualities of the Threes and actually have none."

"Ah," said the Doctor.

During his first weeks of treatment, at the suggestion of Dr. Kahmstetter, Alexander stopped measuring his nose and scrutinizing it each morning in a magnifying mirror, and tried instead to take only cursory glances at himself in large, full-length mirrors. It was during this period that he discovered the existence of other patients, most of whom seemed to be Twos and Fours. Some of these he learned, came to doctors because, like himself, they believed their noses were growing larger. Others came because of a fear that their noses were growing smaller. And still others, with undeniably enormous or infinitesimal noses, were taking treatments to persuade themselves that their condition did not matter.

"You see," Dr. Kahmstetter remarked one day, "it isn't so much the nose but why the nose should be this important to anyone. Many people, after all, have far worse problems than an imagined—or even a *really*—large nose, but this does not prevent them from living."

"I am aware of that," Alexander said, making a secret, burning note that the Doctor apparently, considered his problem imaginary. "Quite aware of it," he added sharply, for he had begun to suspect Dr. Kahmstetter of seriously underestimating his intelligence.

"I mention it," the Doctor said, "only because you yourself have talked of almost nothing else."

"The fact that I have *talked* about my nose," said Alexander, "doesn't necessarily mean it's my most serious problem."

"But isn't that exactly what I was just saying?"

Alexander searched without success for a glimmer of malice or triumph in this remark.

"Isn't that what we have to examine?" Dr. Kahmstetter added.

Alexander declined to answer.

The more he declined to answer Dr. Kahmstetter, the more time Alexander seemed to spend discussing his problems with other patients. They, he was gratified to learn, were not too disturbed about their condition. Most of them, in fact, considered themselves in a better position than people who were not patients. This was a point of view he took pleasure in expounding to certain Fours, who smiled uneasily as he did so or sometimes stared pointedly and tastelessly at his nose.

"Let us assume, for example," he said one afternoon to a young Four with a rather small nose, "that somebody imagines his nose is growing larger." He paused and looked carefully over the Four's head. "Or perhaps someone imagines that his nose is growing smaller." The Four winced slightly. "There *are* people, you know, who believe that their noses are disappearing."

"Really?" she exclaimed with a bright, fixed smile.

"Yes," Alexander said. "I have known people to be so obsessed with ideas of this kind that they have gone to doctors for years and years."

"How astonishing," the Four said.

"Well, actually," Alexander told her, "it's not astonishing at all. The astonishing thing is that anyone could get that upset about a nose." He raised his head, and his eyes took on the unfocussed look of a public speaker. "After all, lots of us may imagine we have something wrong with our nose—may really *have* something wrong, for that matter—but it doesn't prevent us from living."

There was a flicker of recognition behind the Four's bright smile.

"The important thing," Alexander continued, "is to try to find out why people get so upset about their nose."

"How long have you been taking treatments?" the Four asked suddenly, with such unstudied interest that Alexander's head swung toward her like a falling weight. "I ask," she said, "because you've changed so much in the past few months. You seem less guarded. I have the feeling," she added shyly, "that you don't secretly dislike everyone quite so much anymore."

Was it possible, Alexander asked himself when he was alone again, that the Fours had always been aware of his secret contempt for them? This could hardly be the case, he reasoned, for it was their *un*awareness, after all, that he hated. But suppose that their unawareness had never existed; what was it, then, that he had been hating?

"Could it be something in yourself that you have been hating?" Dr. Kahmstetter suggested. The Doctor's observations sometimes struck Alexander as unbearably stereotyped.

Out on the street, he held an imaginary conversation with the Doctor. "If the object of my hatred is myself and not the Fours," he said with elaborate dignity, "does this mean the Fours are lovable or not lovable?" The fantasy Dr. Kahmstetter seemed to wilt under his scrutiny. "If they are *not* lovable," Alexander continued, "then there is a reason for my not *loving* them. On the other hand, if they *are* lovable, why haven't I loved *them* as I have always loved the Threes?" A faintly perceptible smile played around his mouth as he walked away from the inarticulate Doctor.

That evening, at a supper party, as he tried to catch a glimpse of himself in a full-length mirror, Alexander discovered that he was wearing the same fixed, hypocritical smile he detested in the Fours. He turned to the Four with the small nose, who was standing a short distance away and was watching him with interest.

"The trouble with most people," he said rather loudly, "is that they condemn in others what they are really guilty of themselves." The Four's puzzled expression made him feel a little ridiculous, and he gave her a piercing glance. "You, for example, have a habit of diagnosing people. You told me the other day that I secretly disliked everyone."

"I said you *seemed* to dislike people before your treatments," the Four protested mildly.

"Has it ever occurred to you that perhaps it is really *you* who secretly dislike everyone?" Alexander said with a twinge of pain, for he was beginning to get a headache.

The Four laid her hand on his shoulder with such delicate compassion that he knew she must have copied the gesture from a Three. "I've never seen you so upset before," she said.

"I should say it was very interesting—very interesting indeed," Alexander told Dr. Kahmstetter next day, "that a friend who has known me for several years took pains to tell me last night that she had never seen me in worse condition."

"It is interesting," said the Doctor, "but not quite so interesting as the elation that such a depressing statement apparently causes you."

"But I *am* depressed," Alexander said. He was very depressed, he assured the Doctor—by this and several other things. People no longer admired him, as they once had. He was losing the wit and authority that had made the Fours seek him out. His nose was just as large as it had ever been. He still had not found a Three to love him, and he had paid nine hundred and ninety-five dollars for treatments since the beginning of the year.

His accusations made only small soundless ripples in the deep well of the Doctor's patience. Might it not be wiser, Dr. Kahmstetter suggested, to try to understand why it troubled him so to be unpopular with people he professed to despise? Or better still, to concentrate on the *nature* of his hatred for the Fours. Had he any special feeling about his hatred? Had he ever been close enough to it to see what it was like?

He had never actually seen his hatred, Alexander said, but he had felt it often enough. It was a small, sharp stone in his chest. Dr. Kahmstetter seemed especially pleased with this reply.

For the next few weeks, without telling Dr. Kahmstetter, Alexander spent his time trying to examine the stone of his hatred. It was extremely difficult to touch the stone, he found. Occasionally even the thought of touching it caused his chest to contract in a way that made the effort impossible. The best time to approach the task was when he cared least about succeeding. After a particularly concentrated effort had failed and he was on the point of giving up the whole business in disgust, his chest sometimes relaxed and the stone was miraculously available to him. At last, although each movement filled his body with a thousand shocks, he managed to loosen the stone sufficiently to put

one finger behind a corner of it. What he felt there when he did so
made him scream with fright.

The stone, he announced, trembling and defiant, when he
reached Dr. Kahmstetter's office, was attached to the right side of his
heart.

"But how can you possibly say such a thing?" the Doctor asked,
with the slightest trace of impatience. Alexander's contention that he
felt it there did not impress Dr. Kahmstetter. That was just a way of
refusing to examine the stone, he said.

"But suppose that the stone *is* attached to my heart and that
dislodging it will cost me my life," Alexander insisted.

"In that case," said the Doctor matter-of-factly, "I can be of no
help to you."

Alexander had such a glaring pain in his head when he left Dr.
Kahmstetter's office that day that he could not remember a word they
had said to each other. When he reached home, he went immediately
to the telephone and called the Four with the small nose to apologize
for his conduct at the supper party.

It was perfectly all right, she told him. She knew how irritable a
headache made one feel and, actually, after thinking it over, she had
decided there was some truth in what he had said about her secretly
disliking everybody.

It occurred to Alexander as he hung up the phone that he might
be falling in love with the young Four.

"It's the first time, of course, that I've ever felt this way about anyone who wasn't a Three," he told Dr. Kahmstetter at his next session,
pretending not to notice the Doctor's veiled, approving glance.

"Perhaps you are discovering that people cannot be divided into
categories, after all," the Doctor said with the suggestion of a smile.

Alexander kept remembering Dr. Kahmstetter's smile and his
veiled, approving glance. Once or twice, he even found himself smiling
in this same way at the Fours. When he did so, the Fours' fixed, bright
faces became more fixed than ever, but their eyes shot him looks of
loneliness and longing that amazed him. On a bus one afternoon, he
smiled at a Two who was secretly studying the reflection of his nose in

the window. The look that crossed the Two's face was almost identical with what he had seen in the eyes of the Fours.

Was it possible that the glances he had found so threatening were not really threatening at all? Could all these different faces conceal the same expression? How strange that this had never occurred to him before. The Fours, he remembered suddenly, had never said that they *dis*liked his nose. Even the Twos had never looked at his nose with actual malice. Even the Ones, in their numb, fettered way, perhaps yearned to look beyond his nose. And as final, incontestable proof, there was the young Four herself, whose eyes and voice and smile and hands were as sensitive and comprehending as any Three's.

"Perhaps," Alexander said to himself, "you are discovering that people are not divided into categories, after all."

It was five months after their marriage—a year after he had stopped seeing Dr. Kahmstetter—that the young Four made her startling revelation to Alexander. She was extremely casual about it. That was one of the hardest things to forgive her for, really—her total failure to understand his feelings in the matter.

"The trouble with most people," he was saying when it happened, "is that they live by categories."

The young Four seemed rather abstracted, and Alexander went further than he had intended, to capture her attention.

"I myself believed in them once, you know. There was even a time when I would not have married you unless you had been a Three."

"But my darling," his wife said then, smiling in affectionate protest, her voice gentle and amused, "I *am* a Three."

Knowing how little importance he attached to categories, she could not believe that she had shocked him. Nor could she believe that this aspect of her identity, or the circumstances which explained it, could really fascinate him. One of the things she had always loved most about him, in fact, was his indifference to such matters.

Alexander went immediately to call on Dr. Kahmstetter.

"My wife is a Three. Has been all the time," he said, fighting to control his voice, as he entered the Doctor's office.

"Yes?" said Dr. Kahmstetter.

"But I don't know what to do."

"Do? Why should you do anything?" the Doctor asked.

Alexander's chest contracted in such a strange way at that moment that he could not utter a word.

"This is exactly what you have always wanted," Dr. Kahmstetter continued in his kind, cheerful voice. "If I can help you," he added as Alexander walked mutely to the door, "please don't hesitate to call on me."

For several weeks it seemed as if Alexander might never recover the power of speech. And, indeed, this could very well have been the case had he not taken out his measuring tape and magnifying mirror one day and discovered beyond any shadow of doubt that his nose was a sixteenth of an inch longer.

"The trouble with most people," he said then, with a buoyancy that quite amazed his wife, "is that they don't trust the evidence of their own senses."

19

End of a Game

Nancy Huddleston Packer

Charles Andress once said, and believed, that he and his whole life could pretty well be summed up in eighteen or twenty categories, like sportswriter, husband, father of two, Democrat, ectomorph, WASP and so on. Of course he was not all that simple, but he believed himself to be usual, predictable, lacking in dark recesses. Therefore he was confused and shaken when he finally came to recognize that his wife's breakdown tyrannized over him, that he was unable to sustain even ten minutes without thinking about it.

If everything is all right between us as Caroline claims, he asked, then what could be wrong? With her? Me? His fingers pressed eight keys at once and jammed the typewriter. Answer the question: If everything is all right . . .

"Well now, how's our very own Grantland Red Smith Rice today?"

The face of Caroline, secret, sensual, smug (and sick, don't forget sick) vanished, and Charles looked up. Wilson. A lummox. Face like a pale tomato. A fair man, Charles chided himself that he did not have a quarrel with Wilson, who did not matter. With whom then? If everything is so goddamn all right?

"The boss says any time you say so, the presses can roll."

"I'm not finished," said Charles. He jerked from the typewriter the sheet of yellow paper on which, after a sixty- not a fifty-minute hour, he had written only the heading of his column. "If you think this stuff is so easy to write, try it yourself."

"What'd I do?" asked Wilson. "Pass along a message is all. I'm the boss? What'd I do?"

"You circle," said Charles. "You wait."

On a clean sheet of paper he typed his name and the name of his column: Now In This Corner. And relieved by that he remembered Wilson at whom he had thrown so small a punch. He said, "Sorry, I'm just edgy. I don't feel good. Look . . . " but he said no more and Wilson walked away, not mattering in the least.

As if he had been more badgered than in fact he felt he had been, Charles quickly fought back by writing: By rule this column has never taken sides in personal disputes between a ballplayer and a manager. But sometimes the soundest rule must be broken. This is such a time. The very public hassle between manager George Wain and pitcher Wag Schumpeter promises to wreck our small pennant hope. We must take sides.

Hooked. For taking sides was precisely what Dr. Loeb had done from the beginning. Hid it though. Sleek Loeb, extending a hand . . . of what? Charitable contempt? Pure deception?

"Naturally you are concerned about your wife," Loeb had said. "But of course you must realize that her difficulty comes from many years before your marriage. You are not responsible in that sense."

Charles had shrugged to convey that though he was no psychiatrist, he was no fool either, he understood something of breakdowns. Yet fool, he soon saw, was exactly what he was. It was days after the interview that he thought. My wife's trouble comes from many years before she married me and I am not responsible for it; the difficulty is not the result of our marriage, it is the cause; the difficulty led to our marriage; I am a symptom; I don't count.

If I am only a symptom, he imagined asking Loeb, how can she say everything is all right between us? Can everything be all right when I amount to so little? But if I were the cause, how then could anything be all right? And why, Dr. Loeb, do you who know her so little know her so well while I do not count.

Charles looked across the city room. A vast nervous amphitheater of a room, who could work there? The sports editor wore rimless glasses and weighed one hundred and twenty-six pounds and loved contact sports. Behind those rimless glasses, Charles thought, the harsh gaze was upon him: Can't do the work any more, Andress?

That morning in his unctuous sinister voice the sports editor had asked if Charles had anything interesting for the column. "For a change" hung unspoken between them. Grateful to have an answer, Charles said, Yeah, a good-old-days piece, about Wain saying Schumpeter ought to see a psychiatrist. The editor had said, Better leave that to the medics, don't get in over your head. Charles had said, I guess you think people are more interested in high school basketball? The editor's teeth showed back to his molars. Better make it good then.

Charles wrote, Things have come to a pretty pass when the manager of a contending ball club publicly suggests that the team's only twenty-game winner ought to see a head-shrinker. No, psychiatrist. Thirty years ago many a manager would have said that a guy like Wag Schumpeter ought to have his head examined. Today, it's Go see a psychiatrist. In the first instance, invective, pure and simple, the prerogative of men who nurse ballplayers. In the second, diagnosis, partial but nonetheless first-step diagnosis. The emphasis is altogether different. Now I ask you, if everything was all right between them, what could be wrong? That is, if Wain had properly managed the erratic southpaw.

He had been the one to get Caroline started with Loeb. Hundreds of details had finally culminated in one conclusive episode. The draperies of the house drawn all day, every day, yet not a lamp lighted unless he lighted it. Not one social engagement in months. And the fatigue, too fatigued to go out to dinner with him, to go to a movie or a game, to be with him. And all that silence too, which he, fool that he was, had chalked up to the natural leveling off of a marriage. Well, but she had never complained, never said a word, and the children were clean, fed, happy, miraculously undamaged. And of course there was his deeply held belief that theirs was a family graced by love. They quarreled so rarely, and when they did they were not killers, they split their differences. Oh yes oh yes, graced by love.

And then the one event he could not ignore or misunderstand. He had one day called home a dozen times, to get Caroline to go to the first night game of the season, and he had received no answer. He was not exactly worried, but by the day's end he was irritated that she had not anticipated that he might be worried. When he got home, eager to show off his annoyance, he found her sitting in darkness, while the children played in their rooms. He flipped the light switch, and he saw that her face was quite dirty, with driblets of food around her mouth, her hair was uncombed, and her dress was soiled and misbuttoned. She's off her rocker, he distinctly told himself, and the impact of the nasty phrase brought with it a strangling rush of terror.

Yet in his methodical, workmanlike, competent way, he set about rectifying things as best he could. After she went to bed, before 8:30 (and wasn't that a pattern he should have long since detected?), he called their family physician and got the name of a "very-first-rate man," Rudolph Loeb. Next day he called and made an appointment for Caroline.

That night as Caroline headed for bed, he called her to him. He thought she had worsened even that day. She stood before him like a repentant child, head lowered, eyes averted, fingers twisting. First Charles attempted to enfold her with words of love and confidence. Don't charge in. He pointed out the tensions he knew she suffered, the problems, the boredom.

"You overload the system," he said, laughing hopefully, "and it breaks down, like an electrical circuit." He felt awkward and heavy of tongue, and he thought she ought at least try to help him; she wasn't a deaf-mute. Finally he blurted out, "I think you need a psychiatrist, I've made an appointment for you."

He anticipated wrath and defense. Indeed, her anger would in some fashion have given the lie to his fears about her. But she offered no resistance. "I know I'm sick," she said. "I've known for weeks I was getting worse. I thought you'd hate me for it."

As her quick tears washed grime and powder and yesterday's lipstick down her broken face, he rocked and patted her. He felt very tender toward her, and he thought he had handled the situation quite well. Momentarily he regretted going for outside help without giving himself a chance to help her. But that night he heard her weeping as she slept.

Caroline and Dr. Loeb set up a schedule. She would see him three mornings a week at 11:00. From the beginning, she had improved. Oh, not in a straight, steady line, of course, she pointed out, but more like the business of the spiral. Or maybe three steps forward and two back. At the end of the first week, and with visible effort, she opened the draperies on the side of the house that faced the woods, the private side. Still, going to the grocery store frightened her, and anyway she kept the street-side draperies closed.

For nine months Caroline visited Dr. Loeb three times weekly, one hundred and fifty minutes weekly, seventy-five dollars weekly (forget that, for Pete's sake) plus the cost of a baby-sitter (honestly!) and the operation of the automobile (who minds? who minds?) and how the hell long does it take the cat to climb out of the well at three forward and two back?

I have nothing against psychiatry, Charles wrote. In fact, I sometimes think that every lefthander worth his salt ought to have a few preventive sessions on the sofa. Lefthanders are notoriously unstable, they list the wrong way. I happen to be a fair sandlot southpaw myself, and no harm is meant.

"He's a dear," said Caroline one Sunday afternoon at the end of the first month of treatment. "A funny, old-world little man; you'd expect a thick accent, but he's been in this country since he was six. No accent, but all the rest. Maybe foreign men understand better . . . " She let the sentence trail off, and as if her love of sunlight had never faltered, she threw open the draperies on the street side.

"Don't I understand you?" Charles asked, idly.

"We're married, that's different," she said. She stared at him for a moment, looking stricken and afraid, and then she turned back to the draws of the draperies.

"Leave them alone," Charles said quickly. "I understand you with love, he understands you with his mind. That's the difference, all I do is love you."

"That's everything," she said, "as long as everything is all right between us, that's everything." And joyous, she came to sit on his lap.

"Damn the kids," he said, "Sundays were always the best."

She smiled with teasing pity, flirtatious and tender, a look he had forgotten that she owned, a look that stirred a desire that he had only been pretending to have. "Poor Charles, the kids are as hard on you as they sometimes are on me. Dr. Loeb said maybe we weren't quite ready for all the responsibilities."

"He did, did he? What else did he say?"

"Nothing," said Caroline, standing up, straightening her skirt. "He practically never says a word. Maybe he didn't even say that. Maybe I just thought he might. I do all the talking."

"And what do you say then? I mean, about me."

"Nothing. Just how much I love you."

"That's everything," he said.

That's nothing. Very suddenly, the fact of his immense ignorance erupted in him. He knew nothing about her therapy, nothing about her sicknes, nothing about her. For this important time in her life, he was a stranger, a bystander. For all she apparently needed, she had Loeb. Bitterly he drew a poster: Andress Go Home.

He got up. "I think I'll pull weeds. Somebody has to do something around this place. And you know what else I think I'll do? Go have a talk with your boyfriend. If you don't mind, of course." Impulse had spoken, brilliantly. How marvelous and powerful he was. He grinned at her, a grin that felt like oil around his lips, with a touch of malice.

"No I don't mind," she said. "Dr. Loeb said he'd be glad to talk to you any time." His grin dried to paste.

For the next two weeks, Charles's fantasies broke with increasing insistence into his work and sleep. In the evening following her visits to Loeb, he spent restless, agitated hours attempting to pry out of her what had happened. He hoped he was subtler than he felt. I was thinking about your mother today, he said, meaning were you talking about your mother with Dr. Loeb? We ought really to talk more don't you think? he said, meaning Did you talk about me with Dr. Loeb? I don't feel so good tonight, he said, meaning Do you love me, do you tell the doctor that you love me? And it seemed that what Caroline said in answer was always a kind of precise irrelevance. She told him. Sometimes in detail, but she told him nothing he wanted to know.

Eventually he thought he detected a consciously devised pattern of telling intended to conceal, not reveal. Always she told him something outside herself, mother, friends, father. If he probed more deeply, she said Lord Lord I'll be months understanding that one. That evasion, too, he believed was calculated. But he was not sure.

Finally he decided that Loeb's willingness to talk to him should not keep a grown man from taking advantage of that willingness, and he went to see Loeb. He took his own lunch hour, and he thought he had taken Loeb's. I'll pay for it, he said. I'll pay the twenty-five an hour, just go on and take the rest of our savings. But the money was not at issue, and he denied to himself having thought about it. Other than just joking. A joke.

When he entered Loeb's office, he was unhappy and embarrassed, and he affected a nauseating jocularity not at all his style. Every aspect of his wife's condition was good for humor. When he told the doctor that he had recognized her illness because she was . . . dirty, he laughed. He laughed at his coming to see Loeb, lied and laughed that he was doing it to please the sick little girl (had even called her that). He finished up with a ribald psychiatric joke about the coarse sexual fantasies of a woman patient. He didn't think the joke was funny. Never had.

The sleek owl sat with hands lightly touching, the index fingers tapping on the bridge of his nose, rocking and twirling his large, blue serge buttocks in the pea-green swivel chair. The smile that was not a smile, not sympathy, but removed, distant, powerful understanding brought forth from Charles an abject question, a sudden pleading surrender.

"What am I to do?"

The chair swiveled sideways and in that moment of silence Charles saw the bulging eyes, the beakish nose, the mobile, full lips. In a flash of rage, he asked himself why Caroline could not see all that vulgarity and egotism and sensuality. He came to his feet, his hand raised to forestall Loeb. "I'll just grin and bear it. Sorry I took your time." The decision was all his own.

"Just a moment, please," said Loeb. He motioned for Charles to sit. Sullen, nervous, Charles sat down, and instantly he believed that Loeb was about to tell him that Caroline was divorcing him. Why else had they wanted him to come? Why, if not to tell him this final irrevocably damaging thing, that Caroline did not love him? Why else had they connived to get him here?

"We never know," said Loeb, "why at any given moment a particular personality has what might be called a collapse, a breakdown. Sometimes there are more likely reasons than at other times. Naturally you are concerned about your wife, but of course you must realize that her difficulty comes from many years before your marriage. You are not responsible in that sense."

Shrugging, Charles gestured for Loeb to go on, he wasn't a fool, he understood the etiology. Momentarily he thought it would be fun to share with Caroline the asinine fantasy he had had that she was going to divorce him. But then he thought he would not share this with her when she would not share anything with him.

"Treatment," Loeb went on slowly, "is often very alarming and undermining for the whole family. In many cases it's a good idea for the wife or husband of the patient to have some supportive therapy. To help him through the trying months."

A key slipped in and turned a lock. Charles stood. "So that's it, so I'm the nut now."

Loeb was imperturbable. "Not at all. I only meant if the strain gets to be too much . . . "

"Look," said Charles, thumping his chest with his index finger, "I'm a measly sports-writer on a measly newspaper in a measly town. I have four mouths to feed and four bodies to clothe and four heads, at least at last count, to shelter. Bus fare is fifteen cents each way. Insurance, one hundred twenty a quarter. Retirement pension is twenty-five dollars a month, but what's twenty-five a month when it's twenty-five an hour. Savings? Going fast."

Loeb interrupted. "I'd be happy to arrange for payments over a period of years. It is not uncommon . . . "

"It isn't the money, it isn't the money," Charles shouted. "If I woke up and found myself curled up like a baby sucking an inkwell, I still wouldn't indulge myself in these little chats with you. Maybe you ought to take up golf, that would kill a lot of time."

Dr. Loeb's face showed neither anger nor amusement nor even recognition. He said, "I didn't mean treatment with me. It's unwise for a therapist to have two patients from the same family."

Charles' taut spirit went flabby, but he gamely concluded, "Just don't you and Caroline get to planning anything for me, I'm a big boy, now. I don't think I could get sick if I wanted to."

Dr. Loeb stood in a posture of dismissal. "Of course it's purely up to you, Mr. Andress." And days later Charles thought, I am a fool, I don't count, but I am not sick.

Charles wrote, If Schumpeter put himself in the hands of a psychiatrist, then quite obviously control of the team would shift from Wain to the doctor, at least when Schumpeter was on the mound. The psychiatric relationship permeates all others. Put it this way: If George Wain husbands the team, the doctor is—no, for God's sake scratch that. Let no man put asunder the relationship between a ballplayer and his manager. Christ. Take the case, the real case, of James Piersall. Scratch out Christ, but keep Piersall. Charles reconstructed the case of James Piersall. It took two full paragraphs. That was nice. Facts, facts.

"I know you got more important things on your mind," said Wilson, "but these are times that try men's souls."

"What?" asked Charles.

"The boss says, 'See what's with Red Smith over there.' I see, I believe it's dolls. But Charles, friend, the out-of-town edition goes to bed in thirty minutes and you know it don't sleep good without that old Andress hot water bottle to snuggle up with."

"How do vultures know, Wilson, the precise moment to quit circling and go for the flesh? Smell? Sight? ESP?"

"How would I know?" said Wilson.

"The human counterpart," said Charles, "can spot a weakened condition ten desks off, knows a wound when it sticks its finger in one. You keep circling my desk and I'll begin to think I'm sick, dying, dead." I am sick, he thought.

"You sure talk sick," said Wilson. "Thirty minutes."

Charles said to himself, Thirty minutes. He wrote, All joking aside, it is not in the purview of the sportswriter to comment on psychiatry, pro or con. I am only pointing out the ramifications of Wain's contention. The real point is that when any manager goes outside the normal channels of communication between players and himself, he is only admitting that the battle is already lost. Time for a change?

He closed his eyes. Could he run it? Would they print it? Was it that much worse than yesterday's, that much better than tomorrow's? Would there come a time when he could not write at all? And so what? I'm dying, I'm going home.

He clipped together the two sheets of yellow paper, folded them lengthwise, wrote his name on the outside like a student, put on his hat, gave Wilson an ugly wink and floated out of the city room. Dolls, he thought. Oh to be Wilson, say to be racing home now for a quickie. Andress, ardent lover. Yet lover, he thought, was a role he played but rarely now, and with painful, unreleased, unsexual tension. It mattered too much now. Each occasion of their coming together he thought was an opportunity for a miracle, to reestablish them where he once had thought they were, graced by love. As each miracle failed, he felt farther from her, less her lover, profoundly desperate. And in a strange turnabout of their roles, it became Caroline who pursued him and with an apparent disregard for everything except pure sexual pleasure.

Ah darling (he pretended that he heard her say), we had such a good session today, Dr. Loeb and I, but don't ask what. Want me? Go to bed with me? Now now now. Thus the excitement engendered by Loeb found fulfillment with Charles. He was degraded. Even so, even

so, he attempted to turn these seemingly unguarded moments into occasions for prying her secrets from her. With her wariness brought low
by lust, what might he not elicit from her?

Answer: damn little. Even then, there she mastered him. He
feared for himself: how long before the effort broke him?

Out of the aborted interview with Loeb had come his compulsion
to trap Caroline into admissions she would not know she made. At the
beginning, his little traps — suitable for snarling lies as well as truths, for
separating them — snapped shut often before he was fully aware that he
was at that moment attempting to trap her. Innocently he asked a
question; guiltily he listened. But eventually nothing was accidental;
he knew exactly what he was about, was ashamed of it, and was
exultant.

That first night after his visit to Loeb he had said, "Went to see
your boyfriend today." He felt an acid anger, remembering the nasty
phrase *supportive therapy.* "Maybe I will, maybe I won't."

"What?" she asked. "Maybe you'll what?"

In the mirror he watched his face, turned it right and left. "You
know," he said. Conniver, name it. The first trap was thus set.

"No I don't," she said. "Tell me, tell me. He wants to send me
away, doesn't he? Away some place."

Her mouth moved in the circular motion of her anxiety and her
face grew haggard. Thwarted, stung, soft with love, he went to her.

"No, nothing about you. Me. He thought it might be a good idea
if I get some supportive therapy. That's all." In the quiet moments before sleep that night he recalled Caroline's tears and he wondered if
they were real or were the dishonest agents of the conspiracy with
Loeb. He touched her shoulder and forgave himself.

Frequently in the following weeks when he thought he was at the
point of an important revelation, she broke into tears. Her timing was
superb. Please, Charles, please, what do you want, what are you after.
The sad, broken, harrowed face. Always he was deeply ashamed and
vowed never again to harass her. But even as he vowed, he saw forming
on the edge of his awareness a new, more intricate plan. And when

that too failed, brought on its accompaniment of tears, he roared with injury and anger, and planned anew.

Hearing the baby cry out in sleep one evening, Charles said, "I guess the kids really get their lumps in these sessions with Loeb. They sure can get on my nerves." He tensed, waiting.

She appeared thoughtful. "Well, today I told him we were getting a two-wheeler for her birthday. I guess I'm still uncertain about it. She's so little."

After a pause Charles asked, "What else did you say about her?"

"Nothing."

The trap snapped the air. Injured, he said, "Two-wheelers, the most important thing about your kid is a goddamn two-wheeler. For twenty-five an hour you sit talking about two-wheelers. You don't bother to say whether you love her or want to pinch her head off. You have a nervous breakdown, you say you have a nervous breakdown, and your children don't count enough to even discuss them except two-wheelers."

She held out her hand. "Charles," she said.

"Or me either, I guess. What's the most important thing about me? That I'm a lousy sportswriter and you and your boyfriend are having a lot of sport on my twenty-five dollars?"

"Please don't," she said.

"Well what do you say then? What do you tell him that I'm too dumb to understand? What's he give you I don't? What are you trying to do to me?" When the echo of his anger died away, he heard her weeping.

"I love you," he said, searching out a talisman to quiet her. "Even when I think I'm losing my mind, I know I love you, Caroline."

"But you don't know that I love you," she said in a drowning voice.

"That too, mostly." He went to her and began to touch and pat her, tentatively as a small child touches and pats a baby.

In bed that night Caroline said, "You mustn't mind too much this getting angry."

"You just get well and I'll be all right."

"I think I am getting better," she said. "Of course it's a backward and forward thing. Dr. Loeb says . . . "

Dr. Loeb says. Charles sang out: Take me out to the ballgame, set me out in the crowd, buy me some peanuts and crackerjacks. I don't care if you never get well.

Like the traps, the explosions developed their own patterns, as if he were caught in a rhythmic cycle. Try as he did, and he did—smiling larger than he ever felt, talking desperately of other matters, even admitting his anguish to Caroline as if naming would relieve him—he could not control his outbursts. Nor could he confine them and his anxiety to his home. Shortly the quality of his work declined so that even he noticed. He turned in a shorter and shorter and duller and duller column later and later. His colleagues looked at him, puzzled. Look, he told the sports editor, my wife's not well, give me a break. This department rode me for three years, I was the only one anybody was reading and you know it. Can't I ride a while? The sports editor said, Buddy you been riding, what's the trouble, you splitting up with the wife? Hell no, said Charles, hell no, she's just sick. He walked hurriedly away, sickened.

For among the many visions that obsessed him was that of her having left him. Deeply grieved, he lived alone forever. Others found him tragic. Now that, he said to remind himself that he still had his good old sense of humor, is what I call funny. The scene shifted to comedy and Caroline and Loeb scampered off. The owl and the pussycat go to sea in a beautiful pea-green swivel chair. Floating amidst the high waves. Drowning. No. Danced by the light of the moon, the moon, they danced by the light of the moon.

Good thing he still had his sense of humor. Could still laugh at his wife. His sick wife. In the sudden inner quiet he heard the dying of laughter, and he longed to say, But what of me?

As he reached home, walking the block and a half from the bus stop, he heard the carillon of the Episcopal church sing out 12:00. As he put his hand on the doorknob, the significance of the hour came to him: Caroline would be bidding goodbye to Dr. Loeb, the small, soft fluttering hand held overlong in the moist, throbbing hand of the doctor.

"Hello," he called out when he opened the door. Silence. The house was empty. He thought he had never felt such emptiness before, as if it had been not simply departed but irrevocably deserted. In a rush of panic and passion, he went in a running walk from room to room, seeking out signs of the final leave-taking. He found the kitchen as he had left it that morning, cream-sodden cheerios plastered on the sides of the bowl, a gnawed, damp piece of toast, a half-filled coffee cup, a nearly empty bottle of curdling milk on the drainboard. Caroline had left the mess to him. In her desperate desire to leave him, she had not had the consideration, that dreg of love, to clean up after their last meal together.

Methodically he set about straightening the kitchen, dropping the contents of plates into the disposal, rinsing, stacking, scraping fried egg off the formica table top, wiping indefinable nastiness from the high chair, and saying over and over to himself, This is really funny.

When he heard the front door open and close, he was not surprised. He knew he had been only challenging a toy disaster, only playing a game of tragedy. Whatever else was wrong, Caroline was not capable of an act at once cruel and calculated. He was very touched by this knowledge.

"Nap time," he heard her say. "You've had a lovely morning and it's time to rest, both of you now."

Charles lay flat against the wall. He did not want to see his children. He did not want to weigh them into whatever course he intended taking. What was it anyway? Why had he come?

When Caroline came out of the bedroom, he was standing in the hallway. She looked a question: Why are you here. Indeed. He shrugged: Just am. Mildly perplexed and expectant, she slipped her arm around him and they walked into the living room.

"Where's everybody been?" he asked.

"The sitter was sick." She explained that she had taken the children to a friend while she kept her appointment with Loeb.

"How was it?" he asked.

"Fine. They ate lunch and apparently had the time of their lives."

Charles gave her his rigid back to look at. "I meant Loeb."

"That was fine too. Why are you home so early?"

"And why are you evasive so early? And so late?"

Caroline looked puzzled. "Evasive?"

"Evasive," said Charles. "It won't work any more, Caroline. I want to know what's going on, I have that right. And I don't mean two-wheelers. I mean you. I mean me. Don't try to evade it. What did you talk about today with Loeb?"

"The grocery store," said Caroline evenly. "Why I still have to get there when the doors first open. Do you mind telling me what's going on?" She sat down.

Charles closed his eyes. Was he nauseated, or only imagining it? Was he dizzy? Sick? "Do you mind telling *me* what is going on? I'm home so early and so late for you to tell *me* what is going on."

"Tell you what?" she asked in a pinched voice. "Minute by minute? Word for word? 'Good morning, Dr. Loeb,' I said. 'Good morning, Mrs. Andress,' he said. 'Nice day,' I said. No, he said that. I said 'Yes isn't it.' "

"Laugh," he said.

"I'm not. But don't you see I just can't tell you bang like that? I don't even understand it myself yet. You're not a psychiatrist."

Charles sighed, for her benefit. For himself, he wept. "What did you say about me?"

"Your name didn't come up."

"I don't count," he said. "My name didn't come up. I don't matter." When Caroline started to stand, he shoved her back in the chair. The roughness of his gesture surprised him. He said, "Please, Caroline, help me. Don't you see?" With clenched fists, he was a supplicant.

She looked closely at him. "What is it you want?"

"What is it you want?" he mimicked her. "You don't even know there's anything wrong, do you? If I had both legs sawed off like bleeding stumps, you'd be more concerned with a pulled muscle in your little finger."

"I don't know what you're talking about," she said. She seemed puzzled, but oh so well, so reasonable.

"This: I have a wife and she prefers a stranger to her husband. I have a good job but I can't get the work done right any more. Don't you see what's happening? It's simple: we have got to start thinking about me for a change."

He stopped, waited, expected her sudden tears. He feared them and he desired them. Waiting, momentarily he saw clearly that her crying gave him a kind of respite, meant she cared. Then cry.

"I think of you all the time," she said quietly. "I know this therapy is difficult for you . . . "

"Christ," said Charles. "You're not sick, you're not the sick one. I am."

"I love you," she said.

"Don't try that, I invented that trick myself. Love excuseth all things."

"I'm getting better," she said. "Please be patient. Please don't make it hard on me now."

He closed his eyes, felt the drumbeat of his eyeballs. "You don't care if I'm sick or well. I don't count." Action presented itself, a course of action sang clean, through all the noise. He opened his eyes and laughed close to her face, and he felt a tinny jingling excitement. He walked over to the telephone in the front hall and dialed the newspaper office.

Caroline came to stand beside him, her hand making tentative gestures of affection toward him. He ignored her. "What are you doing?" she finally asked. "At least tell me what you're doing."

"I'm quitting my job. I can't make it any more."

"Don't, Charles, please. This isn't good. Are you teasing?"

Teasing, did she dare ask teasing? "Wilson in sports," he told the switchboard, thinking that it was fitting and proper to give the satisfaction to Wilson who also did not count at all. Heat rose in his face and filled his head and eyes and he felt tenderly sorry for himself. "You and Loeb, you and your boyfriend, you never gave a damn what you were doing to me. Well now you know."

Just before Caroline brought her hands to her eyes, he saw her face begin to sag and break. Never mind about that, he'd not fall for that again. She walked away. He looked beyond her to the living room. The sunshine was too bright, unpleasant, dust motes swam in the glare. But the pursuit of darkness was Caroline's way, not his. He would not close the curtains, he would choose another way. As he waited for Wilson, many books and stories, many case histories and even ancient family legends, pictures and fantasies of chaos and misery crossed his memory, and in each Charles Andress was the star. Yet none quite suited him, and so, waiting, he wondered on what downward spiral he would set himself—how, if not in her darkness or another's shriek, he would find his own escape. What awfulness awaited him? What safety?

But at once he faltered, for already he began to hear the sound of his wife's weeping, her shattered sobs. Not fair, not fair, he protested, this is my time. As Wilson said "Who is this?" Charles vowed he would not hang up the telephone, not surrender. But of course he did. All games must end for Charles. After all, he was who he was, and neither mockery nor longing changed that. Regretfully, he acknowledged that he was unable to desert himself or her.

She did not look up at the bang of the telephone. Her face was against her knees, her hands raised as if warding off blows.

"I'm sorry," he said. "I love you, Caroline."

Later, he thought, a small lie to his boss would tide him over, provide an excuse for his strange behavior. I thought I had something serious, he imagined himself saying, but it was only a bellyache. And tomorrow words would surely fall more easily upon the yellow paper, more quickly, better words, for surely today he had finally come against the limits of himself. And yet tomorrow night perhaps—he had to face this—he would again attempt to ensnare his wife in revelations; but his attempts would be half-hearted, useless, would not persuade even himself. And he would no doubt be furious again at his failure just as he had been today, but not so furious as today. He would again grow quiet as now he had, and sooner quiet than today. Eventually he might even forbear, since no other course was possible for him. He was, after all, a limited man. Limited. Momentarily he ached with that knowledge. And then he bestirred himself to go to his wife, for it was she who was sick, before whom opened darkness and flux, who needed him, toward whom he had a duty to perform. Whom he loved. Gently he stroked her cheek and allowed himself to ask silently, Well, she is sick, isn't she?